DRINKING

DRINKING

JACK B. WEINER

W·W·Norton & Company · Inc ·

NEW YORK

Library of Congress Cataloging in Publication Data

Weiner, Jack B   1929–
  Drinking.

  1. Alcoholism.   2. Alcoholics.   I. Title.
HV5035.W33   1976   362.2'92   76–19035
ISBN 0–393–08749–2

This book was set in Bulmer and Times Roman
Designed by Jacques Chazaud
Manufactured by Vail-Ballou Press, Inc.

2 3 4 5 6 7 8 9 0

For all my friends in the Fellowship of the Spirit,
with gratitude and love.

Contents

DRINKING

1

"No, Not Me..."

One sultry September midnight in Los Angeles, a motorcycle headlight pierced the leafy blackness of Benedict Canyon Road, a winding and scenic highway linking Beverly Hills and the San Fernando Valley. Astride the cycle were television actor James Stacy and his companion, Clair Cox, both unaware that another vehicle was speeding toward them from the opposite direction. At the wheel of the onrushing 1968 sedan was Carter Gordon, thirty-four years old.

For one blazing instant, the headlight beams converged. A fraction of a second later, Gordon's car veered suddenly across the double yellow line, broadsiding the motorcycle at 80 miles per hour. There was a bone-grinding crash, then silence. After what seemed like an eternity, powerful police spotlights began to crisscross the bloody and shard-strewn road, coming to rest finally on three severed human limbs.

Carter Gordon miraculously escaped injury; he was immediately booked on a charge of felony drunk driving. The charge was changed to felony manslaughter when, nine hours later, Mrs. Cox died in UCLA Medical Center. James Stacy survived, minus his left arm and leg.

"I thought I was okay and tried to stand up," Stacy recalls. "Then I realized I didn't have a left leg, and it was kind of a shock. Death I thought I could take, but being maimed wasn't part of my plans. Lying there on the road, I kept thinking, 'No, not me.' ''

Those last haunting words could provide a terse epitaph for 30,000 men, women, and children who, like waitress Clair Cox, are slaughtered yearly in alcohol-related traffic accidents on America's streets and highways. "No, not me." Those same words could, in fact, be the theme phrase for an astronomical 500,000 other victims who, year after gory year, are injured and possibly disabled as a result of alcohol-impaired drivers and drunken pedestrians.

Yet, staggering as both these figures may seem, they are merely the bare bones of a grisly panorama. They say nothing about the fact that alcohol is involved in half of *all* traffic fatalities, that drinkers with chronic drinking problems cause a full two-thirds of the alcohol-related deaths, and that, incredibly, far more Americans die in drunk-driving accidents than from acts of outright homicide.

Nor do the drunk-driving death and injury statistics begin to describe the immense costs in property damage, medical expenses, insurance costs, wage losses, and immeasurable human misery. Says actor Stacy, who once played professional football, "I've been getting a lot of amputee scripts lately."

Several days before Christmas in 1973, on a side street of Calumet, Oklahoma, a nineteen-year-old Cheyenne youth tossed an empty bottle of Golden Pheasant shaving lotion into the gutter. He staggered drunkenly to an abandoned garage, slumped down in a dark corner, and, with a single-edged razor blade, methodically sliced through the arteries in his wrist. He died within thirty minutes.

That same evening, six hundred miles to the northwest in Denver, Colorado, a middle-aged woman suffocated her infant son in his crib during an alcoholic blackout.

Just hours later, still farther north in a suburb of Great Falls, Montana, drunkenness caused a father of three children to choke to death on a three-inch piece of sirloin steak.

Early the next morning, some two thousand miles due east, in

Augusta, Maine, two young girls and their mother were rushed to a hospital emergency ward with second-degree burns on their backs and arms. The mother, a widow, had passed out while drinking. Her cigarette had dropped between the cushions of the living-room couch, smoldering until it touched off a fast-spreading blaze.

Viewed separately, none of these seemingly isolated events would be cause for national alarm. Yet those pre-Christmas traumas in Calumet, Denver, Great Falls, and Augusta must be viewed together, for each is linked inextricably to the others by twin bonds of alcohol and violence. In their macabre togetherness, the events symbolize an ongoing continuum of alcohol-related human devastation almost beyond belief. Daily and repeatedly, literally hundreds of similar and often identical events occur in cities and hamlets from the Atlantic to the Pacific.

The stark facts are that half of all homicides and one-third of all suicides are alcohol-related—accounting for almost 12,000 deaths yearly in America. In that tragic regard, the Cheyenne youth and Denver housewife were hardly alone.

Alcohol-related family violence, exemplified by the "battered-wife syndrome," is so commonplace that it defies quantification. As for accidents such as fire-related deaths and injuries, falls, drownings, and electrocutions—during the Christmas season or at any other—the majority of these traumas, too, can be directly attributed to alcohol.

Food inhalation is a primary example. Though often misdiagnosed and infrequently publicized, food inhalation is ranked by the National Safety Council as the sixth leading cause of accidental death in the United States. Thousands of Americans die each year when they choke to death on a piece of meat, as did the young father in Great Falls, Montana. "Alcohol is the main culprit," says R. K. Haugen, a Florida pathologist who has researched the phenomenon for more than a decade. "These people often don't realize quite what they're doing and they don't bother to cut their meat into small pieces."

Alcohol is also the main culprit in a wide spectrum of nonviolent "criminal" behavior. In fact, nearly half of the 5.5 million arrests yearly in America are directly related to the effects of alcohol. Specifically, drunkenness accounts for some 1,400,000 arrests, while "disorderly conduct" and "vagrancy"—(euphemisms, in many communities, for the public drunkenness charge)—account for another 665,000. Intoxicated drivers make up the remaining 335,000 arrests.

Actually, the numbers add up to *more* than half of America's 5.5 million total annual arrests. The reason is that they reflect the "revolving door" procedure found in most communities, whereby homeless alcoholics are arrested, jailed, released, and arrested again, until many actually die.

An example of this syndrome occurred on September 12, 1969, in Seattle, when sixty-five-year-old Wayne Jacob Hill was unceremoniously dumped into the receiving cell of the city jail.

Known as the "test case drunk," Hill had spent a long time arguing that alcoholism is a sickness. Earlier in 1969, at an alcoholism treatment center in southern King County, the diagnosis of Hill's condition left little hope for recovery; tests revealed severe organic brain damage brought about by twenty-five years of heavy drinking.

Wayne Hill made a final point on the subject at 6 A.M. on September 12, when he died in his sleep in the receiving cell. The next arrest would have been his one hundred and fifty-fifth.

No less tragic and all the more ironic is the fact that such arrests, trials, and detention cost American taxpayers an estimated $100 million annually—an amount almost six times greater than the total 1970 budget for federal alcoholism programs.

One steamy June afternoon in Manhattan, John Vairo eased a mud-spattered green Plymouth from its parking space on East Third Street near Second Avenue. As he moved into traffic, Vairo became uncomfortably aware that the car's back seat was soiled with human excrement; he angled the vent window so that air blew directly across his face. It was Vairo's third run of the day, cruising Bowery side streets in search of comatose alcoholics urgently requiring medical assistance.

A New York City policeman, John Vairo is assigned to the Manhattan Bowery Project's rescue squad. Weekdays, he is accompanied by a recovered alcoholic "civilian"; each Saturday, lacking staff, thirty-six-year-old Vairo handles the job himself.

The unmarked patrol car moved slowly through Hester Street, tires crunching glass fragments. In doorway after familiar shadowed doorway, squalid forms were slumped. Outside the 101 Bar, the Bowery East, and the Uncle Sam flophouse, dozens of men, some unconscious, lay sprawled on the hot sidewalk. Occasionally a voice croaked a greeting to plainclothesman Vairo. He responded each time, usually addressing the man by name; after more than three years on the Ninth Precinct rescue squad detail, he knows most of them.

"Howya doing, David?" David, a Juilliard graduate and onetime concert pianist, lurched toward the Plymouth, and Vairo scanned his face and body for visible damage: bleeding, broken bones. Only three beds remaining tonight, Vairo remembered; no, he decided, David isn't ready.

Soon another man staggered to the car. Unable to speak, the derelict motioned violently toward a hallway. Vairo set the parking brake and walked quickly to what looked like a pile of filthy clothing. Gently, he shook the limp form. The man's body jerked and rolled away in panic. The face turned upward finally, one eye blinking wildly at the bright sunlight. The other eye was half out of its socket and crusted. Vairo noticed, too, that the man's shirt was stiff with dried blood, his pants damp with excrement and possibly more blood.

"What happened, Mr. Hansen?" Vairo asked, propping the man against a wall. "Do you recognize me, Mr. Hansen? This is John. Do you want to go to the Fourth Floor, to detox? You remember the Fourth Floor? Your *eye,* Mr. Hansen . . ."

Hansen received emergency medical treatment at the Manhattan Bowery Project's fourth floor acute ward, was bathed, deloused, and, that same evening, transported to St. Vincent's Hospital for eye surgery. Chances are, at this writing, he has returned to the streets and doorways of New York's lower East Side. Even more likely, he is dead.

"This is strictly a lifesaving operation," a Manhattan Bowery Project nurse told me, gesturing outward from the nurses' station to the twenty-eight-bed acute ward on that "Fourth Floor" at 8 East Third Street. "These are men in the final stages of a terminal disease." The young nurse, herself a recovered alcoholic, added quietly, "We don't even talk about recovery rates, because most of these men won't make it. In this place, numbers don't mean a damned thing.''

There is no denying the bitter truth of that rueful last remark. Yet paradoxically, as that MBP nurse is the first to admit, *one* skid row–related number should be of quintessential importance to every American affected directly or indirectly by alcoholism. And that is the fact that skid row alcoholics, although perhaps most visible, comprise fewer than 5 percent of *all* alcoholics. The other 95 percent can be found in every walk of life, since the illness is not the least bit respectful of color, sex, economic status, profession, or any other demographic or sociological codification.

Indeed, most alcoholics are employed or employable family-oriented people. Their numbers range into the millions— somewhere between 15 and 20 million, it is estimated. The overwhelming majority of them live in respectable neighborhoods, send their kids to school, belong to clubs and attend church, pay taxes, and continue to function—more or less effectively—as industrial workers, homemakers, business people, executives, editors, actors, salespersons, farmers, office workers, teachers, clergymen, lawyers, physicians, and judges. From that standpoint, as another recovered alcoholic wryly puts it, ''Skid row is between the ears.''

That may well be. Yet even as the highly visible skid row alcoholic spirals downward toward a seemingly inevitable death, he becomes a beautifully convenient foil—the Great American Cop-Out, if you will—for the other 95 percent. Pointing figuratively (and sometimes literally) to the limp derelict on New York's Bowery, Seattle's Pike Street, or Oklahoma City's Reno Street, the other 95 percent will articulate words or thoughts to this effect: *''That's* the alcoholic. That's not *me*. I have a house, a car, a family, a job . . .''

It was snowing heavily in Chicago early one Monday morning as crane operator Bill Partee backed his van into a parking place outside the sprawling auto assembly plant where he had worked for nine years. Partee remembered little of his weekend binge, save for the fact that he had not been home since Friday morning. Red-eyed and exhausted, he reached under the front seat for the pint of vodka that would relieve his hangover and quiet his shakes. He swallowed deeply, glancing absently at the rearview mirror. A stream of first-shift workers began to straggle slowly toward the plant's main gate. Partee leaned back and took another swallow, beginning to relax. At 6:50 A.M., the plant whistle blared its ten-minute warning, jarring him from his reverie. Time enough to finish the pint, Partee reasoned, vaguely wondering if he would have any trouble getting past the guard this time.

At 8:17 A.M., disoriented and perspiring profusely as he sat in the movable crane cab high above the metal-stamping department, Bill Partee pulled the wrong lever. Three tons of coiled steel crashed downward, slamming into a giant hydraulic press and crushing two young workers to death.

Although the crane operator's name is fictitious, the incident is real—horrifyingly real and all too common. Accidents such as this and alcoholic employees like Bill Partee cost American industry an awesome $15 billion a year—an amount more than sufficient to provide a free, brand-new Ford Maverick to each of Partee's 3.3 million neighbors in Chicago.

However, on-the-job accidents, like drunk-driving fatalities, comprise but the visible tip of the industrial alcoholism iceberg. Less obtrusive but hardly less damaging are such alcohol-related problems as absenteeism and tardiness, reduced productivity, sick leave, inefficiency, friction with co-workers, lowered morale, ruinous executive decisions, and poor customer and public relations—not to mention the loss of valuable employees and the enormous expense of training new employees.

It is estimated that one out of ten employees in private industry is an alcoholic. In the case of General Motors Corporation, for example, simple calculation makes it quickly evident that some 55,000 of GM's 550,000 United States employees are alcoholic. Clearly, business and industry have a tremendous stake in the "alcohol problem"; one can hardly imagine anyone in business disagreeing with the premise that programs to help alcoholic employees are just good business.

Fortunately for General Motors and those extrapolatory

55,000 employees, that giant corporation is meeting the problem head on these days. In June 1972, after many false starts, GM finally implemented a workable program offering sick employees treatment through its Employee Alcoholism Recovery Program.

Indeed, business in general is beginning to learn that a pragmatic, carrot-and-stick approach—with performance as the index and job security as the goad—can result in long-term recovery rates exceeding 70 and sometimes 80 percent. A major California oil corporation, for example, requires alcoholics to enter its twenty-one-day treatment program—or be fired; effective in eight out of ten cases, the program has saved hundreds of thousands of dollars in lost work time. Illinois Bell, similarly, estimates that in five years it saved $459,000 in wages through its treatment program for alcoholic employees. The savings were figured as the product of a decrease in sick leave for 402 employees after they underwent rehabilitation.

The large fly in the ointment, unfortunately, is that such success stories are the *exception* rather than the rule in America today—despite the proven fact that an employer can generally save an estimated $10 in losses for every $1 he invests in an alcoholism program.

There are more than 1.5 million corporations in the United States, yet fewer than five hundred—less than one-hundredth of 1 percent—have *any* sort of alcoholism programs. Worse yet, the majority of existing programs tend to exist on paper alone; the woeful fact is that only a few dozen American corporations have instituted truly meaningful alcoholism programs.

On a day-to-day basis, consequently, during this juncture of the mid-1970s, the unwritten policy of most U.S. firms goes something like this: "This company will pay a high economic premium in lost time and accidents to conceal alcoholism from the attention of labor and management. When alcoholism reaches the stage where it can no longer be concealed, the employee will be fired."

In a Baltimore classroom one December afternoon, public school teacher Mary Spencer drew the window shades, hushed her two dozen students, and flicked the start switch on a motion-picture projector. She sat back expectantly, wondering how her fourth-graders would react to the unusual film she had chosen impulsively from the catalogue. "It was Christmas, and I was looking under the 'A's for a film on Austria and 'Silent Night,' " recalls Mrs. Spencer, a recovered alcoholic who today is program director of the Washington Area Council on Alcoholism and Drug Abuse. "I suddenly saw the heading 'Alcoholism' and, needless to say, I decided that 'Silent Night' could wait."

No sooner had the film ended than an eight-year-old boy walked quickly to the teacher's desk. He pointed to a raw bald spot above his ear, explaining that it was the result of rubbing his knuckles against his head "most every night" when his alcoholic father and non-alcoholic mother "started fighting and screaming and throwing stuff."

The next morning, the same boy and his brother came to the front of the room. They opened their shirts to show Mrs. Spencer a grouping of welt marks; in a drunken rage, their father had beaten them with his belt buckle. During the classroom discussion that followed, still other youngsters vividly detailed not only physical abuse, but also severe emotional abuse received at the hands of drunken parents.

By her own description, Mary Spencer is hardly "thin-skinned," yet she almost fled from her own classroom that day. "It was like seeing the scars of some ghastly epidemic," she says, shaking her head at the memory.

In this instance, the greater tragedy is that yesterday's memory is indistinguishable from today's reality; the "ghastly epidemic" still rages unabated. The brothers with the welts and their bruised classmates have counterparts beyond number in every American city, for it is a well-documented fact that every alcoholic adversely affects at least four other persons, not the least of whom are America's "forgotten children."

In that sense, at least figuratively, the illness of alcoholism is virulently contagious; of all the illnesses which affect family life, none is more devastating than alcoholism. The steady sense of security, love, and warmth necessary for a child's adequate development is so often lacking in the alcoholic home that such children find it all but impossible to develop tools for successful living—trust and confidence in themselves and others.

If statistical evidence is needed, 30 to 40 percent of all delinquent youths come from homes where alcoholism exists—whether in Baltimore or Big Sur. Statistics aside, however, what is glaringly obvious is that alcohol-related child abuse in the United States is creating an ever-growing army of real-life little Harvey Wallbangers and Bloody Marys—traumatized children who, more often than perhaps the vodka advertising experts realize—do indeed become "breathless."

Not far from Houston's Astrodome, a thirteen-year-old girl is walking to school. Two blocks short of her destination, she ducks into an alley, looks quickly about, and reaches tremblingly into her lunch bag for a plastic container filled with vodka. Gagging at the first warm mouthful, she persists until she is able to swallow some of the clear liquid. She leans against the building and stands quietly for a moment, waiting for the warm glow to work downward. Then she tilts her head back, drinks deeply, drinks again, and finally puts the flask back into the bag.

She will drink half of the flask's remaining contents later, in the school washroom, finish the rest during lunch break, and, somehow, try to get through the day. She will repeat the ritual tomorrow and the next day, just as she has been repeating it since the start of school in September, for she has been addicted to alcohol since her eleventh birthday.

Incredible as this capsulized case history may appear, it is not at all unique. The Houston schoolgirl is but one of almost 750,000 American teen-agers and grade-school children who are actually hard-core alcoholics. And that huge number of alcohol-dependent children is rising ominously, creating a nationwide pattern that is almost surrealistic: pre-teens passing around dad's bourbon at slumber parties; children in school cafeterias spiking lunch milk with gin and Scotch from miniatures; hard-drinking pre-teens and teen-agers sharing bottles of heavily advertised 18-proof "pop" wines, chug-a-lugging such favorites as Red Rooster, Ripple, and Annie Green Springs during recess, at casual after-school gatherings, and in the bleachers at school sports events.

Clearly, alcohol has become the new drug of choice for American youth. The switch is on, partly because of alcohol's relative inexpensiveness, accessibility, and social acceptability; partly because of new state laws lowering the legal drinking age; and partly because of saturation TV advertising campaigns with calculated and obviously effective youth appeal—campaigns that skyrocketed "pop" wine consumption from $3 million worth in 1969 to a whopping $33 million worth in 1973.

Now that pop wines seem to have lost that once phenomenal appeal, young people are being wooed with what liquor industry officials call "moo-moos," alcoholic beverages not unlike milk shakes with a kick. These fast proliferating new concoctions—given such fanciful and innocuous-sounding names as Malcolm Hereford's Cows, Snowshake, Icebox, and Aberdeen Cows—combine some form of flavored milk with a substantial amount of grain neutral spirits; their alcohol content is 15 percent, compared with the 9 percent of pop wines.

The most important reason for the burgeoning and potentially catastrophic increase in youthful alcoholism, however, can be traced back to the parents themselves. Recent national surveys reveal that the vast majority of American parents mistakenly comfort themselves when their children switch from other drugs to alcohol, viewing the shift as a "healthy change." In fact, many parents are relieved when their children get "into booze" rather than "*real* drugs" from the start. Hence they often look the other way; to be sure, the parents themselves are usually drinkers, and, not infrequently, alcoholics.

The real-life typification of this prevailing social attitude is succinctly expressed in the words of another Houston youth: "It's like, your dad finds some condoms on your dresser and thinks, 'Wow, the kid's becoming a man; he's makin' out.' And when you come home drunk, it's the same thing: 'The kid's really growin' up, boozin' and all . . .' "

On Memorial Day 1974, in the sleepy waterfront town of Fort Walton Beach, Florida, Walter Wade and Eugene Cole agreed that a drinking contest was the manly way—indeed, the *only* way—to settle a heated dispute over their respective liquor capacities. The men had already been drinking when they asked bartender Claude Kidd to referee a "gin duel" in Kidd's bar after closing hours.

The mood was convivial as the men downed drink after drink, keeping "even." The watchword was "cheers" as fifty-two-year-old Kidd doubled in brass, keeping score and providing refills with alacrity. Finally, when neither Wade nor Cole could drink any more, the contest was called off. Each man had consumed between thirty-two and forty-eight ounces of gin in less than an hour.

Early the next morning, thirty-two-year-old Cole was found unconscious on a street near his home and booked on a public drunkenness charge. He died in jail. Wade, thirty-nine, died the following day in the intensive-care unit of a local hospital. Three days later, bartender Claude Kidd died of a heart attack, apparently brought on by grief. "It came as a shock to him when he heard the news," said Kidd's widow, Catherine. "He couldn't hardly believe it."

For all its disastrous ramifications, the Fort Walton Beach "gin duel" is hardly unusual. Not a month passes during which similar incidents do not occur in one city or another across the United States. In October 1975, twenty-three-year-old John Davies drank himself to death during a period of thirty minutes. The occasion was an initiation ceremony for the Sundowners, a social drinking club of male students at the University of Nevada.

What *is* surprising—considering that alcoholic beverages have been made and consumed by nearly every people on earth since prehistoric times—is how many experienced drinkers are relatively ignorant of alcohol's nature and effects. In that respect, one is saddened not only by the waste of three lives in a western Florida beach town, but by the poignant admission that even a professional bartender could have been unaware of the drug's potentially lethal effects. As Catherine Kidd put it, "Claude couldn't see how they could have died just from what they had in his place."

The point is, of course, that although alcohol is indisputably America's most widely used drug, it is also the least understood and, in the final analysis, most misrepresented. Because, for the most part, companies within the $30 billion-a-year alcoholic beverage industry sell *not* liquor, wine, and beer, but, far more palatably, the siren songs of sexuality, status, happiness, and self-confidence. The advertising images are familiar: gleaming sports cars; dashing young men inches away from lovely, soon-to-be-seduced young women; mountain climbers; water skiers; gift-givers; and so on.

From that standpoint, one must view Walter Wade, Eugene Cole, and Claude Kidd as naïve victims of a spectrum of deeply rooted myths (the equation of heavy drinking with manliness, for example), perpetuated not only by society in general, but, in larger measure, by the alcoholic beverage industry quite specifically.

It is hardly likely that America's alcoholic beverage purveyors will ever show a sports car in flames after a drunk-driving fatality, or a less-than-alert mountain climber (hung over from celebrating yesterday's mountain) tumbling headlong to a new life as a paraplegic. It has been suggested, more realistically, that the liquor industry has a social responsibility to assure the non-destructive use of its product—just as the automobile industry has a responsibility to assure the safety of its automobiles.

For the sake of future "duelists," one can only hope that beverage alcohol labels and advertisements will at least be footnoted someday with such data as this: "Caution—high concentrations (0.30 percent or greater) of alcohol in the blood can lead to shock and death."

San Francisco was blanketed with fog early one summer morning in 1974 as an ambulance raced along the city's deserted waterfront. Siren wailing, the ambulance careened around a corner, skidding to a halt outside a hospital emergency entrance. "She's in labor!" the driver shouted to waiting orderlies. "And she's convulsing!" Inside the emergency room, a physician injected the pregnant woman with an anticonvulsant and quickly checked her vital signs. "Where'd you get her?" he asked, not waiting for a reply. "She's in DTs and she's in heavy labor. Up to OB, *fast!*"

Half an hour later, the woman gave birth to a baby boy, tiny and malformed. In his medical log, the doctor made note of the infant's incomplete eyelid folds, abnormally small head, and underdeveloped upper jaw. The doctor noted, too, that the infant had limited elbow motion, altered crease patterns in its palms, a heart abnormality, and what seemed to be impaired motor function.

Finishing his report, the doctor turned to the OB nurse. "I've read about malformations like this," he said quietly. "Ten to one the mother's a long-time drunk. Her liver is enlarged. And did you see her legs and fingers? The bruises and cigarette burns?"

That same month, three thousand miles cross-country in the uptown Manhattan office where he conducts a private practice, Dr. Nicholas Pace logged his diagnostic observations of a thirty-six-year-old male alcoholic. Pace, who is medical director of General Motors Corporation in New York City, spoke rapidly into a tape recorder, occasionally explaining technical terms for the benefit of a visiting journalist.

"The patient came up to the medical department of GM short of breath and with severe chest pain. My nurse called and said, 'I think a patient is having a heart attack.' I found this man with labored breathing, acute chest pain, and covered with beads of sweat. When we examined him, we found that he had fluid in his lungs, he had an enlarged liver, he had fluid in his belly, and he had three-plus pretibula edema, or fluid in his legs.

"On X Ray we saw a heart that covered the entire chest plate. The heart was huge. We made a diagnosis of beriberi heart disease with congestive heart failure. The patient gave me a history that he was not eating, and that he was drinking thirty-six cans of beer a day."

Bizarre as these separate occurrences may seem, they are neither unusual nor unrelated. Each reflects the fact that alcohol—taken in large doses over long periods of time—can prove disastrous, reducing both the quality and length of life. Prolonged heavy drinking adversely affects virtually every organ in the body; alcoholism is a known cause of death from liver damage, brain damage, and heart disease, and has been implicated as a causal factor in numerous other pathological disorders ranging from bleeding ulcers to hypoglycemia.

It has recently been determined, moreover, that maternal alcoholism can cause serious aberrant fetal development; researchers now say, in fact, that a "fetal alcohol syndrome" may be as compelling a reason for ending a pregnancy as better-known genetic defects.

Nor is that all. Although alcoholism, cirrhosis of the liver with alcoholism, or alcoholic psychosis are the stated causes of death on 11,000 death certificates annually, many times that number of other alcohol-related deaths go unrecorded. Cases in point, in every major metropolitan area, include those alcoholics who die as the result of exposure to the elements, those whose drunkenness masks the symptoms of natural diseases such as pneumonia and peptic ulcers until it is too late, and those who fall victim to what doctors now call the "sudden death" syndrome.

In the District of Columbia alone, such sudden deaths among post-binge alcoholics constitute at least 10 percent of the total case load of the Medical Examiner's Office, says Chief Medical Examiner James L. Luke. Dr. Luke, who shudders at the thought of extrapolating that staggering statistic nationally, is convinced that such deaths dwarf in numbers the combined aggregate of alcohol-related violent deaths. "The sad truth," he says, "is that precious little is understood, from a metabolic point of view, about the biochemical dynamics of fatalities of this sort."

What *is* understood—indisputably so, according to the American Hospital Association—is that 15 to 30 percent of all adult medical-surgical patients in metropolitan hospitals, *regardless of diagnosis,* suffer from alcoholism. Doctors at one such facility, Mount Zion Hospital in San Francisco, say that about 50 percent of all fracture cases result from drunkenness.

Yet, all of this appalling data notwithstanding, the supreme irony is that only recently has alcoholism begun to emerge— *barely* so—as a "respectable" illness. The average American physician invests upwards of eight to ten years in studying for his career, but seldom receives more than token exposure to the critical health problem of alcoholism. Especially revealing, in this connection, is the recent determination that the percentage of alcoholics among America's 356,000 physicians is conservatively estimated at an enormous 18 percent—three times the percentage of alcoholics found in the general population.

More often than not, physicians book alcoholism patients into hospitals under other diagnoses; indeed, until recently fewer than half of America's hospitals would *accept* a patient whose primary diagnosis is alcoholism. The point is angrily affirmed by San Francisco's Dr. Jack D. Gordon, who says, "I've actually heard fellow physicians shout at nurses, 'What's that drunk doing in this ward? These beds are for *sick* people!' " Consequently, adds Gordon, the patient had to be admitted for problems of heart, liver, lungs, or stomach. And in most communities, the alcoholic is *still* jailed without referral for treatment.

It is little wonder, then, that the "closet alcoholic" is no mere figure of speech in America; to this day there remains something abhorrent and disgraceful about alcoholism and its victims. Hence, in a very real and frightening sense, to be an alcoholic in America is not only to suffer from a potentially fatal illness, but to bear an often *un*bearable stigma. To be an alcoholic in America—or the spouse, child, relative, friend, employer, or employee of an alcoholic in America—is to be stigmatized.

And that stigma works in baffling and powerful ways. Within alcoholic individuals, for example, it fosters and nurtures *denial,* creating the paradox of a killer disease whose primary symptom is its victims' refusal to acknowledge their affliction.

On a broader scale, among the public at large, the stigma fosters and nurtures an attitudinal climate—affecting the citizen and legislator alike—that has relegated America's number-three killer and number-one health problem to the very lowest level among national health priorities.

Ostensibly, priorities are the name of the game in public health. Yet, according to the Department of Health, Education, and Welfare, alcoholism remains the nation's most neglected disease—despite the fact that alcoholism costs the nation upwards of $25 billion a year and continues to carve a pandemic swath of death, destruction, and misery across the entire mosaic of American life.

That, in essence, is the reason for this book. Clearly, it is a book about pain and pathos; more important, however, it is about courage, hard work—and hope. For the curtains have begun slowly to part on the pageant that is alcoholism in America. The spotlights have begun to pick faces and forms from the darkness. It is my earnest expectation that this book will further illuminate the vast stage.

A stigmatized "95-percenter," I, too, denied my alcoholism for a quarter of a century. I was convinced, as I pointed to my homeless, jobless brethren in doorways or vacant lots, that *"there's* the alcoholic; that's not me."

At the end of that quarter of a century, in 1970, a more plaintive phrase echoed across the vacant lot of my own soul. My illness had progressed rapidly into its acute stage; that year, I almost died of my alcoholism. Only then could I concede my powerlessness over alcohol. I have not found it necessary to take a drink since.

I began this book in the third year of my sobriety, during Cherry Blossom Week in Washington, D.C. It was a time of renewal and budding, which seemed especially appropriate for a fast-blooming three-year-old. It was also the time of the National Council on Alcoholism's annual meeting, in the cavernous Shoreham Hotel. There, tape recorder at the ready, I haunted meeting rooms and waylaid scores of other recovering alcoholics who would help me chart the pathways of my journey.

At week's end, I trailed NCA founder Mrs. Marty Mann to her New York office on lower Park Avenue. She told me about her personal recovery, sharing her own unique and insightful view of alcoholism in our nation. She also helped me plot the first leg of what eventually would become a 75,000-mile hopscotch odyssey across the length and breadth of America.

As I said goodbye that day, Marty scribbled the word "HALT" on a slip of notepaper, reminding me that as recovering alcoholics we should never get too *H*ungry, too *A*ngry, too *L*onely, or too *T*ired.

In the months and miles that were to follow, I would become all of those things. Prowling the streets of New York's Bowery, I became *A*ngry that very afternoon. I was to become even angrier during the next several months, on other streets across America.

In time, however, that anger was assuaged, giving way eventually to understanding and hopefulness. The process began in a tiny, twelve-bed skid row detoxification center named, portentously for me, Starting Point. And the process is continuing.

2

Skid Row:
Myths and Realities

I am weary of this torment—
Can there be no peace—
And I find myself just wishing—
That my life would simply cease—

I found this poem on a graffiti-festooned wall in Philadelphia's Intermediate House, a transitional facility for skid row alcoholics. The lines rang personal bells for me, as they would, I suspect, for other sober alcoholics unable—or unwilling—to forget what it used to be like. They rang the same bells for Bill, a recovering alcoholic who is resident manager of Intermediate House. "I don't know who put it there," he said, shrugging, as he squinted at the words and crayoned drawing. "I don't know if it was a man, woman, or what, or how long it's been up there. It's just there."

Bill wondered aloud if the anonymous artist's wish had been granted. If I put the poem in this book, he suggested, maybe someday the person would read it and get in touch with me. That would be good, we agreed.

In a Detroit detoxification center, I picked up an orange-bordered wallet card which reads: "TO WHOM IT MAY CONCERN: I am on ANTABUSE (disulfiram) therapy. If I am disoriented, too ill to give a history, or unconscious, I may be having a serious ANTABUSE (disulfiram)-alcohol reaction. *Do not administer alcohol, paraldehyde, or any mixture with an alcohol content.*"

Outside the fourth-floor shower room of New York's Manhattan Bowery Project, similarly, I pocketed the small-print instruction sheet for A-200 Pyrinate Liquid, a malodorous medicament used to kill crab, head, and body lice and their eggs. Held close to my nose, the paper brings back scenes and sounds; it brings back the sight of a medical aide helping to delouse a newly admitted and still intoxicated patient, getting sopping wet in the process, and shouting repeatedly, ''Jesus, man, be careful of your eyes!''

The memory evoked by the instruction sheet's faint aroma is, of course, far more gut-wrenching than the coolly descriptive words themselves: ''BODY LOUSE (fig. B). Usually body lice are somewhat larger than head lice but have a similar general appearance. They lay a great many eggs. Two female lice, in one experiment, produced ninety eggs in six days, all of which hatched in from five to ten more days, and these were soon ready to start their own breeding cycles.''

Some weeks later in Washington, D.C., I ferreted through dusty files for very specific memorabilia. In a basement room at 1330 New Hampshire Avenue, N.W., in the offices of the Washington Area Council on Alcoholism and Drug Abuse (WACADA), I found some faded hospital bills for a homeless alcoholic named DeWitt Clinton Easter. The bills, dated December 1965 and January 1966, were from D.C. General Hospital. They showed that DeWitt Easter had been admitted, released, readmitted and released—over and over again—from the hospital's psychiatric unit, at a charge of $34.75 per day; one bill, for seven days in January, totaled $243.25.

There was a sense of history in those bills, letters, and receipts; later in 1966, DeWitt Clinton Easter—''a white male, age 44, Presbyterian''—had become the victorious plaintiff in a landmark Federal Appeals Court decision (*Easter* v. *District of Columbia*). The decision (along with another—*Driver* v. *Hinnant*) held that conviction of alcoholics on charges of public drunkenness was tantamount to convicting sick persons for displaying symptoms of a disease, and consequently unconstitutional.

Before the 1966 decisions, DeWitt Easter had been arrested more than seventy times since 1937 for public intoxication or other minor violations directly attributable to his alcoholism. Joe Driver's record showed over two hundred arrests; for nothing more than public intoxication, he had spent two-thirds of his adult life in jail.

In subsequent years, a flurry of other legal developments has followed: criminal cases; civil cases; U.S. Crime Commission reports; state intoxication and alcoholism legislation; model and uniform legislation; and, finally, federal legislation—including the Comprehensive Alcohol Abuse and Alcoholism Prevention, Treatment, and Rehabilitation Act of 1970 and its 1974 amendments.

Teeth-rattling headings to the contrary, the majority of that legislation has focused and continues to focus on the so-called "public inebriate"—derelict habitués of the skid rows that blight most American cities. The primary thrust of most of the legislation, in turn, is refinement of the dictum originally established in the Easter case, whereby the disease of alcoholism was officially "decriminalized."

However, as recently as 1971—a full five years after the historic Easter decision—then U.S. Attorney General John N. Mitchell was forced to admit, "In all but a few of the states in the Union, public drunkenness is an offense punishable by a fine or jail sentence or both. In other words, our knowledge in the field far surpasses our action." At this writing, moreover, a paltry sixteen of the nation's fifty states have enacted legislation which would, in fact, provide alternatives to jail for homeless alcoholics arrested for public drunkenness.

In short, little has changed for the residents of America's skid rows. A visit to Philadelphia's Fourth Street, Los Angeles' Main Street, or Dubuque's Front Street provides graphic and ample affirmation of that lack of change.

One of the things that *have* changed is that the "public inebriate" has recently been "discovered" by the intellectual research community—by sociologists, statisticians, urban planners, environmentalists, and other multi-degreed academicians intent on regaling their peers with jargon-sprinkled dissertations on the skid row "way of life." Not surprisingly, such studies tend to be created—and consumed—within the bloodless confines of government-funded think tanks; to be generous, they offer little of pragmatic value.

Here, for example, is a key conclusion of one such study, published early in 1974: "Full entrance into the skid row world implies that the skid row way of life has been fully embraced and a former lifestyle and commitments entirely eschewed in its favor. While unintelligible to those of us who are still in the mainstream of American society, the skid row way of life facilitates regular social participation and permits meaningful interaction among those confronted with similar problems."

What has also changed, far more significantly, is that the "public inebriate" has become a national political football of sorts. Several years ago in Dallas, for example, a revised city charter at long last authorized funds for decriminalizing alcoholism and treating indigent alcoholics. In fairness to "Big D," a few programs have since been developed; as the city fathers grudgingly admit, however, Dallas has yet to come to grips with the problem in a comprehensive and meaningful manner.

True, the political gears finally began to mesh when federal funding became available in 1970. Even then, it took Dallas a long four years merely to organize a consortium of public and private agencies. In 1974, after countless meetings, the consortium itself eventually managed to obtain funds from the Texas Commission on Alcoholism.

The funds, however, were not to treat alcoholics, but to finance the preparation of a $1 million grant proposal to the National Institute on Alcohol Abuse and Alcoholism (NIAAA) of the Department of Health, Education, and Welfare. Assuming that the grant will be approved, only then will contracts be negotiated with various agencies for counseling and treatment programs in Dallas.

In the meantime, moans Police Chief Don Byrd, 50 percent of all Dallas police hours are still spent on public drunks. In 1973 alone, it cost Dallas some $600,000 for the arrest-trial-jail sequence—more than half of the amount being sought in the grant proposal to NIAAA.

Nor does Dallas stand alone in this regard. In Colorado, similarly, a new law calling for comprehensive treatment for alcoholism went into effect in July 1974—without sufficient funds. The legislature funded only $545,000 of a program that had planned to spend $7 million in the state. As a result, police departments around the state have instructed patrolmen to continue to deliver "public inebriates" to the drunk tank, just as before. The only difference is that when policemen pick up drunks on the street and deliver them to jail, the formal booking process is omitted. The drunks are allowed to sober up in jail and walk away the next day without a police record—and with no counseling or other assistance for their drinking problems.

Even in Washington, D.C., where the DeWitt Easter case was initiated and won, the skid row alcoholic remains lost in a morass of legislative and political wrangling. Recently, for example, WACADA has gone back to court with a suit demanding implementation of the District's 1967 Alcoholic Rehabilitation Act, which required alternative facilities for alcoholics other than jail and the work farm.

In preparing the suit, WACADA representatives visited the District's primary alcoholism treatment facility—Rehabilitation Center for Alcoholics (RCA), in Occoquan, Virginia. They were shocked, as I was, first, by the fact that the facility—formerly used as a workhouse—is still physically attached to adjacent Lorton Penitentiary. It is impossible to determine when one has passsed through the hospital-prison boundary, descending in status, as it were, from patient to prisoner; the gate between the minimum security wing of Lorton and the RCA buildings remains open, and the view is dominated by a prison patrol tower complete with uniformed, armed guard.

No less chilling is the realization that "talking" appears to be systematically forbidden throughout the facility; from the doorway to the women's residence, for example, one is greeted by a large warning sign: "NO VISITING ON THE WALKWAYS."

Perhaps most disturbing, says WACADA's Eleanor Edelstein, is the RCA edict, "If a patient on pass has a drink, she must be kicked out of RCA and cannot return for ninety days." In reality, argues Mrs. Edelstein, the patient is still being punished for exhibiting symptoms of the illness for which she is being treated. "When," she asks rhetorically, "does alcoholism cease to be a crime in practice as well as in theory?"

The same point was angrily made by Jack Roak, the late embattled alcoholism program director of Philadelphia's Diagnostic and Rehabilitation Center, a treatment and referral service for that city's skid row alcoholics. Roak, himself a recovered skid row alcoholic, doubted that skid row habitués seeking help are even considered "patients" in most American cities.

"Alcoholism is just a bit more socially acceptable than heroin addiction, but not a hell of a lot," Roak told me. "Can you imagine a cancer patient, reporting to radiology for cobalt treatment, and the doctor saying, 'I'm sorry, I'm not going to see you, you missed an appointment last week.'? But they can tell a guy who has alcoholism, and is on public assistance, and being treated by virtue of medical assistance, 'I'm sorry, you have to leave the hospital today, the state says you should be well.' "

The American skid row alcoholic as "non-patient" and political football was revealed to me most clearly in the state of Washington and, most particularly, in Seattle. It was in Seattle, incidentally, that the phrase "skid row" originated, derived from the Skid Road down which freshly hewn logs were sent hurtling into Puget Sound. Noted for its ubiquitous Boeing factories, overcast skies, and now fading frontier spirit, Seattle today provides a sharply microcosmic view of the social attitude described by Eleanor Edelstein and Jack Roak, along with correlative political realities throughout the Evergreen State.

The primary political reality in any American city or state is, of course, the Almighty Dollar. And, as often as not, availability of that Dollar seems to create as much political dissension as its *un*availability. That point was emphasized to me repeatedly in Seattle, at all levels in the city and county alcoholism field. "There's nothing quite like money to attract all the crumbs in the world," said Jim Heath, executive director of the Seattle–King County Commission on Alcoholism. "Jesus, they just crawl out from under rocks."

Heath was my first contact in Seattle. We sat together in a park late one afternoon, both of us recovered alcoholics. He laughed as he described the community's reaction to a recently awarded $1.7 million alcoholism grant—the largest such grant ever received in Seattle–King County. ''It was like throwing one thousand-dollar bill out between two brothers. All of a sudden, they're not all that close. Even the people who are friends began to fall apart, and it was really unnerving to watch. It's still going on,'' Heath continued, ''and it's really, really bad.''

We sat quietly for a moment, watching two old men pass a bottle of muscatel wine back and forth. Nodding in their direction, Heath said, ''The idea of the grant was to bring the community together in open forum and say, 'Here, gentlemen, here's a pie, and let's cut it up in such a way that we do the best for the suffering alcoholic.' '' Laughing once again, so loudly that he startled the two old men, Jim Heath concluded, ''Well, the person that really thinks that way gets run over in the stampede.''

Several days later, high above Pioneer Square in Seattle's venerable Smith Tower, I talked with another young recovered alcoholic—Charles Kester, head of Seattle–King County's Central Alcoholism Agency. Even with the new money, Kester said sardonically, ''the jackpot is, what the hell do we do with these skid row guys after we dry them out?''

I asked Kester to be specific, and he elaborated, ''We've got a lot of treatment programs around here, but they're a disaster, because guys are coming and going, and in all but one they're not really getting any treatment.''

''Why?'' I pursued. ''Why the hell are the programs so ineffective?''

''Because they don't get paid anything for the alky,'' Kester answered. ''They get paid about $140 a month to keep an alky in treatment by public assistance, and they can't make it on that money.''

Still later that week, I spent the better part of a day at Seattle's Pioneer Alcohol Intoxication Dryout (AID) Center, a fifty-bed facility beset by licensing problems, financial problems, and, again, old-fashioned political controversy. Seated in a circle with director Norman Chamberlain, AID's chief of medical services, and a sociologist, Barbara Gust, I listened while they explored the absurd actualities of skid row alcoholism in Seattle.

"We're under pressure to get the guys out of the drunk tank," they said almost in unison, "but we don't get the money. To get the guys into treatment certainly requires a lot longer than two days, but if we keep them here more than two days, the drunk tank fills up."

Chamberlain pointed out that even if Pioneer's fifty beds were "turned over" every forty-eight hours, the facility could theoretically handle only about 7,000 skid row alcoholics a year, not counting repeaters as new cases. "There are approximately 11,000 arrests in Seattle each year for public inebriation," Chamberlain continued, "so *mathematically* we can take care of 60 percent of the problem. We need half again as many beds to handle the drunk tank alone."

The result of such pressure, naturally, is that most skid row alcoholics admitted to Pioneer are merely detoxified and then sent back out to the street. A system of convalescent aftercare is virtually nonexistent, hence the so-called recidivism rate (a term more properly applied to criminals than to hospital patients) is astronomical.

Obviously, in that connection, it does little good to remove alcoholism from the purview of the law if you do not substitute a full-dress medical treatment—not only a detoxification process, but a thoroughgoing program aimed at long-term recovery from the illness.

The longer we talked that day, the more acrimonious the discussion became. "We're fighting the legislators all the time," the doctor said bitterly. "The thing is, we're not going to do anything until we change our attitudes. We treat the indigent alcoholic like dirt, and we set our expectations within that realm. So it comes down to zero expectations as far as he's concerned."

"What is it worth to treat the indigent?" Barbara Gust interrupted sharply. "They want to do it cheaper, so they can do *more*. One of the attitudes is, 'Let's get the human garbage off the street.' But indigents are as deserving of hospitalizing as the middle-class patient."

Apparently Washington's legislators think otherwise. A 1972 Washington law "decriminalized" drunkenness, directing cities and counties to devote 2 percent of their share of the state liquor tax to pay for treatment of "revolving door drunks" at detoxification centers. Late in 1973, however, the state legislature passed a delaying bill enabling police to continue throwing skid row drunks into jail, instead of taking them to centers such as Pioneer.

The delaying bill was sponsored by Senators Sam Guess (Rep.) and James Keefe (Dem.), both of Spokane, and Perry Woodall (Rep.) of Toppenish, and was unabashedly designed to pacify Spokane boosters who didn't want drunks cluttering up the city sidewalks during Expo '74. "Expo is right across the street from Skid Road, and we don't want drunks lying in the street," Representative William May (Rep., Spokane) told the House Social and Health Services Committee.

Since tourism is akin to motherhood in the minds of most legislators, and since the sidewalk drunk is *not* a tourist attraction, Washington's state legislature was easily persuaded.

Inevitably, of course, the long-term consequences of such misplaced priorities—in the state of Washington or anywhere else—are that America's skid row jungles will fester and abide long after Expo '74's exhibitors' booths and popcorn stands are stale memories.

For most of us, skid row existence is limited to fleeting impressions of a tottering panhandler smearing our windshield as we pause at a traffic signal; of a prostrate form seen briefly from a passing train; of an alien face observed through the mesh windows of a police van.

The reality of life on America's skid rows is another matter entirely. At best, it is stark and dehumanizing; at worst, it is brutal and, ultimately, deadly. In all respects, it is virtually indescribable and, for most of us, incomprehensible.

I remember, in July 1973, walking through what I then thought was the downtown section of Stockton, California, sidestepping and literally tripping over more drunks than I have ever seen in one area, let alone a single city. I later learned that today's downtown Stockton is miles northward of its rotting former self; city officials apparently decided that if they ignored the fast-spreading decay, the blighted "old" city center would putrefy away into nothingness. As in Spokane, however, the blight abides.

Bordering Market Street are the parks of old Stockton, acre after barren acre where no children romp and no grass grows. That day, those acres were dotted with the slumped and comatose forms of men and women; most of them were alive, I guessed, because there was some stirring and lurching. I recall, too, that twice each day those littered acres seemed to burst into flame; at daybreak and just before twilight, California sunshine angles across Market Street, reflecting the glare of hundreds of wine jugs, thousands upon thousands of iridescent shards of white and green bottle glass.

However, to walk through America's skid rows even as a concerned journalist is still to be merely an observer. The true horror is to be on the inside looking out: to be infested with lice most of the year; to scrape and grub for alcohol and, less frequently, food and shelter and cast-off clothing; to fend off violence and homosexual assaults; to develop ulcerations and pneumonia and tuberculosis; to be jailed and released and jailed again; to be preyed upon and exploited unendingly even as the progression of alcoholism brings you ever closer to the gates of insanity and death.

To be on the inside looking out is not only to exist in a world beyond the ken of most Americans, but to use an esoteric language whose key words bespeak little else than fear, violence, and desperation.

In the morning, craving the alcohol that will delay your convulsion and perhaps quiet your tremors, you might squat cross-legged with several others, blocking sidewalk traffic while urging passersby to drop a coin into your *Frisco circle*. During the day, you will be wary of *jackrollers* intent on stealing your jug or money, assaulting your body, or stealing your shoes. Fleeing a jackroller, you may trip, *take a header,* and break your leg or arm or nose. At night, if you have a spare dollar or so, you will *flop* in a tiny triangular cubicle, hopefully oblivious of roaches, rats, and nocturnal jackrollers. If you don't have the *freight* for a flop, you will *carry the banner*—sleeping in a doorway, an alley, an abandoned truck, or a piano crate.

On Sunday or after hours, if the bars and liquor stores are closed, you may search out a *Doctor* who will sell you an eighty-cent pint of wine for $1.50. If you are fairly alert, you will try to make certain that the jug seal is intact, and that the wine has not been diluted with water.

And if you stay on skid row long enough, you will become *mokus*. Then, myths of skid row camaraderie notwithstanding, your drinking buddies will avoid you like the plague, sharing neither cigarettes nor jug nor the time of day. You will be disoriented and unable to speak or even walk; if you do not receive prompt and effective medical attention, you may die.

Today, the odds are that you *will* die. As already indicated, neither erudite dissertations on the skid row way of life, nor legislative decriminalization of public drunkenness—nor even greatly increased public funding for public inebriate treatment programs—has served to substantially change the conditions of skid row existence, or to alter the dismal prognosis for most skid row alcoholics.

In city after American city, even within the sixteen states which have enacted new legislation, revolving-door jail procedures all too frequently give way to revolving-door detoxification center procedures. Additionally, many skid row treatment programs rely heavily on tranquilization—in effect substituting one drug dependency for another—a practice which often compounds the problem by creating a dual addiction.

In sum, the prospects for America's skid row residents seem not much brighter than during pre–Revolutionary War days, when (in Massachusetts Bay Colony and Virginia, for example) public drunkenness was punished by whipping, fines, and confinement in the stocks.

If blame is to be placed, it surely must be shared by most Americans—including, in particular, sizable segments of the legal and medical professions—in short, by all who still look upon the skid row alcoholic as "helpless, hopeless," and worthy only of sympathy. "Sympathy?" bristles one former skid row dweller. "Look it up in the dictionary. You'll find it between 'shit' and 'syphilis.' "

The point is, as we shall see, skid row alcoholics can and *do*

recover. The very concept of "helplessness" and "hopelessness" is but another page in the mythology of alcoholism; indeed, nothing could be further from the truth. In the first place,
the very basis of the decision in the Easter case is that the ill individual is unable to control his behavior even when temporarily
sober; to expect him to voluntarily seek treatment is absurd.

Moreover, as any first-year med student knows, to provide
care only when the patient is in immediate danger to himself or
the community is the poorest medical practice possible, for it
allows the patient to deteriorate physically and mentally long
before he—or she—enters the treatment process. Finally, the
medical profession has a responsibility to treat alcoholism, rather
than to treat only illnesses for which clear-cut procedures exist.

Almost a decade ago, Dr. Paul Travis, direction of the newly
established Rehabilitation Center for Alcoholics in Washington,
D.C., warned his fellow physicians and psychiatrists, "Those
people involved in the treatment process must overcome their
aversion to the initial resentment and hostility expressed by the
newly committed patient. They must also come to accept the fact
that motivation is the responsibility of the treatment process, and
not a prerequisite to therapy."

Foreseeing the hard battle ahead, Travis further cautioned,
"The staff must learn to accept alcoholism as an illness with
recidivism being the rule rather than the exception. Many times,
staff members fail to set limits in their relationships with the patient and end up with the 'I worked so hard and he let me down'
syndrome."

Still, there is an iconoclastic, outspoken new alliance of medical professionals and paraprofessional recovering alcoholics.
One of those people is Dr. Robert G. O'Briant, youthful director
of the Alcoholism Rehabilitation Center of San Francisco's Garden Hospital Jerd Sullivan Rehabilitation Center. A charismatic,
intense man with boyish good looks, O'Briant wastes little time
in letting visitors know where he stands. No sooner had we
shaken hands than he gestured to a series of grim photographs
lining the walls of his office.

I peered closely at three large photos, each of a man chained
to a metal-framed hospital bed. The faces of the men were gaunt

and deeply lined, their bodies wasted. "Each of those men suffered from the disease of alcoholism, and they were put in chains," O'Briant said with quiet fury.

"When?" I asked.

"In 1971. In a hospital in the United States of America," he answered, turning away. "They're all dead now," he added almost inaudibly. "They died of alcoholism."

On another wall a plaque read: "Robert G. O'Briant, M.D., is hereby awarded the title of HONORARY ALCOHOLIC for his dedication, enthusiasm, and zealous efforts in the formation and advancement of Project F.A.I.T.H., a program for the recovery of alcoholics. October 11, 1970."

We took time out while O'Briant discussed "sleep disturbances" with a group of new and still shaky private patients, then returned to his office and talked for several hours about his successful experiences with skid row alcoholics in Stockton and in another facility farther north. At the end, he gazed into my eyes and said levelly, "There's *no such thing* as a helpless, hopeless alcoholic."

I knew that, of course, but my personal knowledge was beside the point. The point seemed to be the urgency with which O'Briant insisted that I drive up to Stockton. There, I would meet with three recovered skid row alcoholics, now employed as alcoholism counselors, whom he had treated just a few years earlier.

Dr. O'Briant's name was sheer magic when mentioned to Jim Hedger. At Stockton's Town House Motel, Hedger and I ritualistically exchanged before-and-after photos; my own photo on an out-of-date driver's license, revealing unmistakably in bloated cheeks and despairing eyes what it used to be like for me; Hedger's two color photos, taken twenty-five days apart at Bret Harte Hospital, Dr. O'Briant's pilot alcoholism treatment facility about seventy miles north of Stockton. "They took your picture when you got there, then they took another the day you left," Hedger said. "Like I was there twenty-five days, and goddamn, what a difference!"

In his early fifties, Jim Hedger is a short and wiry man with calloused hands from "fruit tramping, carrying hod, longshoring, you name it.'' He was born in Missouri, in the small, hard-shell Baptist farm community of Slater. He drank hard for thirty-five years, got drunk every single time he drank, and went directly to skid row when he was kicked out of the army in 1948.

Hedger recounted the physiological and emotional deterioration that had taken place, from the early days in the Civilian Conservation Corps to the last years on skid rows all across the United States. In the very beginning, he drank home brew with his dad because it made him feel like a man. ''As I got into my swing,'' Hedger added, ''I was drinking because I could meet people easier, especially girls. If I had a few belts of booze, hell, I could talk a mile a minute. And if I didn't have a few drinks, I couldn't say a damned thing.''

In time, he *had* to drink, and was drinking for a totally different reason. His body craved alcohol, and it got ''worse and worse and worse.''

The ashtray filled up quickly. We opened the motel room door for a time; outside, the big diesels roared by on North Wilson Street. Hedger paced for a moment, telling me he had never related any of his problems to alcohol, not until he went to Bret Harte Hospital in 1969 and ''started thinking a little bit sober.'' Ruefully, he added, ''Damned near everything bad that ever happened to me was booze-related. Any job that I ever had and lost in my life was because of booze. Any time I ever got in jail, it was because of booze.''

We talked about some of those jails. Hedger estimated that he had been locked up seventy-five or a hundred times, making jail in every town for the last fifteen years that he drank. He talked about his many alcoholic convulsions, hallucinations, and hospitalizations, about sleeping in doorways and freight yards.

''Well, what happened?'' I baited him. ''I thought skid row drunks were helpless and hopeless. What made *you* stop?''

Hedger grinned and then his forehead creased. ''I don't really know what happened at Bret Harte. I suppose just being there with other alcoholics and being able to talk about this thing and finding out that you didn't have to be ashamed of being an alcoholic. Where I come from, the town drunk is a disgrace. I guess subconsciously I just couldn't put myself down there, you see?''

When he found out what alcoholism is and heard for the first time that it is considered a disease, Jim Hedger was tremendously relieved. "If you want to use one word to describe the look in an alcoholic's eyes when he's in that condition, it has to be 'defeat.' Because I'd accepted the fact that I was a goddamned drunk. And that's the great thing about being involved in a program of this type—finding out that, goddamn it, people do live different, that there is a way to live."

The room was hazy with cigarette smoke, and we opened the door again. Hedger began to boil some water for coffee. "I think one of the great things that happened to me at Bret Harte— seeing these sober alcoholics and hearing them talk, and realizing, you know, that at one time they were right where I was: setting there and shaking like a dog shitting peach seeds, all screwed up, confused, and scared. You kinda see a ray of light or something."

Today Jim Hedger works as an alcoholism counselor, sharing that hope with other recovering skid row alcoholics. He's still in Project FAITH and says of his life today, "I don't have to be lonely any more. God, there isn't enough time in the day now to do everything that I want to do and see everybody that I want to see. The great thing about it, as far as I'm concerned, is that it's the best life I ever had in my life."

That same week in Stockton, I met with Eugene Harris, another Bret Harte "graduate," who had actually been born on skid row. Today, Harris works the graveyard shift in a small non-medical detoxification center called Starting Point. There, partly by dint of his own previous bouts with furry creatures of the darkness and "talking, two-headed snakes," he nurses other alcoholics through withdrawal. He keeps a dim light burning at night, Harris explained, and he tunes the radio to a station that broadcasts soft music. And sometimes, he told me, gesturing with his scarred and muscular black arms, he literally croons patients back from the brink of delirium tremens.

I met other recovered skid row alcoholics in Stockton, as well as in practically every city I visited. In Baltimore, for example, I broke bread with a young man named Riley Regan. Regan once spent a lot of his time in a maze of concrete sewer pipes under

Baltimore's main-line railroad tracks. In that foul-smelling refuge from the world, he gulped forty-cents-a-pint wine and, eventually, almost died of alcoholic convulsions. When I last saw him, in the summer of 1974, then sober almost eight years, he handed me a new business card: ''Riley Regan, M.S.W., Assistant to the Director for Area Programs, National Center for Alcohol Education.''

I look at that card today and think back to the night Riley tried to hold up a Safeway supermarket while stuporously drunk, accidentally shooting himself in the leg; or the morning when he awakened to find that someone had dyed his hair orange; or the afternoon when a phone call jarred him from unconsciousness, angering him so that he ripped the phone from the wall and tossed it over the motel balcony into the pool. ''The only thing was,'' Riley told me in all seriousness, ''I didn't let go. I went over the balcony, too, and landed on my head. Christ, I often wonder that I'm alive.''

The more I talked with recovered skid row alcoholics like Riley Regan, Jim Hedger, Gene Harris, Jack Roak, Jim Heath, and so many others, the more often I heard that last phrase. The more I realized, too, that these same men and women—for so long the ''exceptions that proved the rule''—have begun to destroy the myth of helplessness and hopelessness. And, finally, I became more aware that it seems to take a recovering alcoholic—or at least an ''honorary alcoholic'' like Dr. Bob O'Briant—to effectively help a practicing alcoholic who is truly ''sick and tired of being sick and tired.''

In that regard, I'm reminded of a story told to me by a nurse as I left New York's Manhattan Bowery Project late one summer evening. It had been a long day, and she was tired; she had conceded, earlier, that most of the men being treated in the Project's acute ward ''wouldn't make it.'' But then her eyes brightened, and she told me about a man called John, who had been in and out of MBP many times, and then had been readmitted once again in December 1973. He was in very serious withdrawal and ''badly mokus,'' the nurse said. Several days later, he suffered a violent seizure which lasted a full thirty minutes.

''While we were trying to bring him out of the seizure, the

doctor decided to throw an EKG on him. And while they were running the EKG, John's heart stopped. Cardiac arrest. So they pumped his chest, started his heart again, called the ambulance, and sent him up to Bellevue emergency room.''

The nurse was working nights, she said, and about 2:30 A.M. a man from downstairs came up and said he thought he had one of her patients in the elevator. ''No, I had just made a bed check and nobody was missing,'' she recalled. ''I go out, and there's John, in his little blue city pajamas, no shoes, one sleeve hanging off. He had walked over a mile and a third in his bare feet in 25 degree weather in the middle of December from Bellevue to get here. This was a guy who had *died* that afternoon.''

''We fussed a lot,'' the nurse remembered. ''We wrapped him in blankets, got him some slippers, and fixed him a good hot cup of coffee with lots of sugar. He's sitting there drinking it and he's shaking like crazy, because he's frozen to the bone. I'm fussing over him like a mother hen, and I said, 'John, you came *home;* this is like *home* to you.' But he really couldn't come out and say, 'Yes, I do feel this is really the one place.' He kind of muttered, 'This is good coffee.' ''

The next day, John was sent back to Bellevue, where he was discharged after several weeks. ''About a month later,'' the MBP nurse concluded, her eyes suddenly moist, ''we got him transferred to the Montrose rehab facility, where the last I heard, there's a real change. He's making it,'' she said, knocking wood. ''He's really *making* it.''

Cedar Hills Alcoholism Treatment Center is a scant 220 miles west of Spokane; literally under the noses of the very same legislators who decided that Washington's alcoholics must take a back seat to Expo '74 tourism, Cedar Hills' paraprofessional recovered alcoholics are quietly working miracles among court-referred indigent alcoholics, achieving recovery rates five times greater than the national average.

Cedar Hills treats approximately 500 male alcoholics annually in its 120-day recovery program, and has done so since 1967. ''We're able to account for about 85 percent of our alumni,'' exults assistant director Dennis Murphy, who is not an alcoholic, "and we know that our long-term recovery rate is better than 50 percent. In other words, one out of two walking out of here upon release is going to make it."

As a result, alcoholism professionals from all over the United States and from a dozen and a half foreign countries have converged on Cedar Hills during recent years, anxious to learn the secret of success within the unprepossessing nine-acre site at the southeast end of the Maple Valley city dump.

The secret is that there is *no* secret in the 112-bed facility; the goal is simple and clearly stated, the procedures are effective and time-proven. Director Ronald J. Fagan and senior program counselor Robert N. Truman believe strongly, for example, that alcoholism is a physiological illness, and that the psychological deterioration so often seen in alcoholics is secondary to and derivative of the physiological component; and they believe that the illness is progressive.

"As it is progressive physiologically," says white-haired Bob Truman, now sober more than two decades, "so it is psychologically. On the other hand, and I think this is shown very clearly in Alcoholics Anonymous," adds Truman, who had his own problems with the law, as a direct result of his drinking, "if the alcoholic gets sober, follows a simple plan for recovery and stays sober, he grows well."

Treatment at Cedar Hills is free, and the program (which in 1974 cost about $400,000 to run) is funded through city, county, and state application, under the administration of King County's Division of Health Services.

In contrast to traditional psychiatric approaches to alcoholism, in which, as Bob Truman puts it, "the therapist is concerned with every aspect of the patient's life except his drinking," Cedar Hills' treatment program tackles drinking head on; in short, abstinence is the key word and sobriety is the name of the game. Yet the structured and empirical program is enormously varied, including all combinations of individual counseling, group psychotherapy, didactic lectures, alcoholism films, social casework, group dynamics and psychodrama, Alcoholics Anonymous, pastoral counseling and family counseling where appropriate, as well as education and trade upgrading.

"If you were brought in as a patient, Jack," Truman told me, pushing aside the formal mimeographed brochure normally given to visitors, "you'd learn basically the tremendous problem alcohol is in your life. You'd be shown—if you were going to effect a recovery—that you were going to have to develop a serious desire for change, for sobriety."

Alcoholics Anonymous meetings are held several times weekly at Cedar Hills, and patients are encouraged to associate themselves closely with the AA program following their release. In addition, Cedar Hills provides post-release planning; during the initial transition period, the patient is provided assistance in finding a place to live, a job, and even a food allowance. "Help is available," emphasizes Truman. "We'd be remiss to bring a destitute alcoholic into treatment at Cedar Hills and, after his treatment, turn him back out to the street with no place to stay that night. It would be just perpetuating the revolving-door syndrome. We try, in every way that we can, to direct him into the good sober life."

I wandered about Cedar Hills for hours, imagining myself as one of the court-committed patients, many of whom are felony convictees. Since the facility is neither fenced nor patrolled, I wondered about "walkaways"; I was told that the practice is virtually nonexistent—3.8 percent in 1971, for example, and dropping steadily since then. I talked with many of the patients, sharing breakfast, lunch, and dinner. The food was tasty and high in protein. That particular day, the lunch menu alone included clam chowder, grilled red snapper, french-fried potatoes, green salad, bread and butter, lemon pie, and the usual coffee, tea, and milk.

I walked through lecture halls, storerooms, kitchens, and hobby shops. I discovered a power-tool shop, sheet-metal shop, lapidary shop, branch library, and a classroom blackboard covered with algebra equations. I later learned that the Cedar Hills patients who choose to take remedial high school equivalency courses have achieved a phenomenal 92 percent success rate.

That morning I had asked a counselor about the use of medication. "We're opposed to it," he replied adamantly. "Anyone with an understanding of alcoholism should be opposed to it.

After all, we're helping the individual overcome an addiction to a sedative drug, ethyl alcohol, and if we're substituting some other sedative drug, we're helping him to perpetuate his drug addiction."

Later, Dennis Murphy showed me the janitorial school classroom, where patients work with various kinds of wall coverings and floor coverings, for example, learning how to best use the tools of that trade. Proudly, Murphy also shepherded me through Cedar Hills' landscaping school—its steamy greenhouse filled with germinating ground cover for future use by the Public Works Department, and its neat rows of four hundred small cedar trees that eventually will be used to landscape Dome Stadium.

A man clearly in love with his work, Murphy then compared the men to the nearby greenery, saying, "Boy, it's like a plant coming back to life. When they come in, they look like boiled owls, you know? And two months later you don't recognize them. They start feeling better, and they start taking care of their bodies. We've got about twenty-five joggers around here every night, and these guys are really trimming down. One guy," Murphy added, "weighed over three hundred pounds when he came in. When he left, he weighed about two-thirty and he looked like a business executive."

Bob Truman was still more specific about Cedar Hills' successes, decrying the political absurdities whereby tax burdens are forced to *remain* tax burdens even in the face of workable, effective alternatives. Truman told me of one Cedar Hills graduate, then sober more than five years, who had been behind bars 127 times in the Seattle city jail alone. He told me, too, of other successful graduates who had spent most of their adult lives in penitentiaries. "Two men were six-time losers and one was a seven-time loser. The seven-time loser has been out of here over five years now, and he still has the same job I was able to get him the day that he left here."

Unquestionably, the lessons of Cedar Hills Alcoholism Treatment Center will be learned by other communities across America. Whether they realize it or not, Bob Truman, Ron Fagan, Dennis Murphy, and Cedar Hills' "one-out-of-two" walking success stories are broadening the alliance of enlightened iconoclasts referred to earlier—quietly radicalizing treatment goals, procedures, and, most important, *results* for those 5 percent of America's alcoholics commonly known as skid row drunks. Visitors to Cedar Hills cannot help but carry the encouraging message to their respective cities and facilities.

For the present, though, in most cities of the United States, the jungles remain. Skid row and its victims remain, providing the other 95 percent of America's alcoholics with a visible, sordid, and highly acceptable rationalization for the continuing denial of their own illness.

In his office overlooking San Francisco's bustling Geary Street, Dr. Bob O'Briant had summed it up neatly: "It's very useful for a lot of people to be able to point to somebody worse off than themselves and say, *'That's* alcoholism. That's not me.' "

3

On the Job:
Industry's $15 Billion Hangover

In an oak-paneled General Motors board room not long ago, a GM executive and I were viewing some films on occupational alcoholism. Midway through the screening, the projector bulb failed. As I sat quietly in the darkened room, my mind suddenly flashed back twenty years: to the transmission gear department of the Chevrolet-Cleveland plant where, from 1953 to 1957, I had been employed as a hobbing machine operator . . .

I inhaled the odor of oil emulsion flowing over the machine's sharp-toothed cutters; I sensed and could almost feel the smoothness of steel blanks, which would become gears in countless Powerglide automatic transmissions.

Most clearly, I visualized the overhead conveyor behind me. Its three tiered trays carried blanks, finished gears, and, at various times during the day, four-ounce bottles containing 120-proof "white lightning." My supplier was another hobbing machine operator from West Virginia, nicknamed "Greasy"; for a nominal fee, he regularly purveyed the potent moonshine not only to me, but also to several other practicing alcoholics in the department. During our lunch break each day, we would speed down Brookpark Road to the Airways Bar, hoist boilermakers to feed our addiction, then race back to the plant to punch in at the very last minute . . .

After the projector bulb had been replaced and the final film screened, I confided to the executive that I, also, had once worked for General Motors. Impulsively, I described my ''flashback.'' He looked at me with disbelief, joked about Powerglide transmission recalls, then finally said seriously, ''You've come a long way.''

''So has GM,'' I responded, alluding to the films we had just seen and the company's newly initiated alcoholism recovery program.

For the great majority of American companies, sadly enough, no such beginning has yet taken place; on the contrary, the human and economic toll of alcoholism in business and industry continues to rise and rise—rapidly and unfalteringly. In San Francisco alone these days, alcoholism is costing the business community an estimated $400 million annually. On a national scale, the price tag for lost time, accidents, and related consequences of employee alcoholism has soared to a colossal $15 billion per year. And that figure may well turn out to be a conservative one, the National Institute on Alcohol Abuse and Alcoholism admits, for it is based on 1971 data and does not include a host of imponderables.

One such imponderable is the so-called ''Monday-morning flu,'' commonplace in virtually every American office and factory. Within breweries and distilleries, ironically, that particular phenomenon is not only beyond quantification, but often actually nonexistent, since relief from weekend binges is often ''just a swallow away.'' Certainly that was the way it used to be for Eric Bergman, a long-time recovered alcoholic who recalls first going to work for a brewery in 1946, and is today purchasing manager for the world-famed Rainier Brewery in Seattle.

''This was very nice,'' says Bergman, grinning. ''At a brewery, you don't *have* the Monday-morning absence syndrome, because you can get well while you're on the job. I found it easy to have beer on my breath every day. It didn't occur to me that anybody would be upset about it. It also didn't occur to me,'' Bergman adds wryly, ''that my work performance was so bad that I didn't get a single raise in the first four and a half years of working at the brewery.''

Today, almost three decades later, many more millions of American workers, managers, and executives suffer from alcoholism; the present-day estimate is one out of every ten. Although relatively few have the opportunity to ''get well'' on the job, the majority do indeed remain invisible in the sense that they can and do function for years, even while the illness progresses. For the most part, in fact, employee alcoholism usually goes undetected until such time as impairment becomes strikingly obvious—in the form of chronic absenteeism, drastically reduced efficiency, repeated on-the-job accidents, or even disability and death.

''The general public just doesn't understand that there are early, middle, and late stages of alcoholism,'' says Jack Guest, who is Manager of Employee Counseling at Hughes Aircraft Company in Los Angeles. ''They see it only in terms of the late state—in other words, the skid row stereotype stage.

''When an executive of another company says to me, 'We don't have problems with alcoholics, because we fire them,' '' adds Guest, ''I can nail him to the wall with two very specific questions, based on our experience here at Hughes: 'How *long* did the guy work for you? How much did it cost you *before* you fired him?' ''

As Jack Guest and his associates imply, companies insisting or pretending that alcoholism is ''not a problem here'' overlook the fact that most workers with early- or even middle-stage alcoholism have drinking patterns that, to the casual observer, appear to be identical with patterns followed by social drinkers. In fact, the social-drinking society provides alcoholics with a ready camouflage into which they can blend to avoid the penalties that social stigma inflicts upon them.

Over the long term, consequently, companies that deal with alcoholism only when it becomes highly visible are burdened not just with the usual alcohol-related costs, but also end up losing their most experienced, skilled, and difficult-to-replace employees. In Akron, Ohio, for example, Firestone Tire and Rubber Company surveyed 206 employees with ''alcohol problems'' who in 1973 had become involved in Firestone's new Employee Assistance Program. The average age of the employees was forty-nine; far more significantly, their average seniority with Firestone was a startling 21.7 years.

From time to time, I've wondered about those 206 Firestone employees. Twenty-odd years of seniority is hard enough to come by under any circumstances; as any alcoholic knows, it's damned near *impossible* to come by if your life is being steadily diminished by a chronic and progressive illness.

The fact is that the highest alcoholism recovery rates today are being achieved not in hospitals or clinics, but in a sprinkling of factories and offices across the nation. The recovery rates range from 60 percent to as high as 80 to 90 percent within some companies. And although the various industrial programs differ in some details, they are all based on the proven premise that the fear of job loss motivates an alcoholic toward recovery more powerfully than any other factor. "The simple truth is that most alcoholics work, and industry provides jobs for them. Hence, by threatening disciplinary measures or by making the employee realize he or she must perform according to minimum company standards, industry clearly has at its disposal a highly effective motivational lever," insists Keith Kelley, vice-president and director of United California Bank's program on alcoholism and other drug dependencies. Although Kelley shies away from quantifying the program's economic advantages to UCB, another California-based firm, McDonnell-Douglas Corporation, estimates that its four-year-old alcoholism program has eliminated $4 million in productivity losses.

In general terms, the most successful corporate programs today use job performance as a gauge by which to measure employee output, and to identify those workers who may require rehabilitation. Such programs are based on the recognition that alcoholism—even in its early and middle stages—affects job performance through readily identifiable factors including those already mentioned, as well as poor judgment, excessive spoilage, decreasing productivity, fights, lateness, early departures, customer complaints, and so on. "This is the only yardstick we're interested in," asserts Jesse L. Macbeth of Western Electric Company, which started its alcoholism program in 1949. "We're not going to intrude into the person's private life.

Whether he drinks or doesn't drink isn't really our problem. But when his performance on the job falls below minimum company standards, then it's time for us to sit up and take notice.''

Obviously, in this connection, the supervisor plays a critical role in the identification process. However, since he is not licensed to practice medicine and therefore is hardly qualified to make a diagnosis of alcoholism, his role is restricted to, first, documenting unsatisfactory job performance and, second, offering referrals to qualified professionals who will help the employee determine the medical, emotional, or behavioral reasons for unsatisfactory job performance.

In addition to Hughes Aircraft, GM, United California Bank, and Western Electric, other large companies successfully utilizing this approach today include Du Pont, Eastman Kodak, Burlington Northern, Union Carbide, Equitable Life, Caterpillar Tractor, Allis-Chalmers, Merrill Lynch, American Motors, American Airlines, Kemper Insurance, Employers Insurance of Wausau, and a score of others.

Although their policies specifically forbid supervisors to ''play doctor,'' these same companies, on the other hand, agree that alcoholism be named and dealt with openly and honestly in other parts of their programs. ''This is necessary and vital,'' emphasizes Ross Von Wiegand, director of labor-management services for the National Council on Alcoholism, ''if we're to overcome the unmerited and unjustifiable effects of the existing social and moral stigma associated with alcoholism.''

Yet, overcoming that stigma remains a formidable challenge even within companies that have begun to recognize employee alcoholism as a devastating and costly problem. Executives at Hughes Aircraft, for example, whose six-year-old Employee Counseling Program is considered one of the nation's most successful, well remember initial resistance by top management. That resistance centered on the fact that Hughes is a high-technology company, ''differing'' from other companies in the kinds of people employed and the nature of projects undertaken. The firm's major contracts have included, for example, the Early Bird satellite and the Maverick and Phoenix missiles. Of Hughes' 35,000 employees today, some 13,000 have one or more advanced academic degrees.

"The feeling back in 1968 on the part of management," recalls Employee Counseling manager Jack Guest, "was that we wouldn't be as likely to see problems in that kind of population as we would with another kind of population. You know what I mean, Jack. It gets back to the skid row stereotype."

However, Hughes' management did agree to conduct a survey. And it was quickly determined, to management's astonishment, that the rate of alcoholism among the company's top scientists, engineers, and technicians was no less than 6 percent. It was further determined that the 6 percent rate remained consistent across the board—for *all* employee levels from machine operators to top management itself. "Translated company-wide," says Guest, "it meant we had something like 1,800 alcoholics on the payroll, out of some 32,000 employees at that time."

"Prior to that," he adds, "it was agreed that each alcoholic was costing us roughly $4,000 a year. So if you take 1,800 employees at $4,000 each, you've got a $7 million problem annually. And *that* got management's attention."

During the six years since Hughes initiated its Employee Counseling Program, about 1,100 employees have been referred and treated; 600 of the 1,100 have been diagnosed as alcoholics. The recovery rate among those 600 alcoholics, based on a criterion of at least six months' total abstinence, is up around 80 percent. Cost of the program? Hughes figures it actually *saves* $10 for every $1 it invests.

No less important, Hughes officials quickly emphasize, are the human aspects of the program. Frank Huddleston, who is Assistant Manager of Hughes' program, recalls a woman inspector who tearfully insisted that Employee Counseling staff members attend the ceremony at which she would be awarded a twenty-year service pin. "They saved my life," says the middle-aged woman, who now readily concedes that drinking had always been a problem which she had never really faced. "When they told me I'd lose my job if things went on the way they were going, but they'd help me if I wanted help—well, I went to the hospital for twenty-one days and joined AA when I came out, and they stuck with me all through it. Now I've got a life again."

Those same words have been repeated to me time and again,

in literally dozens of plants and offices across America. Each performance-oriented recovery story is unique, to be sure; in a sense, however, all have a common denominator.

There's Aaron Smith, for example, who worked as a General Motors documentation clerk for six years before he entered the GM Alcoholism Recovery Program and gained sobriety. Smith confided to me without hesitation that he had to "print" in the mornings because his hands shook so violently. "My script looked like the writing of a five-year-old," he says, now seemingly awed at the memory. "If it wasn't for the GM program, I'd be dead."

Thirty-three-year-old GM service engineer Roger Sklee, who began working for the company in 1959 as a mail-room messenger, graphically described the progression of his alcoholism over some fourteen years. His job performance deteriorated to the point where he had hidden a year's accumulation of paperwork in desk drawers and closets. "They just opened one closet and said, 'Holy Christ,' " Sklee said to me, smiling for the first time as he detailed the events leading up to his eventual recovery in GM's program. "My life today? What can I tell you? It's a new ball game."

Within General Motors or any other company truly serious about confronting employee alcoholism, that new ball game begins, necessarily, with a forthright and public statement of company policy—preferably above the signatures of top management. In GM's case, the signature is that of Chairman R. C. Gerstenberg; the widely circulated statement minces no words and tackles such basic issues as alcoholism's stigma, telling General Motors employees, for example, "It is time that we face the problem head-on for what it is, not as some indication of moral weakness, but as a disease."

At Firestone, similarly, the signatures are those of Chairman Raymond C. Firestone and President and Chief Executive Officer Richard A. Riley, who sum up their alcoholism recovery program with the simile of "tough love," making clear that the company's concern with alcoholism "is limited to its effects on absenteeism and work performance, not social drinking."

Lacking such top-management sponsorship and full support,

even well-intentioned programs tend to become exercises in futility. Either such programs are not implemented at all, or they are implemented downward only—from the point at which the policy decision and statement were issued. "If the program starts from the middle-management level down," explains one disgruntled corporate medical director, "from there on *up* nothing happens. So the program misses the most costly employees—including, conceivably, the president himself."

The ball game begins, too, with basic ground rules, including, as of primary importance, a clear and concise definition of alcoholism. Most of the companies mentioned earlier stick closely to the National Council on Alcoholism's recommended definition, which gets right to the point in one succinct, jargon-free sentence: "For the purposes of this policy, alcoholism is defined as a disease in which an employee's consumption of any alcoholic beverage definitely and repeatedly interferes with his job performance and/or his health."

At the same time, most companies with successful alcoholism programs encourage *self*-referral by employees, circulating literature in the form of questions and answers, do-it-yourself "tests," or, most frequently, a listing of alcoholism's warning signs. Both Firestone and Hughes, for example, give all employees a colorful leaflet which asks, simply, "AM I DRINKING TOO MUCH?" The leaflet lists nine signs of alcoholism, concluding, "If you have one or more of these, you may have a drinking problem and should seek treatment."

Today's successful employee alcoholism programs are a far cry, unquestionably, from the earliest trial-and-error programs of the 1940s, which mirrored then prevailing social attitudes. Most people of that time considered alcoholism a self-inflicted disability, as well as a moral problem. Acceptance of the disease concept had negligible acceptance even within the medical profession (only in 1956, for example, did the prestigious American Medical Association "officially" recognize alcoholism as an illness); in line with the skid row stereotype, no one was really considered an alcoholic unless he or she was in what are now known to be the late or final stages of the illness.

As a result, early industrial programs were based on two erroneous assumptions, points out NCA's Ross Von Wiegand, whose experience qualifies him as a "dean" of labor-management alcoholism programs. First, that the "alcoholic" was readily identifiable by the supervisor through simply observing the physical and behavioral symptoms associated with the popular stereotype: bloodshot eyes, shaking hands, alcohol breath, loud and obnoxious conduct, and so on. Second, any employee *not* having such readily identifiable signs could not be considered an alcoholic, and was therefore of no concern to the program administrators.

Still practiced by numerous companies, this approach obviously misses all employees suffering from the early or middle stages of alcoholism; hence the majority of alcoholic employees receive no help from the program, and the company misses out on the substantial economic and personnel rewards obtainable through an effective program.

A second approach, all too common in even recently developed programs, gives *verbal* recognition to the necessity of basing referrals on unsatisfactory job performances, but instructs supervisors to initiate referral procedures only when they "suspect" that the poor performance is due to alcoholism. The difficulty, of course, is that the "job performance" approach is merely given lip service, since it restricts constructive action to only those employees whom the supervisor can identify as alcoholics by his own observation. "The net result," says Von Wiegand gloomily, "is a return to the outmoded forties approach."

The third and only truly successful approach—used today by Du Pont, Kodak, Hughes, and the various other firms already mentioned—focuses exclusively on monitoring job performance, rather than "looking for alcoholics" in witch-hunt fashion. In effect, it's an "ABC" approach whereby (A) employees whose performance drops below acceptable standards are (B) referred to professional and diagnostic services for identification of the employee's problem, followed by (C) treatment, by outside resources, appropriate to whatever that problem may be.

As I traveled across America to explore the realities of on-the-job alcoholism—reminding myself over and over that more than *90 percent* of this nations's alcoholics are indeed *employed*—I focused on companies using that "ABC" approach. It was important for me, inevitably, to get the actual feeling—to contrast today's GM, for example, with the GM I once knew. So I role-played, casting myself as an auto assembler, a tire maker, an aerospace engineer, a banker. Once I had been shown the films, had been given the literature, had been told about the alcoholism program, I hypothesized.

"All right," I told Keith Kelley at United California Bank, "I'm a teller at a UCB branch in Culver City." . . . "Great," I said to Jack Guest and Frank Huddleston at Hughes Aircraft, "I'm a designer of communications satellites and I have a Ph.D." . . . "Okay," I interrupted Dr. Nicholas Pace at General Motors, "Let's get specific. I work for Fisher Body in Detroit, and I'm a metal finisher."

"I'm a middle-stage alcoholic and I work for your company," I told each of them. "I'm missing time, coming in late, taking long lunch hours, fouling up on the job, the whole bit. What's going to happen to me in your alcoholism program?"

The answers were simple and direct; my hypothetical occupation and income bracket seemed to matter not at all. Within the several dozen companies having up-to-date and effective programs, I learned, it would go something like this . . .

My supervisor, who is aware of my deteriorating job performance, suspects also that I'm an alcoholic—because he's been trained by professionals. He confronts me and, without ever mentioning the words "alcohol" or "booze" or "drinking," lays it on the line about my long lunch hours, missed Mondays, and generally poor performance. He *warns* me, and if I "shape up" following his warning, that's the end of it.

If I don't shape up, my supervisor meets with a counselor (or plant physician), and the two of them review my job performance record. By this time, the performance has been monitored and documented; if I try to "con" the supervisor, he can pin me down to specific times, dates, and incidents. The counselor, in turn, suggests that I meet with him and the supervisor to discuss the "problem."

At the meeting, the supervisor spells out the facts of my job performance record, then leaves. I'm then left alone with the counselor, who informs me bluntly that if my work doesn't improve, I'll be disciplined—that is, suspended without pay, or fired. During the one-to-one meeting, the counselor gives me numerous conversational opportunities to discuss my drinking. He's an expert; he knows that alcoholism, in its progression, is a highly predictable illness. Sooner or later, I allude to my drinking problem; with knowledgeable prompting from the counselor, I inevitably talk about it at length.

Once the issue of alcoholism is out of the closet—at the first meeting or a subsequent one—I'm offered help and referral, to Alcoholics Anonymous, a treatment facility, or both. I'm assured that my medical records will be treated no less confidentially than medical records for any other illness, and that there will be no stigma or "moral" judgment made. If I require hospitalization, it will probably be at a facility with strong AA orientation; chances are, too, that all costs will be absorbed by the company's health insurance plan.

At the treatment facility, I'll receive recuperative treatment as necessary, learn about the nature and effects of my illness, and spend a great deal of time with recovered alcoholics who "have been where I'm at," and who will help me learn "not to take the first drink, one day at a time." With total abstinence my watchword, and continuing treatment and support our mutual goal, there is an 80 percent probability that I will return to work with a new respect for myself *and* my job—and that I will remain sober.

In the face of literally thousands of such success stories—documented, most meaningfully, by the words and very bearing of the recovering alcoholics themselves—the paucity of industrial alcoholism programs in America seems, at the least, enigmatic. To repeat, fewer than one-hundredth of 1 percent of this nation's corporations have alcoholism programs of any sort; among that grouping of a few hundred firms, perhaps several dozen have truly effective programs.

I pondered the question with numerous professionals in the field; in San Francisco, for example, I spent a morning with

William Livingston, who is labor-management director of the National Council on Alcoholism—Bay Area. Although Livingston remains encouraged by recent progress in combating on-the-job alcoholism, he agrees that the surface has barely been scratched. He described, for example, so-called "pop-up-toaster" alcoholism programs, explaining, grimly, "When an alcoholic can no longer be ignored or covered up for, and he pops up, you send him down the hall for Joe to take to an AA meeting. You *know* that's not a program."

Livingston described his experience, too, with countless corporate executives who are personally threatened by the very word "alcoholic"; in most executive suites of substantial size, he emphasized, one out of ten is likely to be an alcoholic. "And if you are *personally* threatened, there are lots of subtle ways to kill a program at that high level," Bill Livingston said. "By simply not doing anything, or by saying 'Okay, why don't we just draft a policy and procedure and put it in our personnel manual, and it'll stay there, period.' "

In sum, Livingston and other members of the Association of Labor-Management Administrators and Consultants on Alcoholism (ALMACA) told me, "You might say that corporate alcoholism programs are sort of like motherhood and apple pie—you can't really be *against* them. So the prevailing corporate attitude is, 'We'll adopt the program with such faint acceptance and nonaggressive implementation that it'll simply die a natural death.' "

Rather more vociferously, ALMACA members across the country denounce companies that spend large sums advertising and otherwise touting *alleged* employee alcoholism programs. "What I'm talking about," said one ALMACA official, "is the company that takes full-page ads in *Business Week* or *Time,* for example, saying, "Look, we're among the most aggressive, innovative companies in the country, because we have this program, and we're really proud of it,' when in actuality they don't have a damned thing."

Along the way, in various cities, I heard repeated references to one multi-billion-dollar American corporation that is noted for its extremely effective alcoholism program, yet refuses to officially acknowledge the program's existence, let alone discuss it publicly. Time and again I was told about the program, but always with the admonition, "Well, for your information, since it can't be published, the company is Standard Oil."

"Why the big secret?" I asked, naïvely. "What's Standard's rationale?"

I received this reply from a Standard Oil executive of my acquaintance who, naturally, prefers to remain nameless: "Well, the rationale is—rationale and true reason being two different things, frequently—we are really very paranoid about what will happen, for instance, with stockholders writing in and saying, 'What about all the drunks we employ?' Standard Oil is conservative," the executive added facetiously, "and we really know that alcoholism is a *moral* problem, and if you've got any alcoholics on board, you simply fire them. The fact that we've got three hundred-plus people on board who are old-time Standard employees—recovered alcoholics who are functioning like they haven't functioned for years—we gloss that over."

Of course, such a rationale can be used by any corporation unwilling to take a forthright stand on employee alcoholism. A bank might say: "We can't risk creating a situation which could cause people to say, 'I don't want those drunks handling *my* money.' " Similarly, the management of an airline might argue: "If it becomes known that we have an alcoholism program, people will say, 'I don't want to fly with that airline—you know, that's the one with all the drunken pilots.' "

For what it's worth, Nervous Nellies in business and industry can take heart from the experience of numerous companies; American Airlines and United California Bank provide two examples. After the September–October 1972 issue of *Harvard Business Review* carried an article on American Airlines' alcoholism program (co-authored by American's vice-chairman Marion Sadler and James F. Horst, international executive vice-president of the Transport Workers Union of America), public response was overwhelmingly positive. So, too, has been response to continuing publicity about United California Bank's employee alcoholism program.

Still another straw man often created by companies reluctant to establish employee alcoholism programs is the expectation that hospital and medical costs will soar. Experience has shown, once again, that such apprehension has no real basis in fact; surveys by the National Council on Alcoholism show conclusively that there has been absolutely *no* upsurge in insurance claims among large multi-plant companies that have installed alcoholism programs.

Indeed, executives within these same companies fully expect claims to *decrease* in the long run. Within their alcoholism programs, 60 to 80 percent of the claimants have already achieved long-term, stable recovery; as a result, they are no longer "revolving door" cases, which, as any personnel manager knows, become increasingly serious (and expensive) with the progression of alcoholism.

What is most significant, however, is that the *nature* of the insurance claims has changed markedly among those companies surveyed. As alcoholism-related claims have risen, a variety of other types of claims have declined commensurately; the claims declining in number included upper respiratory infections, accidents, gastrointestinal complaints, and musculoskeletal disorders. The reason for the change? Before installing an alcoholism program, it turns out, each of the surveyed companies had *in fact* been paying hospital and medical claims for alcoholism; in case after case, however, the claims had been *disguised* as "more respectable" types of illnesses.

The centuries-old characterization of alcoholism as a moral weakness, a shameful habit, and, indeed, a sin is exemplified by the following letter, actually written by the Suggestion Plan Manager of the Southeastern Pennsylvania Transportation Authority, in response to an employee suggestion that the Authority set up an employee alcoholism program:

Thank you for your contribution to the employees' suggestion clinic. Your suggestion No. 554 has been reviewed in its entirety by the suggestion committee. Upon investigation we have found that alcoholism is a cardinal sin in the transportation business, and could not be considered as an illness. We hope that the above reason shows sufficient evidence as to why we cannot accept your idea. However, enclosed please find a pen in token of appreciation of your time and effort.

True, it is impossible to quantify the human and economic consequences of such stigmatization. What is clear, though, is that the log jam is at the top—in the minds of those who make the decisions and establish the policies. Within some companies, top management is literally shielded from "unpleasant" realities by middle management. More frequently and certainly of more importance, as ALMACA members emphasize, many top executives find the mere mention of "an employee alcoholism program" personally threatening—in the sense that they are unwilling to take a hard look at their own drinking patterns, or to acknowledge the alcoholism of family members.

Assuredly, corporate executives are no more immune from alcoholism than from such illnesses as diabetes or arthritis. On the other hand, the executive alcoholic is able to camouflage his alcoholism more easily and for a longer time than, say, a machine operator whose behavior can be more readily observed and whose performance can be more accurately gauged. "Identifying alcoholism is an especially difficult task on the executive level," asserts Dr. Luther Cloud, senior associate medical director of the Equitable Life Assurance Society, "because, unlike the line employee, the trappings of office and status become viscous barriers to early confrontation."

In addition to the executive alcoholic's ability to take long and liquid lunch hours euphemized as "conferences," to depart abruptly for last-minute "appointments," or even to travel cross-country to mask extended binges, there is the well-accepted and ritualistic "necessity" of expense-account entertaining. Concurrently, executive alcoholics are in a position to be far more costly to their companies than other employees; an executive alcoholic responsible for investment decisions, for example, can literally lose millions of dollars in minutes.

Nevertheless, executive alcoholics tend to be fiercely protected—not only by loyal secretaries and trusted colleagues, but also by executives of higher rank; the entire protective network seems to reflect a sort of deferential nonobservance of alcoholism when it occurs in high places. As a result, the American Medical Association concluded recently, alcoholics among the financially successful may well be one of the most sizable—

and certainly one of the most seriously neglected—groups in America.

This point was graphically documented for me by Dr. John S. Tamerin, a gifted psychiatrist who was formerly research director of the Silver Hill Foundation in New Canaan, Connecticut. A non-profit psychiatric treatment and rehabilitation center with many years of experience in dealing with the executive alcoholic, Silver Hill's private and luxurious facilities spread across sixty wooded acres and include such therapeutic accouterments as swimming pools, a sauna, and even bowling lanes; the milieu is not unlike that of a posh country inn.

Costs for the two-month-long alcoholism program, which is strongly AA oriented, can run as high as $8,000 or more. However, most patients entering Silver Hill's specialized and intensive alcoholism rehabilitation program are well able to afford the investment; their backgrounds tend to be "upper class" in terms of wealth and power. "What we've found over the years," Dr. Tamerin told me, "is that alcoholism among such individuals tends to be viewed in a sort of 'Emperor's New Clothes' fashion. The whole idea that these wealthy and powerful people can 'take care of themselves' *so well* turns out to be precisely the thing that conceals their illness—until the individual patient may no longer be amenable to treatment."

As we walked across Silver Hill's grassy slopes to the research offices one summer morning, Dr. Tamerin described the long-term organic effects of "concealment," emphasizing that the lack of early recognition prevents detection until irreversible changes have occurred. He described, for example, one top-level executive whose high corporate status enabled him to camouflage his excessive drinking for many years. "By the time he reached Silver Hill," Tamerin said glumly, "he showed clear evidence of organic mental deterioration—even while functioning in his high-level job."

Clearly, this ability of the high-level executive to "pass" is not only commonplace, but tragic; as John Tamerin put it, " 'passing' maintains and exacerbates the problem while postponing detection." To drive the point home more specifically, Tamerin told me that tests conducted among upper-class alcoholics at Silver Hill revealed essentially *irreversible* "organic intellectual impairment" in 81 percent of those tested—that is, 26 out of a sample of 31 patients.

Medical terminology and statistical analyses apart, it boils down to the fact that no one does the alcoholic a favor by pretending that his or her illness does not exist. Quite the contrary, such concealment turns out to be a very real form of cruelty by which countless Americans are literally "killed with kindness" each year—on the job and in the home.

For me, the paradox was best summed up by Dr. Thomas J. Doyle, medical director of Consolidated Edison Company of New York. Describing Con Ed's long-time industrial alcoholism program, Doyle noted that for each new case identified under the company's alcoholism program, disability consideration is granted to another employee—stricken with the *end results* of chronic alcoholism—who had *never been identified*.

"It's the failures who stand out in my mind," Dr. Doyle said quietly. "The failures haunt you."

4

The Woman Alcoholic:
Out of Sight, Out of Mind

In the gymnasium of a Roman Catholic church not far from New Orleans' old French Quarter, a meeting of Alcoholics Anonymous has just begun. It is a regular Thursday-evening gathering that is open to the public; more than two hundred men and women are seated shoulder to shoulder in rows of metal folding chairs. "This is a two-speaker meeting," announces a young man who is the leader. "Our first speaker tonight is Virginia."

A tall, dark-haired woman in her early forties rises from the audience and walks determinedly to the podium. The applause fades and there is expectant silence as the woman takes a deep breath and says, "My name is Virginia, and I'm an alcoholic."

"Hi, Virginia," the audience chants in response.

Virginia lights a cigarette and peers out at the sea of faces. "God, I'm nervous," she confides, with a smile. "There are so *many* of you." She takes a deep drag on the cigarette. "We're supposed to tell what it was like, what happened, and what it's like now," she begins. "All right, what it was like . . ."

I attended that meeting—"the biggest AA meeting in town"—on my second night in New Orleans, at the suggestion of two newfound friends. Not unkindly, they had made it clear that it would be unseemly for me to use a tape recorder. As has been the case so often, though, recollection alone serves more than adequately; the words and feelings expressed by Virginia "M" remain no less vivid today than during that balmy spring evening in New Orleans.

Graphically and uninhibitedly, Virginia traced the progression of her alcoholism from the first high school "beer bust" to the bitter end when, as a mother and housewife, she had become a black-and-blue, falling-down, round-the-clock drunk. From the beginning, Virginia drank for alcohol's effect; usually, she said, it helped her to overcome her shyness, enabling her to become "part *of*" rather than "apart *from.*" It all began rather innocuously, or so it seemed at the time, Virginia told the attentive group.

Eventually, there was college, marriage, two children, and, in no time at all, a full-blown addiction to alcohol. "I began hiding bottles all over the place," Virginia recalled. "You know, I kept a pint in the bottom of the clothes hamper, down under the dirty underwear. I kept another under the kitchen sink, and another behind the hot-water heater. And, oh yes," she added, talking directly to the women who made up more than half the audience, "in that last year I kept a pint inside the flush tank of the toilet. Except I always forgot that I'd put it there." She smiled, saying with mock seriousness, "Now, I know, just as sure as I'm standing here, that none of you ladies ever did *that.*"

The audience exploded with laughter, as they did frequently during Virginia's twenty-minute talk that evening. The longer she continued her "drunkalog," in fact, the more frequent became the head-nodding and nudging, particularly among the majority of women, who, earlier, had raised their hands in response to the leader's question, "Are there any other alcoholics here tonight?"

Virginia talked about "rearranging the garbage," praying that the trash collectors wouldn't notice all the empty bottles. She described her drinking "costume"—a wine-stained muumuu that effectively hid her bloat and bruises. It was so filthy, Virginia said, that if you had boiled it, "it would have provided someone with nourishment for a week."

There were, too, the elaborate yet ultimately transparent ploys used to obtain liquor deliveries from a dozen different stores so that area merchants "wouldn't suspect." She detailed nightmarish alcoholic blackouts and drunk-driving episodes during which she had delivered her sons to elementary school.

In those "bad old days," Virginia never went to sleep or awakened but, instead, "passed out" and "came to." Continuing her description of "what it used to be like," she detailed the humiliating absurdity of filling a steam iron with vodka. "At that moment," she said, grimacing, "it seemed like the *ultimate* hiding place."

I remember our constant and uproarious laughter that night. To a non-alcoholic, our reaction doubtless would have seemed irreverent, if not bizarre. Yet our hilarity was in no way derisive; on the contrary, it was the laughter of empathy and self-recognition. For the women, particularly, it was recognition of their *own* former secretive and furtive drinking patterns—the frantically pathetic processes by which they, too, had been invisible alcoholics, hiding and hidden within begrimed housecoats, in darkened rooms, and, finally, behind shuttered windows and locked doors.

Traditionally, in the shaky statistics of alcoholism, the male column always has shown a much higher aggregate than the female column. Today, in America, however, as that New Orleans meeting demonstrated and as most authorities agree, there are probably at *least* as many women alcoholics as men. Indeed, alcoholism among American women may be far more widespread than is even suspected; for every woman alcoholic who has become statistically visible, numerous others remain wholly *in*visible. Concealed from the world by either personal fear, spousal sophistry, or both, a lonely and growing army of desperate women alcoholics are quietly and solitarily drinking themselves into oblivion at this very moment.

It is true, unquestionably, that increasing numbers of alcoholic women have indeed sought help in recent years. As Virginia "M" told her New Orleans audience, "We're coming out of the woodwork; we're acknowledging our illness; we're saying 'We will get help.' "

Yet at the same time, the ingrained pattern of hidden drinking by America's women alcoholics is no less prevalent today than it was, say, in Prohibition days, when a potent nostrum called Lydia Pinkham's Vegetable Compound was the beverage of choice not only during "that time of month," but *all* month.

Even such a positive thinker as NCA founder Marty Mann, who in April 1974 passed the thirty-fifth year of a sober life, concedes that little has changed for women as far as secret and solitary drinking is concerned. When I last visited her in New York, seventy-year-old Mrs. Mann emphasized the point with a sweeping gesture of her arm, a gesture so vigorous that it seemed to encompass every street and room in New York City. Marty said emphatically, *"Thousands* of invisible women are drinking themselves to an early grave."

Eyes narrowing, Marty Mann stepped backward in time, recalling for me her perception of the very same city—with its same streets and plaster-walled prisons—some thirty-six years earlier. "It was the last year of my drinking," she said. "I was living with my sister and a friend of hers in an apartment up in the East Seventies—and that whole area is big apartment buildings, you know, with hundreds and hundreds of windows. That's where I was when I was waking up at three o'clock in the morning and wanted to jump out the window, and all the horrors that I was having. And I used to look up at all those windows and think, 'How many of those windows are hiding women in the fix I'm in?' "

Countless numbers, we agreed—then *and* now. And the "fix" is worse in smaller communities, where, as Mrs. Mann puts it, "the stigma's heavier and the women just don't get out at all." Moreover, as other recovered women alcoholics will attest, the unique circumstances of suburban living present secret drinkers with still other encumbrances, not the least of which is acquiring a supply of liquor; hence, for the alcoholic woman, the automobile—that lifeline of suburban living—is more than a means of dropping off children at school or going to PTA meetings. It provides a way to purchase alcohol without being detected, a feat less easily accomplished in suburbia than in more impersonal urban areas such as Manhattan or Chicago.

On the other hand, within certain affluent suburbs such as

Grosse Point, Michigan, or Scarsdale, New York, money helps mask the problem to an even greater degree than in big cities. "In a community like ours, it's *easier* to cover up," asserts Marie Fitzsimmons, director of the Alcoholism Guidance Center in the high-income community of Westport, Connecticut. "There's money for liquor, for psychiatry, and for a house-keeper, all of which may work against coming to grips with the reality of alcoholism."

In the final analysis, of course, alcoholism among women is a problem peculiar to no particular type of living—country, suburban, big city, or small town. No matter what their locale, economic stratum, occupation, or ethnic derivation, for most of America's women alcoholics the operative word is "secrecy."

The primary and most obvious reason for secret or "withdrawal" drinking by women is, of course, the behavioral double standard long imposed by society itself. As is well known, such inequality ranges over a broad spectrum of living, adversely affecting women's employment opportunities, wage scales, credit ratings, and the like. However, when it comes to the woman suffering from alcoholism, the classic double standard is augmented almost synergistically by the unique stigma attached to the illness itself.

This reality was underscored, often quite angrily, by dozens of women alcoholics during my travels across America. At the Manhattan Bowery Project in New York City, for example, I casually asked one of the nurses how MBP's skid row patients react to the fact that she herself is a recovering alcoholic. "Even among these alcoholics on this acute ward, you hear them say, 'A woman drunk? There's nothing worse,' " she replied, indicating a group of men whose scarred faces and tremulous limbs left little doubt as to the last-stage progression of their illness.

"My own consciousness has been going click-click lately," the nurse added. " 'Nice women don't drink.' You know, this is a hangover from Victorian times. I think there's definitely a double standard of behavior that's applied to women. A woman alcoholic is branded, *zap*. Tramp, loose woman, whore, you name it."

Almost a world away from Manhattan, across San Francisco's

Golden Gate Bridge in a wind-swept Sausalito cottage, I heard essentially the same words from Florette Pomeroy, a recovered alcoholic who until recently has been executive director of the National Council on Alcoholism—Bay Area. "I did my first drinking during Prohibition, which dates me handily," Mrs. Pomeroy confided, raising an eyebrow, "and I was drunk the first time the night that I graduated from a convent boarding school. All that did for me was to instill a firm resolution that I would learn to 'drink like a lady.' And I worked at that for a long, long time."

When I asked Florette Pomeroy what it meant to "drink like a lady," she responded by first "qualifying" herself—recounting her ascendancy and decline through a variety of high-echelon government positions in the early 1950s. She had a "top secret" security clearance. At one point, she said, she was regional officer for the Office of Civil Defense, responsible for liaison with state OCD departments all over the West.

In the last stages of her drinking, Florette recalled, she was regularly required to travel the "speech circuit" from Phoenix to Sacramento, to Carson City, to Salt Lake City, to Portland, and to Olympia. "On the last trip, I made every one of those speeches, and then got so drunk in each place that I had to be helped to get to the plane to get to the next place. And the reports kept filtering back to the regional office, 'You know, she's a great kid, but don't ever send her down here again because it's too much work for us.' "

Mrs. Pomeroy, now sober more than twenty years, got into "real trouble" in Portland during that last fateful trip, she remembered. "I made my set speech and then disappeared into my room and locked the door. I had three or four fifths of bourbon, and two days later they had to get the house detective and a doctor to find out whether or not I was alive. I wouldn't answer the phone, I wouldn't answer the door—you know, the whole bit."

Coming back to the present as she sipped a non-alcoholic "champagne" concoction in the living room of her snug hillside cottage, Florette Pomeroy said sternly, "I think society of course levels a different kind of indictment at the woman than they do at the man, today as well as during my drinking days. They're far more tolerant of the man who is a drunk publicly than they are of the woman who is a drunk publicly. And I think that leads a great majority of women to be secret drinkers for as long as they can possibly conceal it.''

Concurrently, Florette Pomeroy adds, the woman alcoholic is zealously overprotected by her family—husband, parents, and even children when they are old enough to play a protective role. ''What's more, she suffers from her *own* belief that it's worse for a woman to be an alcoholic than it is for a man, so that when she falls off that pedestal, her sense of shame is deeper.''

The pedestal to which Florette Pomeroy refers is hardly the product of alcoholic hallucinations. It is a very real concept for most Americans, symbolizing not only the hallowed ''sanctity of motherhood,'' but also such a well-worn shibboleth as ''The hand that rocks the cradle is the hand that rules the world,'' coined a century ago by William Ross Wallace.

Digging deeply into what one woman calls that ''hand that rocks the cradle jazz,'' a small group of recovering women alcoholics and I sat around a luncheon table at Silver Hill Foundation in New Canaan, Connecticut. One of the women told me that losing custody of her children tumbled her headlong from the ''pedestal,'' proving its flimsiness in excruciatingly painful personal terms. ''A mother is important, and all of a sudden you're not a mother. That was the worst horror for me. You know, I'm *nothing* now. All my femininity, all my femaleness is gone, because the whole point was being 'mother.' ''

In somewhat different terms, another of the women described the very same feelings. ''Believe me, it's a burden, not a badge,'' she chimed in sourly. ''Even if you're lying in the gutter, you're still *Mrs.* So-and-So. The wife and mother.''

That same day, I spent several hours with Harriet Gibney, another recovering alcoholic and Silver Hills ''graduate'' who is now a key member of the facility's alcoholism treatment staff. ''My mother was an alcoholic,'' she told me at one point. ''But we never ever talked about Mother's 'ailment.' She just ate an awful lot of bad clams.''

Recalling to me that she could never tell whether her mother was drunk or sober, Mrs. Gibney long ago concluded that women are far less likely to show that they're drunk than their male counterparts. ''They don't feel free about being 'high' the way men do," she said. "It's as true now as it was twenty years ago, when the word was 'tight.' As a woman, you didn't show that you were tight. I think women practice this control because they're ashamed of it. And even more devastating," Harriet Gibney added, "is that the husband aids and abets the entire process, because, after all, an alcoholic wife is a terrible affront to the male ego."

A man is certainly far more embarrassed than a woman about an alcoholic spouse, agrees Dr. LeClair Bissell, chief of the Smithers Alcoholism Treatment and Training Center at Roosevelt Hospital in New York. "More often than not, in fact, the wife who wants to hide her problem generally finds a willing aide in her husband," says Dr. Bissell, who is herself a recovered alcoholic.

Additionally, the woman alcoholic who gets as far as a physician or other professional poses special interview problems, points out Dr. Bissell. "For a woman alcoholic, there are unique horrors," she says. "One is waking up in bed with someone you don't know. The other is the joy of carrying a baby, when you don't know the father."

A far more commonplace horror among women alcoholics, however, is that they have a much greater fear of losing their looks than men have. "One of the reasons that it's never acceptable for a woman to be drunk in public, even in these permissive times," emphasizes Marty Mann, "is that it's so unpretty. It's a hideous thing to see a woman drunk. Her makeup slips, her hair falls down, she looks like bloody hell. So when her drinking begins to get out of control, she goes underground. She'll take two drinks at a party, and then go home and finish the bottle by herself."

That harsh truth is elaborated upon by Florette Pomeroy, who believes that female physiology itself accounts for the fact that a woman "goes downhill" faster than a man does. "She lets herself go completely. And because you've turned yourself into an incredibly repulsive being, the sense of total loss, of whatever your femininity is, is so complete that the process of coming back and being confident again that you can act and feel like a woman is extremely difficult. And that means," Florette adds from her own experience, "that women go farther down the path and become sicker before they are exposed, and their families seem to heap an additional level of shame on them.''

Consequently, for the most part, women alcoholics tend to drink longer and harder than do men. Recent medical findings indicate, moreover, that physiological differences do indeed compound the problem, at least to the extent that the progression of alcoholism in women is not unlike the proverbial snowball gathering momentum and increasing in size as it races downhill toward self-destruction.

Medical research apart, it is a certainty that when women alcoholics finally do seek help, they frequently are in truly desperate shape; within a relatively short period of time, often six years or less, their alcoholism has progressed from the very early stage into the beginning of the final stage.

"The worst I ever got," Harriet Gibney told me, "had to be when we were living in Tokyo in 1969. Peripheral neuritis had begun to set in. My hair was beginning to fall out, and my teeth were loose. I later divorced my husband and got custody of the children, and God knows how *that* happened. And after that," she added, "I went on a two-month binge that made *The Lost Weekend* look like a Sunday-school picnic. I was a mess, bloated and skinny at the same time, if you can imagine that. I really looked grubby.''

Today, she is trim, vital, and strikingly attractive—a blond and tawny woman who glows with good health. By her own estimation, she looks at least fifteen years younger than she did in the last days of her active alcoholism. "Before I got sober," Harriet recalls, "I must have had two dozen major hospital admissions in eight years, each ostensibly for a legitimate reason. When I finally got the message, I stopped being sick. I stopped dropping bowling balls on my feet, stopped breaking my bones. You begin to take care of yourself, you know?''

Indeed I do know; the before-and-after difference—among women alcoholics in particular—is very often breathtaking. From an educational standpoint alone, that difference has enormous impact among those women still grappling with the various forms of denial and concealment that in themselves are so symptomatic of the illness.

To be sure, one can actually *witness* the tremendous value of "sharing" by such women as Virginia "M" at open meetings of Alcoholics Anonymous; of Harriet Gibney detailing her then-and-now physical and emotional condition to patients being treated for alcoholism at Silver Hill Foundation; and of Marty Mann, Florette Pomeroy, and others reaching out to countless invisible women alcoholics in radio and television discussions.

Marty Mann delivers upwards of two hundred lectures a year and has appeared on "I can't tell you, Jack, how *many* TV programs about women alcoholics." During 1973 and 1974, Marty's path and mine crossed perhaps a dozen times in various cities. One evening in Washington, D.C., we talked over coffee about the tremendous educational job still facing the National Council on Alcoholism; several women joined us. "Most people don't know a damned thing about alcoholism," said one of the women, a recovered alcoholic singer, "except that it's 'wrong.' And even those who *do* know something—and I mean women especially—are totally ignorant of the insidious progression, the whole idea of predictable stages. One, two, three and you're dead."

Significantly, not long after that discussion, NCA published an important new brochure, entitled *What Are the Signs of Alcoholism?* In checklist fashion, it is designed to help a person learn if he or she has some of the symptoms of alcoholism. Here are those yes/no questions, prepared by NCA's medical department in collaboration with medical authorities around the world:

1. Do you occasionally drink heavily after a disappointment, a quarrel, or when the boss gives you a hard time?
2. When you have trouble or feel under pressure, do you always drink more heavily than usual?
3. Have you noticed that you are able to handle more liquor than you did when you were first drinking?
4. Did you ever wake up on the "morning after" and discover that you could not remember part of the evening before, even though your friends tell you that you did not "pass out"?
5. When drinking with other people, do you try to have a few extra drinks when others will not know it?

 6. Are there certain occasions when you feel uncomfortable if alcohol is not available?
 7. Have you recently noticed that when you begin drinking you are in more of a hurry to get the first drink than you used to be?
 8. Do you sometimes feel a little guilty about your drinking?
 9. Are you secretly irritated when your family or friends discuss your drinking?
10. Have you recently noticed an increase in the frequency of your memory "blackouts"?
11. Do you often find that you wish to continue drinking after your friends say that they have had enough?
12. Do you usually have a reason for the occasions when you drink heavily?
13. When you are sober, do you often regret things you have done or said while drinking?
14. Have you tried switching brands or following different plans for controlling your drinking?
15. Have you often failed to keep the promises you have made to yourself about controlling or cutting down on your drinking?
16. Have you ever tried to control your drinking by making a change in jobs, or moving to a new location?
17. Do you try to avoid family or close friends while you are drinking?
18. Are you having an increasing number of financial and work problems?
19. Do more people seem to be treating you unfairly without good reason?
20. Do you eat very little or irregularly when you are drinking?
21. Do you sometimes have the "shakes" in the morning and find that it helps to have a little drink?
22. Have you recently noticed that you cannot drink as much as you once did?
23. Do you sometimes stay drunk for several days at a time?
24. Do you sometimes feel very depressed and wonder whether life is worth living?

25. Sometimes after periods of drinking, do you see or hear things that aren't there?
26. Do you get terribly frightened after you have been drinking heavily?

Those who answer "yes" to any of the questions, says NCA's medical director, Dr. Frank Seixas, may have some of the symptoms of alcoholism. Taking the questionnaire an important step further, "yes" answers to several of the questions indicate these stages of alcoholism: Questions 1–8, early stage; Questions 9–21, middle stage; Questions 22–26, the beginning of the final stage.

For the reasons already indicated, meaningful statistics on women alcoholics are virtually nonexistent. In turn, it is impossible to even estimate how many of America's women alcoholics would fall into the area indicated by the last five questions of the checklist. However, my own experience, along with the experiences of the many women alcoholics with whom I have spoken, demonstrate that the number is frighteningly large.

It all came into dismal focus for me one gray afternoon in San Francisco. I was sitting in that city's Suicide Prevention Center (SPC) on Twelfth Avenue with a long-time SPC counselor. On a desk in front of us was a bulging, dog-eared folder called "The Death File"; it contains records from 1966 to the present of those people who had called Suicide Prevention Center during a time of crisis and, at some later date, had "suicided," to use the counselor's word. "More than half of the people who suicided," she said quietly, hefting the grim Death File, "were women alcoholics."

No less tragic, on the other side of the ledger, is the utter dearth of recovery facilities for women alcoholics who still cling tenaciously to life. In Stockton, California, for example, there is not a single transitional facility for homeless women alcoholics seeking help. Following a forty-eight-hour detoxification period in that city's San Joaquin General Hospital, homeless women alcoholics are returned to the streets without so much as a fare-thee-well. "They go through detox," says an alcoholism counselor at the hospital, "and that's it. The same night, they're back sleeping in the weeds alongside the railroad tracks."

At the southern end of the state, in San Diego, the situation is even worse. There, the county's 100-bed Alcoholic Detoxification Center admits men only; moreover, it is almost impossible to get local hospitals to admit alcoholism patients of either sex. "About all you can do without medical help is to offer them another drink to stave off the symptoms of withdrawal," says Cheney Mayfield, women's counselor at San Diego's Alcoholism Counseling and Education Center. In one recent year, Cheney Mayfield adds bitterly, three of the women alcoholics on her case load died.

On the East Coast, similarly, a 1974 canvass in the District of Columbia showed that while more than 700 beds are available to males in the religious missions and in District-funded alcoholism rehabilitation programs, there are fewer than 100 beds for women. None of the principal church groups, such as the Gospel Missions and Central Union, has facilities of any kind for women; although the Salvation Army has fifteen beds for females, there is a three-day residency limit. The D.C. Rehabilitation Center for Alcoholics at Occoquan, Virginia, which was opened in 1966, has 425 beds for men; not until 1969 was a thirty-bed women's unit added and later expanded to fifty beds.

Only at three community-run halfway houses—Shalom House, Deborah's Place, and Zaccheus House—can a homeless woman alcoholic find a place to stay in the District of Columbia as long as it "reasonably" takes to get herself together. However, the three facilities have a total of only twenty-eight beds, and two of them, Shalom and Deborah's, opened in 1974.

"The emphasis has always been on helping men, yet the need for helping women is so much greater," says Dr. Veronica Maz, a former Georgetown University sociology professor who quit her academic job several years ago to start the So Others May Eat (SOME) soup kitchen, and who now runs Shalom House. "The crux of the problem is that although there are probably more women than men at the bottom of the heap, the women remain hidden—out of sight, and thus out of mind."

The same point is angrily emphasized by Shirley Fisher, an experienced counselor who runs a halfway house for women that was opened in May 1973. "Society is doing just as little as it can get by with when it comes to the woman alcoholic," she says. "The only time the District responds is when we raise hell."

Most of the time, unfortunately, not even hell-raising does much good. In San Francisco, once again (where, it is estimated, at least half of the Golden Gate Bridge suicides are alcohol-related), that fact was dramatically illustrated for me by Jane O'Toole, a recovered alcoholic who is manager and director of Stepping Stone Halfway House for Women. During the course of what was, for me, an emotion-charged day inside the tidy and homey facility on Tenth Avenue, she shared the personal before-and-after experiences that led to the formation of Stepping Stone in 1963. And she enabled me to see, in grotesque perspective, how the microcosmic successes of facilities like Stepping Stone stack up against the macrocosmic failures of San Francisco and other great American cities that have not even begun meeting the minimal needs of their women alcoholics.

A dark-haired and soft-spoken woman, Jane O'Toole dates her sobriety from June 5, 1951, "one day at a time," as she puts it. She was the first "graduate" of America's first recovery house for alcoholic women, a place in Los Angeles called Friendly House, finally seeking help after a seventy-two-hour stretch in jail. It was the only time she had ever spent in jail and "thank God, the last time."

Earlier, Jane O'Toole's alcoholism had progressed swiftly into the final stage—from "hidden drinking and lying about the drinking and hiding bottles," through divorce and separation from her children, to a period during which she "quickly sank to a level of practically a barfly. And this," she told me quietly, "helped heap more guilt and more remorse and more self-hatred. But I *had* to drink. I was at that point where I had to drink in order to be with me. *I* was completely unacceptable, so I kept drinking."

Following commitment to the psychopathic ward of Los Angeles General Hospital, and then several ninety-day stints in Camarillo State Hospital, Jane O'Toole went on a five-and-a-half-month binge that was to be her last drunk. She lived in constant and total terror during those twenty-two weeks, she said. "I was afraid to cross the street, afraid to go out, afraid to come in.'' Not long afterward, however, she took that giant step from the county jail to Friendly House, where she was taken under the wing of a remarkable woman named Addie.

When she left Friendly House after six weeks, Jane recalled, she asked Addie if it would be wise to visit her children. ''Addie said she didn't think so, because my husband had remarried and she thought it would be too much of an emotional thing,'' Jane continued. ''But she gave me some advice that I'll never forget, because it made a great deal of difference in my life. She said, 'Just hold yourself in readiness, in case you're ever needed.' ''

Jane O'Toole was needed just weeks later when her husband died in a drowning accident. Barely two and a half months sober, she went to court and asked for the guardianship and custody of her two children, then five and seven years old. After several hearings, her petition was granted. But the children's stepmother had also petitioned for the children, and the step-mother's attorney protested the award by decrying Jane's alcoholism. ''And the judge said,'' Jane remembered, permitting herself a smile as she calmly lit a cigarette, '' 'But this woman does not do these things *now*.' ''

The same is true of more than two-thirds of Stepping Stone's seven hundred alumnae, women alcoholics whose long-term, total-abstinence recovery rate approaches that of America's most successful industrial programs. ''For a quick profile,'' says Jane O'Toole, ''the average Stepping Stone resident is a woman of thirty-eight or thirty-nine years of age, a divorced Catholic with two children, and separated from her children. Most of our women are working women, because of the urban setting, and a good seven out of ten are the typical hidden woman drinker.''

The average stay at Stepping Stone is five or six months, and after several weeks the women are encouraged to look for a job. The facility is also strongly AA oriented, and the women are urged to attend outside meetings as well as those held in the recovery house itself. ''We stress home,'' Jane O'Toole says, smiling again. ''I'm well known for my joke in saying I don't run a house, I run a home.''

To everyone's surprise, including my own, it costs only $25,000 a year to operate Stepping Stone, and 70 percent of that amount is provided by $35-a-week fees from residents able to pay. The balance is raised through voluntary contributions, and the facility just about breaks even each year.

However, the catch for most of San Francisco's women alcoholics—literally hundreds upon hundreds who need and want the kind of help provided in a recovery home environment—is that Stepping Stone is the city's only facility of its kind. It stands alone in spite of its proven success, in spite of the fact that San Francisco's alcoholism rate is among the nation's highest, and in spite of insistence by Jane O'Toole and other experienced alcoholism professionals that the city easily needs at least thirteen "Stepping Stones."

The new recovery houses, like Stepping Stone itself, would be virtually self-supporting; the outside funds required would be not greater than perhaps $8,000 annually for each facility. In short, for less than $100,000 a year, San Francisco could quickly take a large step toward meeting the urgent needs of women alcoholics seeking residential rehabilitation.

Not only are such funds being withheld, but an amount almost double that required for twelve more "Stepping Stones" has been siphoned into a project which, snorts Jane O'Toole, "is a duplication of the service the Salvation Army's been providing for a hundred years. It's costing $193,000 and is designed to handle only forty-five women, which is a pretty expensive operation for somebody to go in and take a shower."

All this is not to say that the outlook for America's women alcoholics is hopelessly bleak. There are communities across the nation where vital progress has taken place, and where the outlook for continued advances is rather bright. One such community is Bellevue, in northwestern Washington, an affluent bedroom suburb on Lake Washington reputed to have the highest ratio of women alcoholics in the nation.

"Bellevue is the fourth largest city in the state, and there's more liquor sold here per capita than anywhere else in Washington," says Barbara Starr, a recovered alcoholic who is executive director of the community's Eastside Alcoholism Information and Referral Center. "We know that for a fact, because our liquor stores are state run."

When Barbara Starr entered the professional alcoholism field in 1966, there were six Information and Referral centers in the state; today there are thirty. During the same period, in Bellevue alone, meetings of Alcoholics Anonymous have increased from half a dozen to almost two dozen weekly; moreover, women now substantially outnumber men at the Bellevue meetings. "They're getting the homemakers, the mayonnaise-jar-filled-with-bourbon-under-the-sink crowd," Barbara says knowingly. "I used to belong to that bridge-lunch bunch, too, and, believe me, I know all about that life style."

Most meaningfully, the Eastside Information and Referral Center (whose seven-person staff includes four counselors who are recovered alcoholics) is reaching women with the very early symptoms of alcoholism. "At the beginning," Barbara Starr claims, "every woman I saw needed in-patient care. They were acute chronic alcoholics. Now only somewhere between 5 and 10 percent require in-patient treatment, and that's what's really encouraging."

One key to this early-stage detection and treatment is close co-operation among Bellevue's Information and Referral Center (which is an affiliate of the National Council on Alcoholism), Alcoholics Anonymous, the schools, and the community's six-court judicial system. In Bellevue's public schools, for example, three-session audiovisual alcoholism education programs are held monthly. Similarly, the courts require drunk-driving offenders to attend classes on alcoholism, and they are also urged to join AA. "Probably one out of three newcomers at AA meetings gets there because of DWI [driving while intoxicated]," says the secretary of one Bellevue Alcoholics Anonymous group.

An equally important reason for Bellevue's success in what one alcoholism professional calls "the early warning system" is the intense involvement of recovered alcoholics like Barbara Starr, people who have "been there" themselves, have come back, and now serve as public and living proof that alcoholism can indeed be treated and arrested. Depending on the circumstances, along with her own intuitive assessment, Barbara Starr often tells her own story to shaky referrals and "walk-ins" who are filled with trepidation.

Sitting across her desk from me, Barbara pretended that I was a newly referred woman alcoholic. I was the alcoholic wife of a Bellevue executive, she hypothesized; I had received my second DWI, perhaps while driving my children to school. Barbara first tackled the "skid row stereotype" barrier, telling me about her own middle-class background, her marriage, and four school-age children; she emphasized that she and her husband had been deeply involved in community affairs. At the peak of their involvement, Barbara's husband had been state president of the Jaycees, and she had followed him as state president of the Jaycee wives. "At one point, we were voted the outstanding young couple in the state of Washington," she said somewhat wistfully.

Then, very quickly—still pretending that I was a woman referred by the court—Barbara Starr sketched the rapid and inexorable progression of her alcoholism. "I wound up with bleeding ulcers, so I started drinking moose milk, which, if you don't know, is milk laced with booze. Never thinking, of course, that alcohol had anything to do with it. I got worse," she added, "and my nervous system went to hell. I went to the doctor and he prescribed tranquilizers. So I was drinking and taking tranks, and my husband's drinking was progressing, too. He's on uppers and I'm on downers, and we're drinking, and that really allows for happy living, right?"

The drinking soon began to affect the marriage, Barbara went on; and it began to affect the children as well, to the point where mother and daughter had literally changed roles. "I didn't know who I was," she remembered. "I knew that something was haywire, but it never crossed my mind that I was alcoholic."

For the better part of an hour, Barbara Starr detailed her decline and fall, all the while trying to reach me as the "woman alcoholic" with my own built-in denial system. She talked about playing tournament bridge during alcoholic blackouts—and *winning*—despite the fact that she never remembered sitting at the table. She detailed her late-stage, round-the-clock drinking, including some horrendous episodes on airplanes. "Once, I started out for Los Angeles and ended up in a Palm Springs hospital. I asked the attendant how I got to Palm Springs, and he said they took me off the plane in a wheelchair.''

Then there was what her children now call *''that* summer,''* Barbara Starr recalled, including a Sunday when the police ticketed her for "drunken rowboat driving, if you can picture that. At the end,'' she concluded, "my drinking got to a point where I was neglecting the children and the guilt and remorse were overwhelming, so I began taking more pills and drinking more alcohol to escape.

"Finally, my drinking got so bad that I wouldn't answer the phone,'' Barbara added, leaning forward as if I was a real and very frightened woman alcoholic. "You know, the day you wake up and you can't count on yourself any more is a pretty desolate, horrible, horrible feeling. I was having convulsions every day by this time, and living that miserable hell that every alcoholic knows.''

Hypothetical woman that I was that day, I nevertheless identified with many of the things Barbara Starr described. I identified and I was hooked. Swiftly and deftly, then, Barbara set the hook, looking straight into my eyes. "With the woman alcoholic, it used to be that if you said that you were one, you might just as well print the word PROSTITUTE across your forehead. But that's changing, and there's less stigma today. It doesn't have to be the way it used to be, because the point is that you're *here,* and help is available if you want it, just the way I wanted it and got it.''

Not surprisingly, I was optimistic—in fact, almost ebullient— as I left Bellevue that day. From the airport, I called Florette Pomeroy in Sausalito to share my mood, for Florette had put me in touch with Barbara Starr in the first place. And Florette brought me gently back down to earth, telling me that "we who work in the field continuously'' very often tend to think that there's been a dramatic change in public attitudes about alcoholism. But it's still a dramatic change that affects only a small proportion of the community, she added, implying that places like Bellevue remain, once again, exceptions that prove the rule.

"One of my favorite bits of philosophy,'' said Florette during that phone conversation, "is that until we reach the point where at least 51 percent of the people in the community are firmly committed to the concept that alcoholism is a treatable illness, and that the alcoholic can recover, we really can't expect the majority of *alcoholics* to accept this, because we're profoundly influenced by the mores of the people around us."

So long as the majority of people feel that alcoholism is a sort of unmentionable condition, and really don't know anything about it or learn anything about it, Florette Pomeroy adds, "we're going to continue to suffer from what I call the conspiracy of silence that surrounds the alcoholic and the woman alcoholic in particular."

The delaying mechanism, of course, is society's continuing ambivalence toward the woman alcoholic. On the one hand, women are encouraged to free themselves; indeed, they are exhorted that they have already "come a long way, baby." The liquor industry itself has leaped unhesitatingly on *that* bandwagon, trying hard to capitalize on women's struggle for liberation; chameleon-like, various liquor companies long ago changed the verbal coloration of their ads in attempting to grab the female segment of the drinking population.

J & B Rare Whisky's pitch, for example, is that "you don't have to be one of the boys to like J & B Rare—whisky's not a male prerogative." As long ago as 1968, the same way, Black & White Scotch put it in these terms: "Putting on weight? Stop eating bread and potatoes and start drinking Black & White . . . At least you'll keep cheerful." And finally, there is the more recent Smirnoff Vodka ad showing that not only does drink keep you happy, it also makes life more exciting: "I used to belong to the public library—until I discovered Smirnoff."

On a broader scale and in contrast, as we have seen, society's indictment of the woman alcoholic is far more insidious and deeply rooted, linked to that "hand that rocks the cradle jazz," the "Scarlet Letter syndrome," and a host of other exemplifications of the double stigma confronting women alcoholics in America today.

"Every time I see Foster Brooks or Dean Martin doing their nauseating 'funny drunk' routines on TV," says one woman alcoholic friend of mine, "it strikes me that they would never ever do a 'funny *woman* drunk' on the tube, because that is sacrilegious, man. And it's the same thing with those stupid lamps; you know, the ones with the drunk leaning against the lamppost. Did you ever see one with a *lady* drunk holding up the lamppost? You never will, sweetie, because it's a whole different bag. We have to keep the ladies in their place, and for the lady lush, that place is in the closet."

5

The Young Alcoholic:
High without the Hassle

Friday, September 26, 1969

U.S. Senate, Special Subcommittee on Alcoholism and Narcotics of the Committee on Labor and Public Welfare, Los Angeles, California

The special subcommittee met, pursuant to notice, at 10 A.M., in the Board of Supervisors Hearing Room, 500 West Temple Street, Senator Harold E. Hughes (chairman of the Special Subcommittee on Alcoholism and Narcotics) presiding.

SENATOR HUGHES: The Chair will now call Gary H. I would just like to preface his testimony with a brief statement. Gary is a very young man who had meditated quite some time about coming before this subcommittee with his testimony, and I think he is very courageous in the fact that he is here today. I want you to be perfectly comfortable, Gary, and to proceed without any worry about anything at all and do the great job we know you can do. If you will proceed with your statement then we would like to cross-examine you a little.

STATEMENT OF GARY H., HIGH SCHOOL STUDENT,
LOS ANGELES, CALIFORNIA

GARY H.: My name is Gary H. I am a resident of Los Angeles. I am 15 years old and a junior in high school.

I have done a lot of my growing up on the Sunset Strip.

It is a true statement when I tell you that there is no chemical or drug in my bloodstream. My body has been completely clean for about three months.

I would like to fill you in on my past experiences as a narcotics addict and an alcoholic.

I was in the sixth grade and 10 years old when my experience in drugs began. My first exposure was with tranquilizers and sleeping pills. I found some pills in the bathroom of my home. I did not know what they were and I really don't know why I did, but I took them to my room and took four of them.

In about an hour or so I got a—I don't know if it was physical or mental—but I got a lift from them. I felt good. I felt like I could do things I could have never done before—like I had a powerful command over things. So I thought that if I felt that good, another pill would make me feel better. Anyhow, within a few days the 20 pills were gone, except for two. I saved two of them and showed them to a friend of mine who said he could get me more. He said they were sleeping pills and tranquilizers. That was the beginning and I went on a search for more.

Almost right away I did not only want the pills—I needed them. I used to think of them as my food and water. My body had to have them. I would get sick and shaky without them.

This turned into an expensive habit for me, and so I found alcohol. I heard it was cheaper and with the alcohol I felt that I wouldn't need the pills anymore. However, this wasn't true.

So over a period of time when the alcohol didn't help to cure me, I went back to the pills. I now know that it is all the same thing but in a different form. That is my opinion, but my experience with the pills and alcohol, they are all one. So I began taking them all together.

I was 12, and pretty soon after that I started on other chemicals or dangerous drugs such as marijuana, hash, cocaine, barbiturates, benzedrine, and LSD.

Within a year or so I discovered the wonderful world of methedrine. It was as easy to buy the drug as it was to buy food in the supermarket. At that time it was harder to get the money than it was to get the drugs.

If you want to know how a 13-year-old gets the money to support his addictions, I would have to tell you. I would buy the drugs at the street market cost on the strip from men in white shirts and ties. If one wasn't there, there was always another one around. Then, in turn, I would sell it at a profit to other young users. That's how I supported my addictions. However, there are many other ways to support them.

The important thing I want to tell you is that I couldn't function without the drugs and alcohol. I couldn't function as a musician or an athlete, I couldn't perform well in football without popping 35 to 50 pep pills down my throat. It gave me a sense of security in my music and in football and it gave me a fearless sense of aggression. I could not function without them.

That's my story. My life was completely unmanageable. But now I have found a way to live my life, not run it, and only with the help of many other people could I have achieved this goal. I now choose not to use drugs or alcohol. I have chosen life instead of hell. I could never have done it alone. I have a need for other people.

That is where I am at now. I am one of the lucky ones. I am not unique, but I am fortunate. I saw a girl I knew about 16 years old draped over a curb on the strip. Half her body was on the sidewalk and half in the gutter. She was dead. She never came down from a bad trip. That could have been me. However, I am alive. I have been given another chance to accept the realities of life. For the first time I can see and feel the beauties of the mountains and the ocean. This all came with the hope, confidence, and the love of other people. Like I said before, I was fortunate.

There are many other teenagers such as I that are dying in the streets. That is why I feel this subcommittee's proposals are so vital to the here and now. That is why I am up before you. I am aware of many relatives and friends who might be shocked but I deeply feel you have to understand the problem of drugs and alcohol among young people. There is a need of a place to go when a teenager is so strung out and hopeless they want to die. There could be an answer, and I don't mean a jail or an asylum, but a place in all hospitals with substantial medical aids, like a clean bed and food.

God, as I understand Him, does not withhold His love merely because we are young. I wish people could realize that God has no stepchildren. Thank you.

At this writing, more than six years after his moving testimony in that Los Angeles hearing room, twenty-one-year-old Gary H. remains one of the lucky ones. Unlike Gary, however, many of his former friends are still ''out there''; several have since died as a result of their alcoholism. All across America, in fact, the toll of alcoholism among adolescents has risen sharply, to the ominous point, warns the former director of NIAAA, Dr.

Morris Chafetz, that "the results could be catastrophic for our entire society."

Psychiatrist Chafetz, a sometimes controversial political appointee to the nation's top alcoholism post, adds with uncharacteristic verve, "The tremendous upsurge in drinking among America's youth just blows my mind."

During countless public appearances in the past few years, Chafetz has emphasized over and over that America's youth are clearly forgoing other drugs for alcohol. As he has put it repeatedly, and as the media have echoed, "The switch is on."

In my estimation, Dr. Chafetz and his associates are only half right; my own nose-to-the-ground odyssey in and around America's bars, liquor stores, schools, jails, and alcoholism treatment centers has convinced me beyond any doubt that the switch has long since taken place.

From the Deep South to the Pacific Northwest, I tramped through college and high school and junior high school gymnasium locker rooms reeking of wine vomit; talked with teen and pre-teen "bottle gangs"; saw scores of fast-aging juveniles who had been arrested many times over for driving while intoxicated; watched bota bags replace marijuana roach clips as fast-selling record store and "head shop" sundries.

In city after city, I witnessed the physical and emotional anguish of acute alcoholism among youngsters barely out of puberty. In one large suburb, I was told of the then newly popular "wine enema," a practice far outreaching my own grisly experiences as a teen-age alcoholic. "I don't do it any more," one sixteen-year-old boy told me, "but it really gives you a wild kind of high. And the thing is, they can't tell by your breath."

For official documentation of the skyrocketing incidence of alcoholism among American youth, one can plod through the heavily footnoted NIAAA report *Alcoholism and Health,* subtitled "New Information" and issued by that agency of the Department of Health, Education, and Welfare in June 1974. Under the heading "Trends in Teen-Age Drinking," one reads, for example, "Preliminary findings from the 1974 national survey of junior and senior high-school students indicate that among seventh graders, 63 percent of boys and 54 percent of girls have had a drink. As Figure 3 indicates, the proportion of teen-age drinkers increased with grade to 93 percent of twelfth-grade boys and 87 percent of twelfth-grade girls.''

Unquestionably, such surveys serve their purpose. For considerably less cost, however, any concerned reader with time and the wherewithal for travel can ascertain, with rather more gripping personal impact, that alcoholism is not only rampant among American youth, but appears to be getting worse instead of better.

Occasionally, moreover, surveys can be highly misleading; footnoted or otherwise, cold statistics and initial impressions sometimes tell just half the story. A significant example is the fact that youth-oriented, low-proof ''pop'' wines seem to be losing favor among teens and pre-teens. To the dismay of the Wine Institute, purchases of the high-profit fruit-flavored beverages have begun to falter—after sales bubbled upward from $3 million in 1969 to a heady $33 million in 1973.

A hopeful sign for those concerned about rising teen-age alcoholism? Unfortunately, no. The real reason for the drop-off, young people point out knowingly, is that sedative drugs such as Seconal (known in youthful vernacular as ''downers'' or ''reds'') are expensive and becoming more so; hence, such once popular combinations as ''reds and Ripple'' have increasingly given way to alcohol alone, especially the more potent ''whites,'' including vodka, tequila, and gin.

In many American supermarkets, a half pint of house-brand vodka sells for as little as $1. ''It takes less to do the job,'' one newly recovering teen-age alcoholic told me in Detroit. ''Also whites are easier to hide and carry, in a nail-polish-remover bottle or a Thermos. And there's less chance of getting busted or thrown out of school, like if you're holding reds or weed.''

What's more, as the testimony of Gary H. made clear, legal restrictions on the purchase of alcohol pose no challenge at all for America's estimated 750,000 young alcoholics. Although liquor store managers report few attempts by minors to purchase alcohol, and react to queries with suspicion or noncommittal shrugs, young people themselves say ''it's a breeze,'' noting, for example, that "fake ID cards" are as readily available as bubble gum.

In Bridgeport, Connecticut, for instance, Natalie, seventeen, used to "pile on the makeup and flirt with the clerks" to avoid being "carded," while Carol, fifteen, has her older brother buy her liquor. Although the legal drinking age in Connecticut is eighteen, even pre-teen youths can obtain liquor easily, says Dr. Roland Casperson, coordinator of alcohol services at the Greater Bridgeport Community Health Center. A favorite method is using the local "wino" to buy liquor by giving him the money and tipping him a quarter when he comes out, adds Casperson, who notes with alarm that 10 percent of those in the Center's outpatient program are under twenty.

That same alarm is being voiced across the nation. In New York City, an estimated 60 percent of 1,048,000 city youngsters between twelve and eighteen years of age use alcohol, asserts Joel Bennett, president of the New York Council on Alcoholism. "Approximately 36,000 adolescents here now have early symptoms of alcoholism and alcohol abuse," he adds.

In Florida's Dade and Broward counties, similarly, a survey by Resource Planning Corporation found 23,000 adolescents aged fourteen to seventeen who were intoxicated ten or more times in 1973. In those same counties, more than 10,000 youths in the fourteen-to-seventeen age bracket drink every single day. "Two years ago alcohol was no problem," says Dade County school board member Dr. Ben Sheppard, a physician and long-time director of drug rehabilitation programs. Sheppard needs no survey, he adds, because 40 percent of the youngsters being brought to his clinic—by parents or guardians—"are into alcohol, mostly tequila."

Still another report, in Delaware, warns that "adolescents constitute a disturbingly large segment of the state's population of problem drinkers," that several thousand of the state's teen-agers have already become heavy drinkers, and that heavy drinking among adolescents is sharply increasing, particularly as a substitute for various illegal drugs. Of the state's 56,200 heavy drinkers fourteen years of age and older, in fact, almost 4,000 are teen-agers. Considered in the statewide aggregate, the fed-erally financed study adds, "Persons 24 years old or younger constituted 35 percent of all the problem drinkers in Delaware."

"With many of the young people," the report concludes, "alcohol does not enjoy the status of a drug. Instead it is looked upon as a totally innocuous substitute, with little potential for ul-timate harm."

It is becoming manifest, of course, that just the opposite is true. The morbid day-to-day consequences of rising teen-age al-coholism can be seen in countless hospital emergency wards, au-tomobile junkyards, and, inevitably, mortuaries from coast to coast. At this writing, six out of every ten alcohol-related high-way deaths in America involve a person sixteen to twenty-four years of age. And the carnage, hand in glove with youngsters' alcohol dependence, is becoming ever more widespread.

In Massachusetts, for example, the number of alcohol-related traffic fatalities involving young people has jumped 22 percent since the state lowered the drinking age to eighteen from twenty-one in March 1973. "The increase was sharp and drastic and di-rectly attributable to the lower drinking age," says Richard E. McLaughlin, secretary of the Department of Public Safety, who analyzed highway fatalities during one year.

Specifically, reports McLaughlin, drivers between eighteen and twenty years of age caused 222 of the 972 fatal accidents in Massachusetts during the twelve-month period; of the 222 driv-ers, 74 had been drinking—twice as many as during the preced-ing twelve months, when the legal drinking age was twenty-one. And those 74 young people brought about the deaths of 89 peo-ple: themselves, their passengers and other motorists, and pedes-trians.

In Florida, where the legal drinking age was also reduced from twenty-one to eighteen in 1973, the situation is much the same. Less than a year after the new law went into effect, the Department of Highway Safety and Motor Vehicles conducted a survey of convicted drunk drivers. "We were shocked at what we found," says Don Keirn, chief of the Bureau of Driver Im-provement. "Before legalized drinking was reduced to eighteen years of age in July 1973, teen-agers were involved in one percent of the drunk driving cases. Now it's ten times worse. Ten percent of our drunk drivers are eighteen, nineteen, and twenty.''

A less obvious but perhaps longer-term consequence of the upsurge in youthful alcoholism is described by one mother of an alcoholic. ''It's especially debilitating for the adolescents to drink,'' she says, ''because when they do they fail to cope with the problems of adolescence. They don't grow and mature emotionally. They also tend to lose school time, learn more slowly, and become involved in crime.''

Then, too, there is the ''sudden death syndrome,'' described earlier, whereby alcoholics experience one or two days of sobriety following a two- to three-day binge, and then suddenly die. The phenomenon is especially critical to people under the age of thirty, warns Dr. James Luke, Chief Medical Examiner for the District of Columbia, who says the deaths are usually caused by a piece of excess fat loosened from the liver.

Young people also seem especially vulnerable to the muscle and bone deterioration that alcohol can cause, deterioration that can weaken the heart and heighten susceptibility to bone fracture. ''People are very fragile,'' adds Dr. Luke reflectively, alluding to teen-agers in particular. ''It doesn't take much to harm them.''

That fragility has begun to express itself in a condition known as ''instant alcoholism,'' which appears to result from young people's previous dependence on drugs other than alcohol. ''They turn this dependence on this drug to the liquor, and after just a few drinks they're hooked,'' says Sara Whitley of the Dallas Council on Alcoholism.

For Allan Luks, who is executive director of the New York City affiliate of the National Council on Alcoholism, that phenomenon is especially frightening. We talked about it at length one sun-drenched afternoon in Denver, during a coffee break at NCA's 1974 annual meeting. Youthful himself, perhaps in his early thirties, Luks observed that young people today were either ingesting alcohol at a faster rate than their parents did, or had another addiction before turning to alcohol. And although the percentage of alcoholism among the young is still a relatively low one compared to that among other segments of the population, he said, the very fact of *any* percentage is significant, because alcoholism usually takes years to develop.

"There are signs that it's now becoming a disease of the young, instead of the middle-aged," Luks told me. "Our New York office gets about 4,500 calls a year, and 2,500 of them result in referrals for treatment. It used to be that the number of teen-agers and young adults was almost zero. But in 1973 we had 24 referrals for treatment under nineteen years of age, and 109 in the twenty-to-twenty-five-year-old category."

What about the ones who *don't* call? "They go on drinking," Allan Luks said quietly. "Their alcoholism progresses, and some of them die before they're old enough to vote."

And some of them get married and have children, it occurred to me later; as alcoholic parents, they then bring into the world a new generation of emotionally handicapped offspring—in much the same manner as they themselves were handicapped, in so many instances, by the alcoholism of *their* parents. Hence, the circle remains unbroken.

"Although the children of alcoholics are the principals in a hidden tragedy, they tend to be totally ignored by the professionals treating the alcoholic parents," stresses Dr. Willem G. A. Bosma, who is director of the University of Maryland Hospital's Division of Alcoholism and Drug Abuse. "And yet," he adds, "research indicates that the alcoholic's children, the most plastic and impressionable members of the family, are most subject to the destructive influence of an alcoholic parent."

Dr. Bosma continues determinedly, "In this part of Maryland, of 128 male adolescents on probation after court conviction, 82 had at least one alcoholic parent. And a survey of successful adolescent suicides showed two-thirds of the adolescents to have an alcoholic parent. In our own adolescent suicide clinic," he concludes grimly, "we treated twelve attempts in adolescents ranging from twelve to seventeen years old. All had made an attempt, and one had succeeded at the second suicide attempt. Of the twelve, ten had an alcoholic parent, while one had a parent who drank heavily."

The point, clearly, is that neither the alcoholic father nor the alcoholic mother can adequately fulfill the role of parent; the result, as venerable alcoholism specialist Dr. Ruth Fox puts it, ''is that there are gross failures of identification in the growing child, a condition which can warp all his future relationships.''

For me, as perhaps for the reader, the conclusions drawn by Drs. Bosma, Fox, and others become far more meaningful when they are expressed in terms of everyday realities. I was particularly struck, for example, by these excerpts from actual dialogues between social worker R. Margaret Cork and several traumatized young children with alcoholic parents.

''The worse times are when Dad hits Mom,'' said twelve-year-old Jerome. ''One time when he was hitting her, I ran up and hit him as hard as I could with one of my toys—I don't even remember what it was—and after that it was all a blank. I don't remember what happened.''

''Which is worse, the drinking or the fighting?''

''The fighting. Even when I'm in bed I hear it. You can't ever get away from it, but sometimes you have a rest from the drinking.''

''How does the fighting make you feel?''

''Mad and pretty scared,'' Jerome answered, hanging his head. ''Usually I start crying.''

''There's just always screaming in our house,'' ten-year-old Judy told Margaret Cork. ''It makes me get all funny inside—frightened like. The little ones get mad at me because they have to mind me when Mom can't manage them. Mommy always screams at me because I keep forgetting to do all the things she tells me to do, and I can't keep the little kids quiet enough when she has a headache. I can't talk to Daddy or Mommy about how I feel—they just get madder. I always dream it will be better, but I know it never will.

''I keep wishing my parents were like other parents,'' Judy continued wistfully. ''They're so unhappy. I keep worrying what will happen to me if Mom gets sick—she just has this one lung—and Daddy keeps having to go to jail. I feel so awful I keep thinking of dying.''

Sadly, such traumatization is commonplace within literally millions of American households, leading to the frightening alienation that, in turn, becomes a primary reason for eventual alcohol dependence by the emotionally and sometimes physically brutalized adolescents themselves. In discussion after discussion with alcoholic young people—some still suffering from active alcoholism and others, like Gary H., on the road to recovery—that particular feeling became an almost predictable refrain.

"I drank the first time because I wanted to be part *of,* instead of apart *from,*" I was told in city after city. "I drink because it makes it easy for me to talk to other kids, to do the things I'm too scared to do when I'm not high. Like talk to a girl, or dance, or just be with other kids. To be loose. You know, stuff like that."

If parental alcoholism plants the seed for the same illness among the young—and if, as many experts now suggest, genetic predisposition prepares the soil, in a manner of speaking—certainly society itself provides a climate conducive to that seed's germination and maturation.

Indeed, few young people—no matter what their background or genetic makeup—can initially resist the attractions of a beverage with such remarkable and seemingly magical properties as the ability to induce euphoria, sedation, intoxication, and narcosis. Rare is the impressionable teen-ager who would summarily reject an elixir promising personal ease, peer group acceptability, instant manliness or womanliness, freedom from fear and anger (or what one writer calls "the amalgam of both, known as anguish"), in addition to "a sense of security . . . and a fearless sense of aggression," as Gary H. told the Senate subcommittee when he was just three months sober.

Unlike other drugs, as we well know, alcohol is not only legal but readily available (even when, for minors, it is *il*legal). Moreover, as subsequent chapters will demonstrate in greater detail, alcohol (otherwise known as ethanol) is advertised and marketed less as a liquid with the chemical formula of C_2H_5OH than as a means for achieving status, success, instant happiness, and heightened sexuality. Radio and television commercials for those youth-oriented "pop" wines are ubiquitous cases in point. One TV ad for a low-priced wine shows an overstuffed, bearded monarch pointing to a bottle of his product, saying that anyone who drinks it is "real smart." By implication, therefore, anyone who doesn't use it is "real dumb."

Too, something in our culture and conditioning keeps most of us from realizing that alcohol is in fact a *drug;* the use of the word "real" for other drugs is probably the most revealing aspect of contemporary social attitudes. And those built-in attitudes are so strong that one wonders if Americans will ever become as concerned about the use of alcohol by teen-agers as they were about the so-called "dangerous" drugs such as LSD, Methedrine, and heroin.

We laugh at drunk jokes, send drinking-oriented "bon voyage," "get well," and "happy birthday" greeting cards to friends, chuckle at drunken behavior, sanctify cocktail time, and generally tend to think of someone with alcoholism as "different."

Nor is that all. Drinking has come to represent one of the few "rites of passage" in our society; in addition to the almost mandatory use of alcohol at weddings, graduations, funerals, wakes, confirmations, and so forth, there are the military's traditional "wetting down" ceremonies and, even more commonplace, sports-page photos and film clips of champagne-puddled locker rooms following World Series or other championship victories.

Morris Chafetz claims to have learned from college students, also, that "other drugs tend to make you introspective, contemplative of your own navel, whereas alcohol tends to make you contemplate others' navels. In our society," he adds, not quite so facetiously, "where we give a lot of value to being socially facile, alcohol tends to win out."

Certainly alcohol wins out among parents of young people who have switched from "real" drugs to the one that is socially acceptable. One could almost hear the enormous sigh of relief breathed collectively by parents across America as they became aware of that "big switch," grateful that "all the ruckus last night was only because Linda and her friends were into the Scotch, and it wasn't drugs, thank God."

To be sure, that sigh of relief results as much from many parents' unvoiced concern about their *own* drinking patterns as from ignorance about the illness of alcoholism and its deadly progression. And the same sigh is echoed subliminally by the young people themselves, who are now able to ''get high without the hassle.''

At the Division of Alcoholism and Drug Abuse of the University of Maryland Hospital, Dr. Willem Bosma told of one case which, in its own bizarre way, seemed to sum up the almost universal attitude of parents and even educators to the excessive use of alcohol by youngsters. In his clinic, Dr. Bosma treated a boy of seventeen who had been drinking for fifteen years and who had been ''high'' since the age of five. ''He had grown up with an alcoholic grandfather who didn't eat very much and who fed the boy beer and whiskey.''

When he first saw him, Bosma said, the boy was quite well physically. ''But mentally he was in dire need of all kinds of treatment. He didn't have the time to develop mechanisms to cope with the world, since he was always anesthetized.''

Dr. Bosma simply couldn't believe that school authorities had been unaware of the boy's alcoholism, so he personally checked classroom records. ''The records never mentioned alcohol,'' he said, ''but noted he was unsteady on his feet, impulsive, and loud. He couldn't do any gymnastics because he fell all the time, and he had a speech impediment. And these reports,'' Bosma added, ''were from every teacher in every grade the boy was in. Nobody ever mentioned that he smelled of alcohol, which I'm sure he did. Even the speech therapist, whom he visited regularly for his 'speech impediment,' didn't notice that he just had a thick tongue.''

The point, Bosma concludes incredulously, is that ''we don't *want* to see. We don't want to see that there are an awful lot of children who have problems with alcohol, and that the children of alcoholics themselves have an awful lot of problems.''

In that extremely important sense, alcoholism remains first and foremost a *family affair*. From the standpoint of education and prevention, at one negative extreme are those parents who consider it ''cute'' to give a five- or six-year-old a sip of their martini. After all, what could a few sips do? ''Well, a sip or two doesn't do anything to a man who weighs two hundred pounds,'' says one alcoholism counselor, "but a child who weighs forty or fifty pounds can get quite high off a few sips of anything."

Then there are those parents who feel a few sips will calm a "nervous" child when all else fails. "Well, I'm trying to help a fourteen-year-old who got so much medicinal alcohol that at the moment she's usually too drunk to even make it to school in the morning," says alcoholism counselor Carolyn Buren in Dallas. "It got so she started taking the drinks herself when she was feeling bad. No one thought to try to find out *what* was making her feel bad until it was too late."

At the positive end of the spectrum, in sharp contrast, are nationwide campaigns being conducted by the National Parent-Teacher Association and Jaycees—in cooperation with NIAAA and NCA—designed to draw attention to the problem of alcoholism among the young. NCA urges, for example, that teenagers discuss "the drinking question" with their parents, pointing out at the same time that "alcohol cannot help you solve personal problems, overcome personal fears and inferiority, or to be popular with the crowd." Don't be afraid to say, "No, thanks, I don't drink," if that's your choice, one NCA pamphlet concludes.

National PTA literature, in turn, is directed to parents, comparing, for example, responsible family drinking patterns with "invitations to drinking disaster." Most low-risk groups of drinkers have these patterns, points out PTA: If they drink, parents present a constant example of drinking responsibly and in moderation—without lecturing or preaching; they teach by example; "ground rules" for using alcohol—or not using it—are well established in the family, agreed upon by all; excessive drinking is not acceptable to the family; overindulgence is not looked upon as comical; drinking is considered by parents to have no moral importance—to them, it's neither virtuous nor evil; drinking is not viewed as an escape, a proof of adult status, or anything else; drinking is not engaged in for its own sake, but as a part of other activities; no pressure is placed on a family member or guest to drink; no social significance is attached to a person saying "No, thank you, I don't drink."

In contrast, PTA's campaign brochures emphasize, problem

drinkers generally come from families that show far different practices, beliefs, and attitudes: The family "ground rules" for drinking are vague and inconsistent; one set of rules holds for men, another for women; often, one parent favors drinking, the other opposes it; if children have been using pep pills, marijuana, and similar drugs, some parents seem relieved when these children turn instead to alcohol use.

The results of such practices and attitudes, PTA cautions: Children experiment with alcohol in their mid- or late teens, usually away from home; young people become accustomed to drinking on irregular occasions (such as the weekend "beer bust") and to drinking large amounts on an empty stomach, rarely drinking mainly with meals; children see both adults and young people drink to escape from emotional and uncomfortable situations, and they adopt these practices themselves; children see pressure placed on others to drink, and to them not to drink is scorned as a sign of cowardice or unfriendliness; young people boast of their drinking prowess; young people drink to win acceptance from their peers, or to prove something—their manliness, glamour, sexual equality, or independence from their parents; intoxication is viewed as comical or socially acceptable; the message that children get from parents is, "Drink as I say, but not as I do."

Considering "where we are now compared to where we were," says Marty Mann, amazing progress has been made. Nationwide, for example, Mrs. Mann and other authorities point out, there has been a sizable increase in attendance by young people at Alcoholics Anonymous meetings; in the larger cities such as New York, Chicago, and Los Angeles, moreover, literally dozens of Young People's AA groups have been established in the past several years to accommodate the influx.

The remaining and seemingly unassailable challenge, however, is getting community alcoholism education programs started. "Everyone is still so worried about the drug scare," fumes one Texas doctor, "that alcohol just isn't considered. I tried going to one school principal to talk about it, and he told me to leave well enough alone. Parents consider alcohol education programs to be moralizing."

The same point is made by an alcoholism specialist at Rutgers University, who feels that "if we really went at this thing, it would require a social revolution." In his view—one with which a great many alcoholism professionals heartily concur—"We really should start now on a program that gives every child from kindergarten through college factual, unbiased training about alcohol. Then in a couple of generations we'd see fewer problems. Most people would have learned to drink responsibly."

Seemingly, everyone agrees that the challenge is primarily one for parents. In my own experience, a neighbor literally punched his son black-and-blue when he found him smoking marijuana. Weeks later, when the boy threw up on the living-room couch following an all-night binge, the father seemed rather proud; he confided to another neighbor, in fact, that pot was just a "stage," and that the youngster was going to turn out "just fine."

A far more empirical appraisal comes from Dr. James Luke of Washington, D.C., who has supervised autopsies on the corpses of numerous young alcoholics. "We aren't born needing a drink," he says. "We're *taught* to drink. The answer is subtle, and it will take a long educational process and significant social change to correct the problem."

6

"What Shall We Do with the Drunken Sailor...?"

On a sunny Monday in February 1975, several dozen uniformed men and women gathered together deep within the confines of the Naval Regional Medical Center in Long Beach, California. Many were already sitting as I entered the nondescript room. A Navy nurse caught my eye and motioned me to an empty chair beside her.

"It's 1300," a young lieutenant commander announced, adjusting the focal length on a Kodak Carousel slide projector. "For God's sake, let's get started so we don't have to be here all night. Can someone get the lights?"

The projector mechanism clicked and a photograph of an overweight, middle-aged Navy chief appeared on the screen. His expression was glum; his eyes were averted from the camera.

"This guy is really scattered," said a voice from the darkness. "He's so full of denial, it's unreal. I can hardly pin him down to what his name is. It's going to take a long time for this man."

The next photo was of a young black sailor. His hands were in his pockets and there was an enigmatic smile on his lips. "This is Jesse, who's going back to duty on the twenty-sixth of February with a good prognosis. I feel that he's made one hell of a lot of progress. When he came in here, he had so much brain damage that I thought he was retarded. But he isn't. He admits he's alcoholic, and it came out in group that he's been drinking alcoholically since he was ten. He's making a lot of progress on his own and doing a lot of work on his own, and I feel that he's really caught on to the program."

"He had a hell of a pill problem, too, didn't he?" said another voice.

"Yes, poly-addicted," replied the first. "A real chemical gourmet."

My eyes had become accustomed to the darkness. I could see the computer printout held by the nurse in the next chair. The paper was headed "ARC PATIENT LISTING 02/21/75 REMAINING"; it listed name, rank, service number, and other data for some fifty patients.

The photos and brief case histories continued. "Mike is also going back to duty the twenty-sixth of February, with a fair prognosis. I feel that he's made a lot of changes, has accepted his alcoholism, but I feel also that he's inclined to fall back into his old ways unless he gets a strong AA program . . .

"Alice is moving, but she's moving slowly. She has a lot of remorse and a lot of guilt about her alcoholism, which she covers up. She's really on the bottom. She'll smile a lot, but inside she's really hurting. So she's gonna take a little while . . .

"Bill is new in group, and he admits he's an alcoholic. He has a lot of memories that go back to 1962 in Great Lakes, when he was thrown into a padded cell for alcoholism. I have high hopes for him. You should have seen this guy's face when he first came into the group Saturday, and then again today. The difference is unbelievable . . ."

That's exactly it, I thought, aware that I had become transfixed by the photos and progress reports. The difference *was* unbelievable. There I was, sitting among a group of recovered alcoholics, each a counselor in an Alcoholism Rehabilitation Center (ARC) within a giant naval hospital; all had been sober for two years or more, and most had achieved their sobriety in Long Beach or similar facilities under the official aegis of the U.S. Navy, by top-level fiat, and with aboveboard funding procedures.

Within the U.S. military, of all places, alcoholism was finally being treated as an illness rather than as a disciplinary problem. The photos on the screen were of first-class citizens sharing a malady no less respectable and no less acceptable than coronary insufficiency or arthritis.

I sat back and thought briefly of my own ill-fated military career during the Korean war; I recalled a court-martial hearing for drunken assault, and yet another for wrecking an Army ambulance during an alcoholic blackout.

As the lights came on, I remembered some of those bad old days—in Fort Dix, for example, and in countless bars along the main street of nearby Wrightstown, New Jersey. As a twenty-one-year-old practicing alcoholic, I had bellied up to those bars with the best of them; I had torn up enlisted men's clubs and my own barracks with the best of them, too. And, in the final analysis, it had been all right with my commanding officer, my first sergeant, and my peers.

It had been all right because it was not only expected and tolerated, but even encouraged; indeed, my behavior had meshed perfectly with age-old military shibboleths equating hard drinking with manliness. In retrospect, that malignant equation had damned near killed me—as it had damned near killed the glum-faced Navy chief and the young black seaman on the screen and so many, many others.

In a broad sense, the military is, of course, but a subculture of the larger society itself. Thus it is in no way surprising that military drinking customs are founded on such bedrock myths as the hard-drinking, fearless frontiersman who drinks straight from the crock and never gets crocked; the two-fisted, rock-jawed tiger of an aviator who can chug-a-lug all night and fly all day; the foot-weary infantryman who can hold his booze like a man and for whom, consequently, a thigh-slapping, whiskey-filled canteen is *de rigueur;* and the notion, commercialized by marketers of decorative wall plaques for home bars, that one should "Never Trust a Man Who Doesn't Drink."

However, the military has also long nurtured drinking practices, rituals, and traditions of its own. In the pioneering days of the United States Navy, for example, it was standard practice for every departing ship to take on board far more rum than water. And when, in 1913, Secretary of the Navy Josephus Daniels decreed that the service would henceforth be "dry," the idiomatic expression "drunk as a sailor" was soon replaced by "drunk in every port"—a phrase that quickly became far more factual than figurative.

"As every Navy skipper knows," says Captain Joseph A. Pursch, who now heads the Navy's Alcoholism Rehabilitation Center in Long Beach, "once his ship hits port, the intoxicated sailor becomes his number-one problem."

A flight surgeon, psychiatrist, and self-proclaimed "workaholic" with more than a decade of experience in alcoholism treatment, Joe Pursch is a dedicated and highly skilled professional with little patience for the strictures of past practice. We spent hours together at the Long Beach ARC, and dug deeply into a host of military traditions and rituals associated with drinking.

On a daily basis, alcohol has become a veritable staple of life for most of us, Pursch maintains. "From a psychological standpoint," he says, "we use it to control almost any shift in our emotions. We also use it to assuage psychic pain, loneliness, uneasiness, to celebrate, and to mourn. In terms of its intended chemical effect, we tend to use alcohol as a stimulant, antidepressant, sedative, analgesic, tranquilizer, aphrodisiac, and soporific."

Warming to his subject, Joe Pursch describes the constancy of drinking as he has personally observed it over many years in the military, using his own field as the primary example.

"In Naval Aviation, we drink at Happy Hours, after a good flight, after a bad flight, and after a near midair collision (to calm our nerves). To celebrate our first solo flight, we traditionally present our instructor with a bottle of his favorite liquor and, if we successfully bail out of a crippled airplane, we express our thanks to the lifesaving parachute rigger with a bottle of his preferred spirits.

"We drink when we get our wings, when we get promoted (wetting-down party), when we get passed over (to alleviate our depression), at formal Dinings In, change-of-command ceremonies, chiefs' initiations, and at 'Beef and Burgundy Night.' At birthday balls, we drink our door prize if we have the lucky ticket.''

In much the same fashion, Pursch continues, when a diver inspects the hull of the ship, he is given medicinal brandy, and the same treatment is prescribed for exposure to the elements if a man falls overboard and is fished out of the Caribbean on a hot day in July.

"A night carrier landing sometimes rates medicinal brandy dispensed by the well-meaning flight surgeon. We 'hail and farewell' frequently, and the first liquid that wets the bow of a newborn ship is champagne. In short,'' concludes Pursch, ''we drink from enlistment to retirement and from teenhood to old age.''

Harking back to his own enlistment, Joe Pursch recalls, "It was very difficult to have a feeling of belonging if you didn't at least drink a good bit. And it's unfortunate,'' he adds, ''because this feeds right into what many a young person will want to do in order to escape from the nervousness that comes with having to learn to adapt to a new environment, to be away from home and all that.''

Earlier that day in Long Beach, an ARC counselor had similarly described his early days in the service. ''The first thing you learn is about the social functions and your obligations connected with them. And if you're an officer, they even have a book out called *Welcome Aboard* that includes the cocktail hour. It also includes a very detailed description of the 'Dining In.' ''

"Dining In,'' I learned, is an age-old armed forces ceremony during which officers gather together as ''officers and gentlemen,'' sans ladies; in an extremely formal and ritualistic manner, they eat, drink, smoke, and toast various people. One elaborate ritual involves a large jug of wine, which is passed from hand to hand and never allowed to touch the tablecloth.

Then, too, there is the ubiquitous "Happy Hour,'' a euphemism for the knock-down-drag-out, bargain-rate boozing bouts that take place in enlisted men's and officers' clubs on U.S. military installations the world over.

"In my outfit,'' one retired Army major told me, ''you just

didn't think of *not* going to Happy Hour. Happy Hour is a drinking contest, and it's understood there that the guys who are the real men drink a lot. And you do this by showing that you drink a lot; you don't just talk about it, you actually do drink a lot.''

Not long ago in Bethesda Naval Hospital, as a classic example, a ''pressure cooker'' game was held daily in the Officers' Club. ''It took place in a big room with a bar,'' a former participant recalls. ''The rule was that as long as people walk in and have a drink, and are buddies, and so on, Happy Hour prices prevail. But the minute someone leaves, the prices rise to the customary level. Naturally,'' he adds, ''two or three of the most chronic alcoholics—comedians and heavy boozers—will sit by the door. In a joking manner, but not *really* joking, they restrain you from leaving.''

Considering the prevalence of such long-standing attitudes toward drinking in the military—attitudes which, like old soldiers, only slowly fade away—it follows that misbehavior connected with drinking is condoned, expected, or, at the very least, understood.

''I've seen this time and again as a doctor,'' says Joe Pursch. ''If a guy comes up for a captain's mast, the charges are always Drunk and Disorderly, Drunk and Absent, Drunk and Refusing a Direct Order, Drunk and Assault, Drunk and Destroying Government Property, Drunk and Asleep on Watch, and so on.

''Very seldom,'' he adds, ''is there anything without the 'Drunk and' part. If you destroy government property or whatever *without* being drunk, you're in deep trouble, and then you go to the nut ward. If you're AWOL without being drunk, you're a deserter. And if you pinch the admiral's lady on the fanny or take a leak on the admiral's lawn and you're not drunk, my God!''

Because the military is in many respects a cross section of American society, it is generally assumed that at least one out of every ten men and women in uniform is afflicted with alcoholism. However, a raft of recent studies indicate that the incidence of alcoholism among military personnel may, in fact, be substantially greater than among the civilian population.

According to one such study—a carefully documented Bureau

of Naval Personnel (BUPERS) survey of 1,603 Navy officers and enlisted personnel—39 percent of enlisted men and 23 percent of officers reported having experienced "unfavorable consequences" from drinking. More important, over 15 percent of those surveyed reported a *significant* drinking problem—one impairing duty performance, personal life, or both.

When one extrapolates that 15 percent to include U.S. military personnel the world around—from, say, Sasebo, Japan, to Adiak, Alaska—the total is nothing less than staggering.

The magnitude of the problem can be more easily grasped by narrowing one's perspective, viewing the incidence of military alcoholism in terms of an individual Army division—or perhaps a single aircraft carrier. By happenstance, my own perspective was narrowed and my own focus sharpened during the summer of 1974. The aircraft carrier U.S.S. *America* had dropped anchor in Chesapeake Bay, just off the coast of Norfolk, Virginia; under way with all its aircraft squadrons aboard, the *America* carries 4,800 persons.

At the time, I was visiting the Alcoholic Rehabilitation Center at Norfolk Naval Base, then under the command of Alfred J. Croft. Al Croft had just returned from the *America,* where he had lectured about alcoholism, and I recall asking him very specifically, "How many of those 4,800 men have drinking problems, or are alcoholic—by your estimate?"

Croft, who is himself a recovered alcoholic, replied without hesitation, "Conservatively speaking, you'd have between three hundred and five hundred on that ship alone."

What do you do with those drunken sailors? Until recently, that hoary drinking-song refrain was answered by terse and cold-blooded administrative fiat: "You let them go down the tubes." This has meant, of course, separation from the service and expulsion into the civilian world. Not unlike a rudderless torpedo laden with unstable explosive, the alcoholic serviceman has found himself ejected into an environment no more receptive to his condition or knowledgeable about his illness than the hostile environment from which he had been unceremoniously expelled.

The net result? For countless decades, many of the military's most skilled and highly trained enlisted men and officers were either separated prematurely and punitively or, in the words of Joe Pursch, "were nonchalantly or forceably retired into invalidism."

As but a single contemporary case in point, alcohol-related disorders in the nation's VA hospitals doubled between 1965 and 1969 alone; to this very day the wards of America's veterans hospitals are dotted with jaundiced, cirrhotic men in the terminal stages of alcoholism.

Worse yet, the military has mirrored the rest of American society by attempting to "cover up" for the suffering alcoholic; the woods are full of misguided commanding officers who, for months and sometimes years, have looked the other way so that "good old Joe" could complete the last mile of his twenty-year hitch and thereby become a pensioner. The motivation is invariably altruistic, yet the result is inevitably disastrous; since the cover-up enables Joe's alcoholism to progress untreated into its terminal stage, good old Joe is literally killed with kindness.

The practice has become so widespread and damaging that, like Watergate, the cover-up can no longer be covered up. As long ago as 1971, for example, a study entitled *Alcoholism among Military Personnel,* prepared by then U.S. Comptroller General Elmer B. Staats for Senator Harold Hughes' Special Subcommittee on Alcoholism and Narcotics, blasted the U.S. Department of Defense, charging, "Because the military services often deal punitively with alcoholism, there is a tendency to cover up the problem throughout the chain of command and there is little incentive for an individual to come forward openly and seek help. The problem is hidden and covered up as long as possible by the man himself, his family, or a sympathetic commanding officer so as not to jeopardize the serviceman's career."

The generally unpublicized report went further still, stating, "The situation is similar to that which existed many years ago for venereal disease, until regulations were modified so that it was no longer considered misconduct."

In what ultimately amounted to a scathing indictment of the entire U.S. military, the report summed up then existing Department of Defense policy, noting, "Little has been done by the military establishment to deal with the problem of alcoholism unless an individual has become at least partially ineffective in his duties or has committed one or more punishable offenses, such as being absent without leave. . . . Some individuals stated their belief that a man should be allowed to drink until he gets into trouble. Most of the bases that we visited had no regulations on how to handle an alcoholic or a problem drinker."

Generally speaking, until recently the alcoholic serviceman has been handled—or, more accurately, *mis*handled—in one of three ways. He has been left alone or "carried," as it were, by sympathetic commanding officers until retirement time; he has been transferred repeatedly and literally passed from one command to another; or he has been punished—in the form of reprimands, extra duties, reduction in rank, loss of security clearance, or separation from the service.

In short, as the Department of Defense itself finally has begun to recognize, traditional military attitudes toward alcoholism have been, at the least, anachronistic and, at the worst, barbaric; along a spectrum ranging from major physical disability to death itself, the toll has been appalling.

Yet perceptive line officers as well as military lawyers, chaplains, and doctors have known this all along. "They have seen the drinker's hangover at captain's mast," says one Air Force major. "They have seen his deteriorating career at courts-martial, his suffering wife in the confessional, his broken jaw on the orthopedic ward, his bleeding ulcer in the operating room, and his shrunken liver at autopsy."

Human misery apart, one can hardly ignore the gargantuan economic drain resulting from the military's traditional approach to alcoholism. According to one exhaustive study conducted in 1972 for the Department of the Army by Information Concepts, Inc., "Duty time lost because of absence related to drinking problems will cost the Army 2,200 man-years (one division-month) and $17 million in pay and allowances alone in 1973, in addition to over 16,000 man-years of duty time at reduced efficiency because of drinking."

Similarly, the aforementioned U.S. Comptroller General's

study estimates that the potential annual cost to the government is about $48 million "for each one percent of alcoholism incidence in the military."

Money talks, and big money talks loudly; fortunately, that being the case, the military has begun to listen. The point was colorfully illustrated for me by Dick Jewell, a recovered alcoholic and retired Navy commander who was instrumental in getting the Navy's alcoholism program off the ground back in February 1965. Today Jewell is senior alcoholism counselor at Long Beach Naval Hospital. A loving and much loved friend to literally hundreds upon hundreds of recovered Navy alcoholics all over the world, he recalled for me a recent visit to the Long Beach Alcoholic Rehabilitation Center by Major General John Singlaub, who is in charge of the U.S. Department of Defense's Drug and Alcohol Abuse Program.

"I was the only guy around, so I was high man," Dick Jewell said. "General Singlaub asked me, straight out, 'How much is this facility costing the service?' "

The rest of the conversation, by Jewell's recollection, went something like this:

JEWELL: How much does it cost to train a Marine major helicopter pilot?

SINGLAUB: Hmm. About $350,000.

JEWELL: Okay. And a major, Air Force?

SINGLAUB: He comes a little higher. Say $500,000.

JEWELL: What about a lieutenant commander, academy graduate, who's gone through flight school and is now a major? What would it cost to replace him?

SINGLAUB: About $350,000.

JEWELL: Okay, now add them up. Because besides the chiefs and all the other officers and everything else—and I mean about 1,500 guys of all ranks and grades—we've given the Navy back *these* three guys. And with these three alone, the way an old Okie figures, we've paid our way *forever*.

SINGLAUB: Hmm. I see what you mean.

Earlier that week, I had spent several hours with Dr. Gene Purvis, who is a flight surgeon, pilot, and psychiatrist. Purvis is also a recovered alcoholic, sober more than a year at this writing, who initially achieved his sobriety at Long Beach ARC. At one point, I asked Gene Purvis to estimate the Navy's investment in him during his seventeen-plus years of active duty.

The young doctor leaned back and scratched his head. "Let's see. First there's aviation training. And I dropped lots of bombs and shot lots of 20-millimeter cannon shells, which is expensive. Also, I was carrier qualified. I flew 1,200 hours in a jet. I guess they had over a million dollars invested in me at that time.

"I was actually a drunk back then," Purvis said reflectively. "I remember passing out in the hotsy bath of the Imperial Hotel in Tokyo, and one of my buddies gave me artificial respiration. But that never even got my attention. I was drinking Akadema wine, so I figured I shouldn't drink *wine*. That's how I rationalized that," he added with a grin. "Anyway, with the aviation training, plus the investment in medical training and psychiatric training, I'd say about two million dollars."

Today, Gene Purvis is depot psychiatrist for a Marine Corps recruiting center in San Diego and, moreover, has volunteered to head an alcoholism treatment unit within that vast facility. Thus, for a pittance of a rehabilitation investment, the military has not only preserved its $2 million stake in Dr. Purvis, but has enabled him to return that stake many times over by helping restore others suffering from alcoholism.

In that very real sense, recovered alcoholics like Purvis are today among the military's most valuable human resources. "We're still dealing primarily with crisis situations," says one enlightened Department of Defense official. "We've hardly begun to scratch the surface of education and prevention. But we'll eventually get into that, too, because attitudes are changing. And they're changing because of the impact made by the recovered alcoholic—the sober officer, the sober chief, the sober serviceman who leaves a facility like Long Beach ARC today and goes back out to the U.S.S. *Cutty Sark* and reports for duty."

The military's secret weapon is, of course, the fact that it can actually coerce an alcoholic into accepting treatment, because a serviceman can be "ordered" to an alcoholism rehabilitation facility on an either-or, shape-up-or-ship-out basis. The military is much the same as industry in that it controls a highly effective motivational lever. As noted in an earlier chapter, poor performance alone activates the lever, while threat of job loss and ultimate separation from the service provide the goad.

As might be expected, the long-term recovery rates of effective military programs parallel recovery rates of effective industrial programs: about 70 percent of all Navy, Marine Corps, and Coast Guard members treated at Navy rehabilitation centers are being returned to effective duty.

One such officer is Navy Lieutenant Commander Jack M. Jackson, a naval aviator who not long ago returned to a high-level job at the Pentagon after spending eight weeks at Long Beach ARC. Jackson was the two-thousandth patient admitted to the facility and, for that reason, the subject of a Department of the Navy press release. He was in desperate shape when he arrived at Long Beach and, in fact, had to be carried off the plane.

"It's not like being healed after a long sickness," Jackson says today. "In my case, it's more like a resurrection, because when I came to the center I was more dead than alive—and I'd been dead for a helluva long time."

Like many others, Jackson went through an intensive eight-week program that includes constant group involvement, daily Alcoholics Anonymous meetings, and even recreational psychotherapy. The morning-to-night schedule also crams in films, chalk talks, group therapy, psychodrama, and one-to-one sessions with counselors and other staff members.

Captain Joseph J. Zuska, MC, USN, now retired, along with Dick Jewell, fought tooth and nail for the Navy's alcoholism program. The essence of the treatment is to: 1) Detoxify the sick individuals; 2) assist the patient in overcoming his denial; 3) free his brain from alcohol toxicity; 4) educate him about his disease; 5) re-educate him to a more mature way of coping with life's problems; 6) expose him to a group, such as Alcoholics Anonymous, which offers fellowship, hope, no need to drink, and an opportunity to help others; 7) recognize and treat the effects of the illness on the family.

"But abstinence is only the first step toward recovery, and in and of itself doesn't result in recovery," emphasizes Zuska. "Sobriety, which is a state of being comfortable without drinking, takes a year or two to achieve, and is *necessary* for recovery. The final step is involvement with other alcoholics, and the desire to help them. And this results in a much stronger state of sobriety and well-being."

If the group is the springboard from which the recovering alcoholic serviceman is set firmly on the pathway to long-term sobriety and well-being, the group counselor is its mainstay. An active-duty, recovered alcoholic with two to ten years of sobriety, the group counselor serves as a role model—that is, as a supportive but firm example for identification.

"It quickly becomes apparent to all patients," points out one Long Beach ARC staff member, "that although the average counselor has had most of the troubles and bad breaks that the patient has had, he now stands tall, looks confident, and smiles easily. The patient also learns," he adds, "that the counselor's car is paid for, his family is happy, that he has money in the bank, that he has many things that he could only dream about during his days of self-destructive drinking, and that he now is a non-drinking, sober, highly respected member of his community. So the counselor becomes a tremendous source of inspiration to the system and visible proof that the system works."

While the counselor is the mainstay, the group therapy sessions and AA meetings are where the gut-level action takes place. "I came to group and spent three weeks being absolutely furious," recalls Gene Purvis. "I was the most highly trained, and they knew that. There were cooks and engineers and chiefs in my group, and they knew I was a doctor and an ex-jarhead fighter pilot, and they tore me apart.

"You know, as a psychiatrist," Purvis says, "I'm pretty adept at getting at people. But they had ways I had never tried of uncovering and stripping denial away. And that's beautiful, because they were just sitting there being honest.

"They'd say, 'Doc, you're full of shit.' Or, 'Doc, you can't get by with that. You drink too much, you *know* you drink too much, and you're scared. I can see it in your eyes, 'cause you won't look at us.' Boy, they were all over my case. But I'll tell you,'' Purvis concludes adamantly, ''it's the best thing that ever happened to me. It saved my life.''

At Navy ARCs, lifesaving comes in many forms. As one counselor puts it, ''If it works, we use it.''

A striking example is an approach whereby poly-addicted patients—those dependent not only on alcohol, but on such other mood-altering drugs as Valium, Librium, and meprobamate—are dramatically and quickly switched from ''pills to people.'' The switch may start in an ARC hallway, when a newly admitted patient confronts a counselor or doctor and shouts, in effect, ''If I don't get my Librium, I'm gonna explode!''

''If someone says that to me in the hallway,'' explains Dr. Pursch, ''I say, 'For heaven's sake, Smitty, sit down here; that sounds alarming.' And then I look around. The next guy who walks out of the men's room or out of an office or somewhere, I stop him and I sit him down, and I stop another guy and I sit *him* down. And I say to both of these guys, 'My heavens, you know what this man just said? He said if he doesn't get his Librium he'll explode.' ''

Then, adds Pursch, ''the two men look at each other, sort of smile, and they say to the first man, 'Shucks, that's just what I used to say, except I didn't say Librium, I said Valium, and I knew, just like you, that I needed it *bad.*'

''Then I walk away,'' Pursch says, ''and do some work. And maybe twenty minutes later I walk out, and find the guy calmed down and still talking to the other two. In kind of a playacting mock panic, I walk up all of a sudden and say, 'For Chrissake, who gave you the Librium?' And the man is shook up, and he says, 'Honest, Doctor, nobody gave me nothing.'

''And I say,'' Pursch continues, '' 'Well, I could have sworn, because it's twenty-two minutes since I sat you down here, and you're not exploded anywhere, or are you covering it up?' And the man kind of smiles and sheepishly laughs, and I make a point of telling him that maybe for the first time in his life he's realized that he can get over this kind of feeling without Librium, by merely talking about it.''

The switch from pills to people has begun. The patient then

learns that AA and other people can help far more effectively than pills. "Because he didn't explode, he's twenty-two minutes older, a whole hell of a lot smarter, and he's still got a clear head."

The U.S. Navy is obviously light-years ahead of the Army and Air Force as far as effective alcoholism treatment programs are concerned, and those branches of the service would do well to visit Long Beach, or Norfolk, or Great Lakes, to learn the how and why of the Navy's success.

The principles applied at Long Beach ARC are applied no less astutely at other naval rehabilitation centers; one reason is that an ongoing interchange of personnel (and, hence, information and experience) takes place among most of the Navy's facilities. During my visit to Long Beach, for example, I met doctors and counselors from perhaps a dozen different U.S. naval stations. Similarly, during an earlier visit to Norfolk Naval Base, I met alcoholism counselors who had attained their sobriety at Long Beach, at San Diego, and at Great Lakes; I met Navy personnel from Washington, D.C.; Corpus Christi, Texas; and Terminal Island, California, as well as from many points in between.

From the outset, it became evident to me that the unrelenting enemy of every Navy rehabilitation facility and alcoholism counselor is, purely and simply, *denial.* For example, there is denial at the command level that there is a problem on a particular ship, and, more prevalently, denial of personal alcoholism.

"It sometimes takes days," says Al Croft, who until recently headed the Norfolk ARC, "to find out exactly how alcohol is affecting the man's life, and he's pitting his brains against mine. He's trying to minimize the effect that alcohol is playing in his life, and this of course sounds very much like me in the old days before *I* got sober. We have various techniques we use to pull things out of people," adds Croft, who earlier had described his own experience piloting ammunition ships into South Vietnam harbors while drunk.

"All you have to do toward the tail end of a conversation is to look the fellow in the eye and ask him, 'When's the last time somebody told you they loved you?' Or, 'When's the last time you thought about committing suicide?' Then you stand by and pull out the Kleenex.''

The technique may seem harsh and the scene invariably becomes emotional, Al Croft concedes. ''But,'' he says, ''if we can get this out of a person and psychologically get him to this point, chances are from here on in he'll tell the truth, and then this is when we can start.''

As for results, they speak for themselves. Croft showed me a series of personal data sheets used at Norfolk, along with psychological test graphs revealing dramatic ''before and after'' attitudinal changes in ARC patients. He told me of one man whose initial self-image was of ''a weed in a field of corn.'' Weeks later the man perceived himself as ''a strong oak tree,'' Croft said proudly.

I was shown, additionally, follow-up reports of men who had completed treatment at Norfolk ARC and subsequently reported back to duty. On one such six-month follow-up, the man's commanding officer noted that the recovering alcoholic in question ''has invested several hours per day in learning about the main propulsion equipment and systems installed on *Kennedy*. He shows a great deal of initiative and pride in his abilities and has become a highly valued asset to the *Kennedy*'s main propulsion team. He is a very strong and demanding petty officer.''

Still another progress report from the photocopied sheaf in my possession contains these unsolicited remarks from a commanding officer, about a man we shall call John Smith. ''John Smith is the epitome of the man willing to face 'one day at a time.' He has been instrumental in the implementation of the *Forrestal*'s Alcoholic Awareness Program and devotes a great deal of off-duty hours as the volunteer counselor. He is thus gaining personal strength even as he assists others in their attempts to secure sobriety.''

The fundamental lesson to be learned from such reports is that alcoholism is a highly treatable illness. Unlike victims of such often untreatable illnesses as, say, leukemia or sickle-cell anemia, the person with alcoholism does indeed have a choice between catastrophe and good fortune. Sadly, however, this most treatable illness continues to remain the one that is *least* treated in America today.

"Thinking back," says a Navy commander now billeted in Washington, "had the Navy had a program in my early years similar to what now exists, I might have licked the problem before it licked me temporarily. I'll always be an alcoholic, but I'm now considered a recovering alcoholic, thanks to Alcoholics Anonymous and the Navy's alcoholism prevention program."

The commander in question wears gold wings over four Distinguished Flying Crosses, twenty-six Air Medals, two single-action Air Medals, and, among other decorations, a Purple Heart. He recalls flying combat missions with enough blood alcohol in his system to qualify for a drunk-driving charge had he been in an automobile. In graphic understatement, he recalls his "bottom"—the point at which he finally made the choice between catastrophe and good fortune.

"The insidious thing about alcoholism is the way it creeps up on you over the years," the commander says. "For me, it culminated one morning after I'd been relieved as executive officer and ordered to a billet in California. I went to work and discovered that I simply could not cope with daily life. My hands were shaking and I couldn't talk without my lips quivering. I should add that you don't have to reach this point to be considered an alcoholic."

Providentially, such before-and-after success stories are becoming almost commonplace in the Navy. The Navy has by now had so much experience with diagnosing and treating alcoholism that the illness can often be detected and arrested in the early rather than late stages. Among the most valuable tools used at Navy Alcoholism Rehabilitation centers, I learned, is a mimeographed sheet entitled "U.S. Navy Alcoholism Progression Chart." It lists "Observable Behaviors" in the early, middle, and late stages of alcoholism as follows:

Early. Talks a lot about drinking exploits and drink-related activities. Outdrinks most shipmates, does not want to stop when they do.

Drinks before attending situations. Borrows money, sometimes does not remember borrowing. Has other memory lapses after heavy drinking. Much of liberty time spent drinking. Has occasional shore patrol difficulties, usually drink-related. Avoids non-drinking shipmates. Becomes irritable when his drinking behavior is discussed. Is occasionally late, especially after lunch at shore stations.

Middle. Sneaks alcoholic beverages into quarters, or keeps in car. Shows up with visible signs of hangover repeatedly. Avoids all but heavy-drinking shipmates. Rationalizes drinking behavior, refuses to discuss it. Frequent sick calls, usually without specific complaints. Exhibits grandiose aggressive behaviors. Is increasingly late, some other unauthorized absences. Some outstanding work performance, but not always dependable. Frequent requests for special liberty, i.e., payday afternoon. Arguments with shipmates, some fights. Increased frequency of memory lapses. Skips some meals in order to drink, may go "on the wagon" now. Increased shore patrol reports, alcohol involved consistently. Sneaks drinks and tries to calm nerves when upset. Has family and indebtedness problems. Is bleary-eyed at times. Uses alibis to explain drinking behaviors, blames others for his problems.

Late. Drinks in the morning to calm tremors/shakes. Work performance becomes undependable. Increased sick calls, now with real illnesses, i.e., gastritis. Unauthorized absences increase, now usually more than one day. Is intoxicated on duty at times. Liberties become one long "drunk." Bleary-eyed much of the time. Habitually uses breath purifiers. Nervous/shaky unless drinking or taking other sedatives.

I can personally attest to that chart's accuracy, in several ways. Certainly in my own experience as a practicing alcoholic, I exhibited *all* of the symptoms listed, in and out of the military. Additionally, in interviews with dozens upon dozens of recovered alcoholic military personnel during recent years, I was able to see my own former mirror image and, in turn, those same predictable symptoms of alcoholism's progression.

Especially vivid in my memory is a former Marine drill instructor, Staff Sergeant Jim H., who is now an alcoholism counselor at Norfolk Naval Base. A muscularly compact man in his early thirties, with twelve years of military service, Jim has been sober for about four years. His hair is crew-cut and, when we first met, he seemed the epitome of the classically "brutal" Marine DI. Observing a giant scar on his temple, I recall thinking that I would surely hate to meet him in a dark alley.

The scar was the result of an automobile accident, Jim told me later. On the way to his own wedding, blind drunk, he was thrown from his wrecked sports car, skidding headfirst down a cement highway. He told me, too, that he was in trouble with alcohol from the beginning. He drank alcoholically as a teenager, and continued to drink when he came into the Marine Corps.

"It became part of the thing to do, to be a Marine, to drink heavy," Jim says. "I spent time in the county juvenile camp as a result of my incorrigible behavior while drinking when I was a teen-ager, and I got in the brig in the Marine Corps for drinking, and right on through."

In the military tradition, Jim's superiors tended to overlook his drinking as long as it didn't drastically interfere with his job performance. Recalling one incident of unauthorized absence (UA), he said, "I was putting recruits to bed. After I put them to bed, I left the barracks and went out to the bar up on the hill, got drunk, shacked up with some broad, and didn't get in until eight-thirty the next morning. The recruits were supposed to be up by five o'clock, go to chow, and this, that, and the other, and they didn't do it. I wasn't there.

"They charged me with being UA," he recalls. "They knew I was drinking. I *told* them I was drinking—I was honest with them. They busted me, but left me with the same platoon working as a drill instructor. Then I went to work. I worked day and night for sixty-two days, and didn't take a day off, and turned out the highest honor platoon that had been in the field in three years at the recruit depot. And they gave me my stripes back because I was such a good drill instructor. I had to be," Jim adds sardonically, "to cover up for the past mistakes and make up for the ones coming."

And so it went for years, until a near disastrous episode that was to become Jim's moment of reckoning.

"My wife wouldn't give me the checkbook," he told me. "I

picked my daughter up out of the high chair and said, 'You gimme the checkbook or I'm gonna bash her head on the floor.' She gave me the checkbook. She ran out of the house screaming, with my daughter. And I went out and cashed the check and got drunk off my wife.

"It was two days later that the colonel presented me with a discharge. The whole world came down on me—my career, my family, the whole thing. But I remembered the deal with my daughter, and I woke up to it the next morning," Jim added. "I hadn't blacked out during that, and it was painful. Because usually I'd blacked out during my greatest misconduct."

Not long thereafter, Jim H. sought help. He was sent to Long Beach ARC and, during his first afternoon as a patient, sat down in the big assembly hall and listened to a man tell his AA story.

"He had been a Marine," Jim says. "He had done everything I had done, we'd torn up the same clubs. This guy was the first guy I'd ever heard stand up and say, 'My name is Larry, I'm an alcoholic.' He told *my* story, right down to the point of where he had tried to kill a son, and the identification was there, you know. I went to my first AA meeting that night," he adds, "and I stood up and I said, 'My name is Jim, and I *think* I might be an alcoholic.' "

Just days later during the recovery process, Jim attended another AA meeting in Long Beach. He still remembers some of the people who spoke that night, although he doesn't remember what they said. "But I remember sitting in that chair," he reflects, "and I was hurting. Some little gal, looked like a schoolteacher, got up and started talking. She was about my age, and she talked about these things and about the hurts inside and the remorse and guilt and everything else, and I'm sitting there in my chair and I started bawling, and I started shaking, and I was about to fall out of the chair. And this old guy named Dick sat down next to me, put his arm around me, and he just held me. He said, 'It's going to be all right.' "

And the thought in Jim's mind at that time, he remembers, was, "What in the hell do you know about it's going to be all right? But he loved me, and I sat there, and I wanted him to take his arm away but I didn't want him to take it away, and I said, 'Get me out of here.' And the old guy said, 'You sit still now. Sit still.'

''And that gal got done speaking,'' Jim went on, and we went outside and sat in his car, and I said, 'Dick, take me to get a drink, and it'll all go away.' And the only thing I remember about a two-hour conversation is, he told me, 'Boy, sometimes you gotta sit still and hurt.' And I heard that.''

That, Jim concludes, is part of his philosophy today; he applies that philosophy—along with many other things he has learned about alcoholism—not only to his own program for staying sober, but to the therapeutic process in the group he heads at Norfolk ARC.

''Right now,'' he told me, ''I've got a group that's really just in the beginning stages of starting to get into themselves. Most of my people have been here a short period of time. The way I feel today is that a part of me goes out that door every time one of my patients leaves this place, and a part of them stays with me.''

Today Jim H. cries unashamedly when his patients ''graduate'' and leave Building J-50 at Norfolk Naval Base. He is able to love and be loved, which is indeed a far cry from the violent misanthrope he once was. In his view, finally, he is more of a man today than he ever was.

During my last night in Norfolk, just hours after my session with Jim H., I stayed at a third-rate motel on rain-slicked Military Highway. After a ghastly dinner at a place called Sherry's Restaurant, I returned to my room. A drunken, violent party was going on in the room next door; later, a drunken man in another wing of the motel repeatedly phoned me, bewildered that he was reaching a stranger when he was trying to dial his mother at an outside number. At about eight o'clock, I switched on the television set to drown out the noise, only to come face to face with Flip Wilson doing an interminable skit about a drunken bartender. Though the studio audience was hysterical with laughter, I couldn't crack a smile.

Many more alcoholics would have died had it not been for a seed planted over a decade ago by Commander Dick Jewell, a recovered alcoholic who is now senior alcoholism counselor at Long Beach ARC. Jewell, who had been in and out of military hospitals for years, was one of those servicemen forced into premature retirement because of his alcoholism. His last hospitalization took place early in 1965 and, as had been the case so many times previously, the word "alcoholism" was never even mentioned. Not surprisingly, the retired commander remained a very sick man when he was discharged from the Long Beach VA psychiatric ward.

But Jewell had become "sick to death of being sick to death," in spite of eight consecutive misdiagnoses. He finally chose life rather than slow death and abruptly stopped drinking, maintaining his sobriety and regaining his sanity by close interaction with recovered alcoholics who "had been where he had been."

During those first months, it occurred to the retired commander that perhaps the same approach could help shipmates still suffering from the same illness; perhaps, in fact, meetings of Alcoholics Anonymous could be held at Long Beach Naval Base. Still newly sober and more than a bit rocky, Dick Jewell one day cautiously approached the naval dispensary; the officer he had chosen to see was not in, and Jewell was directed to Senior Medical Officer Captain J. J. Zuska.

Like most medical officers, Joe Zuska had for years been unsuccessful in his efforts to treat alcoholic patients. He was a four-striper with a great deal of seniority; he was independent, often outspoken, and, most important, had reached a point in life where he had begun to search for a meaningful way to spend the rest of his Navy career. Zuska listened to what the soft-spoken retired commander had to say. And when he heard that there just might be a way to help alcoholic sailors and officers by enabling them to meet and talk to each other about their problems, he became curious.

Together, Dick Jewell and Joe Zuska persuaded the executive officer of the naval station to let members of Alcoholics Anonymous hold meetings in a conference room. On February 20,

1965, the first meeting of Alcoholics Anonymous Drydock Group No. 1 took place, with three people in attendance. Today a worldwide network of Navy ARCs and AA Drydock groups extend from Great Lakes to Guam and Alaska to Japan; there are rehabilitation units and Floating Drydock groups on the seven seas as well, on such Navy vessels, for example, as the U.S.S. *Bainbridge, Midway, Ranger,* and *Enterprise.*

When I talked to Dick Jewell in his office, the first thing I noticed was a large oil painting hanging above his desk. Done in bright yellow and red, it depicted nothing more than a giant bottle of Ten High Whiskey. ''Some old boy painted it,'' Dick said in response to my raised eyebrow. ''Sort of a reminder of those last days when my daily diet was ten half-pints of Ten High. This was my whole world, me and my jug.''

Jewell wiped his eyes, adding quietly, ''I can't keep from puckering up when I get into this area. It's too damned important, and there's too much at stake. I didn't know back in '65 how they would receive an ex-drunk asking to start up an AA meeting.''

Out of the first thirty patients, not a single one recovered; some, in fact, died. But Zuska and Jewell persisted and, eventually, were given permission to use an abandoned Quonset hut for the meetings. However, since alcoholism was, far more so than today, an unmentionable condition—and because their operation was practically illegal—the pioneer group gradually acquired more opposition than support. Says one old-timer wryly, ''The list of people who covertly or actively opposed their ideas is long and distinguished.''

Success was slow in coming, but it did come, manifested by scores of recovering alcoholics who had been written off as ''helpless and hopeless.'' Finally, in 1967, the Navy's Bureau of Medicine and Surgery reluctantly gave the green light to proceed with the work as a pilot program. Symbolically, the authorization arrived in an envelope marked ''Secret.'' Even with official sanction, the innovative Long Beach model for treating alcoholic sailors and officers remained a clandestine, scorned operation.

''This is evidenced by the fact that between 1965 and 1973, in spite of repeated invitations, not a single doctor from Long

Beach Naval Hospital even came to see what the program was all about,'' says Joe Pursch. ''Housed in a dilapidated World War II barracks where most windows and doors couldn't be shut, let alone locked,'' Pursch adds, ''it remained essentially a bootleg operation—its product more and more widely known, yes, but its location and means of production shrouded in a sinister, illicit fog, like a whiskey still in a dry county.''

Dick Jewell recalls those days vividly. Bouncing up from his chair like a bantam rooster, he says today, ''Captain Zuska had the guts to fight every son of a bitch in the Navy and in the DOD, the whole damned bunch, and he did it. The years between 1967 and 1971 would have killed anyone but Zuska.''

Later that afternoon, Jewell detailed a 1969 appearance by Captain Zuska before Senator Harold Hughes' Special Subcommittee on Alcoholism and Narcotics. Following Zuska's description of the successes at Long Beach ARC, Senator Hughes stood up and said, ''Captain Zuska, do you mean to say you're treating the disease that the armed forces doesn't have?''

And then, Dick Jewell recalls with a sly grin, Senator Hughes pulled a letter from his jacket pocket. It was signed by then Secretary of Defense Melvin Laird and was a response to Hughes' inquiries about Department of Defense policy and activities regarding alcoholism in the military.

''Due to the disciplinary nature of the armed forces, we do not have this problem,'' Laird's letter stated.

''That's when things started,'' Dick Jewell said, handing me a newly published Navy pamphlet. The pamphlet lists such milestones as Public Law 92-129 (''Identification and Treatment of Drug and Alcohol Dependent Persons in the Armed Forces,'' enacted by Congress in 1971); DOD Directive 1010.2 (''Alcohol Abuse by Personnel of the Department of Defense,'' signed in March 1972); SECNAVINST 5300.20 (''Alcohol Abuse and Alcoholism among Military and Civilian Personnel of the Department of the Navy,'' signed by the Secretary of the Navy in May 1972); and OCMMINST 12792.1 (''Department of the Navy Civilian Alcoholism Program,'' signed by the Director of the Office of Civilian Manpower Management in May 1973).

''People started coming down here,'' Jewell added. ''We finally moved from Building 63, the old Quonset hut, into this new hospital. Right here at Long Beach, 2,313 people have been through this program as of today."

"Today" happened to be February 20, 1975—the tenth anniversary of Drydock Group No. 1. From all over the United States and other parts of the world, hundreds of Drydock alumni and their spouses and friends had begun to gather. It was a gala, festive occasion; there were banners and streamers, congratulatory letters and telegrams from Navy brass and President Gerald Ford himself. A huge four-tiered cake had been prepared, elaborately decorated, and lettered with the words, "10th Anniversary, Drydock Group."

As I entered the fourth-floor lobby of ARC that day, a friend introduced me as a guest and recovered alcoholic. I was handed a small birthday candle; its color symbolized my number of years of sobriety, and I was invited to place it on the cake. As I did so, I noticed a giant map of the world with red lines radiating, web-like, from Long Beach ARC to more than fifty Drydock groups, Floating Drydocks, and Alcoholism Rehabilitation units in both hemispheres.

I saw, too, a glass case housing the dog-eared attendance notebook from the first Drydock meeting ten years earlier; I passed a conference room called the "Dick Jewell Room" and, later, attended an AA "marathon meeting," during which recovered alcoholics capsulized their before-and-after stories for newly sober ARC patients. Nine new patients had been admitted that morning, I was told, and five Marines were due to arrive for detoxification that evening.

Evening came, and hundreds of us regrouped at the Elks Lodge, a dome-shaped structure topped with a massive gilded elk. In huge red letters, the marquee welcomed "NAVY DRY-DOCKERS." The multi-tiered cake, soon to be ablaze with candles, had been brought into the banquet hall.

For me, as well as for the many other recovered alcoholics in attendance, it was a proud and joyous occasion. The men wore jackets and ties and the women, mostly Navy wives, rustled from table to table in long gowns. There were speeches, presentations, and plaques.

Later, we danced to the music of Fabio's Big Band USA, the name glitter-lettered on cardboard bandstands against a red velvet backdrop. My lady friend and I sat at a table with a recovered alcoholic retired rear admiral and his Alanon wife, with a Navy pilot and his young wife, who had been sober since 1971, along with several other strangers who very quickly became our friends.

The program opened with a moving invocation, followed by AA speakers. Dick Jewell became tearful when he was given a plaque signed "With all our love from the staff—past, present, and future." Captain Zuska introduced himself by saying, "I'm Joe Zuska, and I'm a friend of Dick Jewell."

And when Zuska was presented with a "secret message," symbolizing the early "bootleg days" of ARC, he said laughingly, "Dick, you're not cleared for this. But I can tell you that it's a message from the Chief of Naval Operations, who says alcoholics *should* be treated."

It would have been easy to leave the Elks Lodge that midnight with the warm feeling that alcoholics are being treated in the military as a matter of course. On the way home, it would have been easy to hum an old drinking song, exulting, "Glory be to God that there are no more of us . . . ." But my friend and I would have been singing that line wholly out of context, for the next line is " 'Cause one of us could drink it all alone."

The unfortunate reality is that the military's recent successes are limited, and that hidden and untreated alcoholics in uniform outnumber those being treated many, many times over. Moreover, virtually no programs have been designed to help the families of alcoholics.

True, those things that can be changed by fiat or administrative order have been changed—more so in the Navy, to be sure, than in the Army or Air Force. The Army is still actively skirmishing with polls, questionnaires, and studies. Yet, as any combat commander knows, there is a world of difference between activity and action. The Air Force, in turn, is only now beginning to evaluate and remedy past mistakes.

"All our programs today are patterned after the one started at Wright-Patterson Air Force Base in 1966," says Major John Murphy of the Department of the Air Force. "But we were in existence on a very small basis back then. And the original program had many limitations as to who they would accept and who they would not accept.

"And those limitations were such," Murphy admits, "that a man pretty well had to be a recovered alcoholic before he even got in the door. He had to have no less than seven years and no more than seventeen years of service. He had to be totally sober for a period of five days before he was accepted at the center. He was not allowed to have any brain damage as a result of his alcoholism, or any liver damage, or any secondary conditions resulting from alcoholism, before they would accept him. Well, you know," Murphy adds, "that the lines were set up so rigidly that they got very few patients."

Fortunately, those Air Force guidelines have now been scrapped. Yet, as the Department of Defense's Major General John Singlaub admonishes, "there's still a war within the military over alcoholism, its prevention, treatment, and rehabilitation." Singlaub predicts it will continue to be so for some time to come.

The objective of that war is to convert the thinking of the entire military establishment. As it has been from time immemorial, the primary enemy is the moral and social stigma attached to the illness. Even as the military ponderously mobilizes its forces, that enemy continues to snipe away at human lives.

A dramatic case in point was provided once again by Long Beach ARC's Captain Joe Pursch, when he introduced me to a hit-and-run victim who had been crossing a street intersection while drunk. The serviceman was admitted to the emergency room of the Long Beach Naval Hospital, where it was determined that his pelvis and both legs had been broken. Casts were applied and "everything was fine," Pursch recalls.

"Not a word about alcoholism was mentioned until thirty-seven hours later, when the guy went into DTs," Pursch says. "Then they called us in a hurry. When we took a more careful history, the nurses reported, 'Yes, of *course* he was drunk when he came in here, but so is everybody.'

"Which is not true," adds Pursch, "but it is true that a lot of people are drunk when admitted. When we questioned the doctor, he said, 'Of course he was smelling of alcohol and drunk, but if we called you guys for everybody who was drunk, you wouldn't have enough doctors. So we only call you for those who go crazy, like this guy.'

"And the reason they called us," Pursch concludes grimly, "is that the patient was starting to talk about how frightening and unsanitary it was to have cats flying through the room. He was having withdrawal symptoms."

7

Physician, Heal Thyself

Physicians of the Utmost Fame
Were called at once; but when they came
They answered, as they took their Fees,
"There is no Cure for this Disease."

—Hilaire Belloc, *Cautionary Tales*

It was dusk in Atlanta. The windows of the medical building overlooked a sprawling shopping center. Beyond the glass, festooned with Christmas wreaths and winking lights, cars circled endlessly in search of parking space. The gray-haired receptionist commented irritably on the horn-blowing, promising me that the doctor's office would be less noisy and that he would see me shortly.

He did appear, finally, assisting a one-legged man into the waiting room. Hobbling past me on a pair of new aluminum crutches, the man cheerily wished me "Happy holidays." I wished him the same, grateful that I was well and whole and, best of all, that December 25 would mark my sixth sober Christmas.

The doctor urged me to relax while he made a phone call. I glanced about the room. Amid the impressive array of framed diplomas, certificates, and commendations was this prayer: "God grant me the serenity to accept the things I cannot change, courage to change the things I can, and wisdom to know the difference."

For a number of reasons, including the fact that the forty-year-old physician was a member of Alcoholics Anonymous, we had agreed in advance to give him a pseudonym. "Considering the time of year, how about Doc Holiday?'' I joked. He laughed and agreed, then plunged into a graphic synopsis of his life before sobriety, or, as he put it, ''B.S.''

Doc Holiday talked that evening of those feelings so painfully familiar to alcoholics the world over; he talked about the guilt, remorse, helplessness, and, ultimately, the terror he had experienced as a practicing alcoholic. Most important for my purposes, Holiday candidly described his attitudes toward patients during those desperate years, as well as his own impaired ability as a physician.

Morning after morning, he recalled, he came into his office bleary-eyed, tremulous, and, toward the end, almost wholly disoriented. Deep breaths of mask-fed oxygen became as mandatory as the early-morning drinks that, predictably, had become necessary to ''start his heart''; during those last tumultuous months, he self-prescribed virtually every tranquilizer, hypnotic, and sedative drug known to medicine. I can still hear him rattling off the names of perhaps a dozen such drugs—Stelazine, Ritalin, Thorazine, Valium, Elavil, Equanil, Demerol, and on and on—sounding for all the world like a hot-shot detail man hustling for a consortium of pharmaceutical firms.

''I remember as a physician,'' Doc Holiday told me in his soft drawl, ''that people actually had to *force* me to deal with their alcoholism. They'd have to say, 'Wait a minute, I don't want to talk about vomiting blood. I want to tell you *why* I vomit blood. I drink two bottles of whiskey a day.'

''And I'd say,'' the doctor added, '' 'That's all right. So you drink a little more than I do.' ''

I murmured something about denial, and Holiday nodded vigorously. ''I had it all figured out,'' he confided. ''As a doctor, I know that the best way to get a drunk off your ward is to wait three days and make him mad. It doesn't take much to make a drunk mad, does it?'' Holiday asked, grinning. ''And on the third day, that drunk signs out against medical advice, and you don't have to take care of him. You know he's just going to go across the street to the bar and get a drink, and then he's not gonna shake any more.

''I've done some of that in my life as a physician,'' Holiday added quietly. "It was hard to get drunks admitted to my ward in the first place, and for several reasons. Because if I admitted them, I had to work them up. But if I worked them up, I had to ask them some questions about drinking. I didn't want answers to any of those questions in my own life. So I avoided it."

Doc Holiday's unwillingness to treat alcoholic patients before the 180-degree turn his life has taken is hardly a unique phenomenon in medical circles. On the contrary, the avoidance the Georgia physician describes is the *rule* rather than exception in most doctors' offices and health care facilities across America today.

Paradoxically, the myth that alcoholic persons are unreachable, untreatable (and, indeed, not worth treating) is in large measure sustained by the attitudes of the very people who are in the best position to help—the nation's health care practitioners.

When one digs below the surface, the grim actuality of such dereliction is almost beyond belief. The World Health Organization recognized alcoholism as an illness a full quarter of a century ago, in 1951; the American Medical Association followed along in 1956, the American Psychiatric Association in 1965, the Department of Health, Education, and Welfare in 1966, the President's Commission on Law Enforcement and Administration of Justice in 1966, and the Department of Defense in 1972.

Yet at this writing, in 1975, at least half the hospitals in this country still adamantly refuse to admit patients with a primary diagnosis of alcoholism.

In medical journal editorials, where words seem to speak more loudly than actions, it has constantly been stressed that "an acutely ill alcoholic person, or the non-alcoholic individual who is acutely intoxicated, should be provided care under medical supervision."

Within the harsh reality of the institutional milieu, however, most hospital officials tend to react in terms of the "typical alcoholic patient," who at admission is often dirty, disheveled, disturbing, and demanding. If the patient is boisterous, it is unlikely that he will be considered sick. Usually, he is viewed as weak-willed and immoral, offensive to other patients, upsetting to hospital routine, and, as the absurd stereotype continues, likely to assault attendants and nurses.

The genesis for such mythology is the major misconception that most alcoholic patients are, purely and simply, skid row derelicts. Indeed, study after study has confirmed that the majority of America's health care personnel hold this view or, at the very least, are prejudicial and hostile toward alcoholics.

One such study, conducted by the authoritative *Quarterly Journal of Studies on Alcohol,* queried 88,302 physicians in private practice in the United States. Some 6,800 general practitioners, 1,200 osteopaths, 3,375 internists, and 1,675 psychiatrists returned usable responses. The study, which was completed in the early 1970s, revealed these prevailing attitudes:

The chief cause of alcoholism was believed to be "personality or emotional" by 83 percent of the general practitioners, 74 percent of the osteopaths, 81 percent of the internists, and 77 percent of the psychiatrists who responded; "social conditions" by 41, 36, 38, and 37 percent; and, very much to the point, "lack of will or morality" by 26, 24, 16, and 7 percent of the GPs, osteopaths, internists, and psychiatrists.

"Largely because of this and other misconceptions on the part of physicians," asserts Dr. Morris E. Chafetz, former director of the National Institute on Alcohol Abuse and Alcoholism, "most alcoholic persons will not be diagnosed and will not be offered treatment until and unless they have dissipated almost all the physical, social, and psychological resources needed to recover from any illness. Such an approach to any other health condition would be indefensible," he adds angrily.

Indefensibility aside, even when physicians do bother to accept alcoholics for treatment—and when hospitals do open their wards to "dirty drunks"—the real problem is often concealed. The fact is that hospitals generally admit alcoholics under diagnoses other than alcoholism, deluding themselves and, once again, helping the patient deny his or her problem.

Similarly, most physicians themselves are hesitant to make a diagnosis of alcoholism—for fear of having made a subjective judgment or, like "Doc Holiday," because the problem strikes too close to home. "The sad fact is," says Dr. Richard L.

Reilly, an Arizona osteopath who in 1974 gave up his medical practice to concentrate on the treatment of alcoholics, "that a sizable portion of every physician's practice is made up of alcoholics, but he either doesn't know it or chooses to ignore it."

All too typically, when physicians have no choice but to hospitalize acutely ill alcoholic patients, they record a diagnosis other than alcoholism—either because the physician himself wishes to hide the real problem (with or without the consent of the patient); because of archaic hospital admission policies; or, to get down to dollars and cents, because the patient's insurance coverage specifically excludes alcoholism.

Of course, such misdiagnosis distorts the statistics derived from hospital records. More significantly, the diagnostic misinformation may misdirect staff members in the management of the illness, putting the admitting physician in the position of either conspirator or ignoramus. A typical example was cited not long ago in the *Journal of the American Medical Association:* An alcohol-dependent patient, not intoxicated when admitted for a surgical emergency, developed delirium tremens twenty-four hours after the operation, utterly confusing a surgical resident who had never seen that condition treated.

Whether that surgical resident was a conspirator or ignoramus is beside the point. The point is far more fundamental, boiling down to no-strings-attached medical care for alcoholics versus Hippocratic hypocrisy. Those on the side of the alcoholics are hardly "dewy-eyed idealists," as I have heard them called; rather, they are hard-nosed pragmatists who base their case on facts—such as the startling admission by the American Hospital Association that 15 to 30 percent of all adult medical-surgical patients in metropolitan hospitals—*regardless of diagnosis*—suffer from alcoholism.

"Half of the people in our orthopedic service are alcoholics," agrees Dr. Joseph Pursch at Long Beach Naval Hospital. "You just don't break any bones in twentieth-century living, hardly, unless you're toxic from some chemical. And the number-one chemical we detect in our orthopedic service is alcohol. It's the same in our medicine ward," he adds. "Probably 40 percent have alcoholism or an illness that their alcohol intake continues to aggravate and therefore is not healing.''

In San Francisco's Mount Zion Hospital, similarly, it has been estimated that about half of all fracture cases result from drunkenness. Parenthetically, although Mount Zion is among the nation's more enlightened health care facilities these days, it should be pointed out that as recently as 1957 Mount Zion's constitution expressly prohibited the admission of alcoholics.

''We had to change the constitution to get the alcoholism program going,'' says Mount Zion's Senior Physician, Dr. Jack Gordon, who helped spur the hospital's reversal of policy. ''The constitution excluded prostitutes, drug addicts, and drunks. They put everything except dogs in that paragraph.''

After rummaging through his desk for a copy of the old Mount Zion constitution that afternoon, Jack Gordon sighed reflectively, ''You know, alcoholism is a field of medicine that *still* carries a heavy stigma. It's sort of like being a VD doctor in the old days, or a hemorrhoid specialist, or an arthritis specialist before all the modern drugs. In other words, a quack doctor. Because doctors thought, and still think, there was nothing you could do about it. It's a moral problem. You know, an attitude to the effect of, 'If he wants to stop drinking, nobody's pushing it in his mouth. So don't bother me.' ''

The prevalence of this view among health care professionals was dramatically demonstrated in Washington, D.C., a few years ago by another well-known alcoholism specialist, Dr. Maxwell Weisman, who now heads the American Medical Society on Alcoholism. ''How many of you would raise your hands with me,'' he asked his audience of doctors, nurses, and other professionals, ''and say that alcoholism is a self-inflicted disease that the alcoholic brings on himself?''

A great many hands were raised that day, surprising Dr. Weisman not in the least.

''That's *nonsense,* ladies and gentlemen,'' he stormed. ''Nobody can maintain that alcoholism is self-inflicted, any more than diabetes is self-inflicted. We don't know the causes of diabetes, just as we don't know the causes of alcoholism,''

Weisman said. "But we do know that we do not hold the diabetic responsible for his diabetes, and we cannot or should not hold the alcoholic responsible for his alcoholism.

"In the emergency room," Weisman added, "when a doctor sees a diabetic in a coma for the third or fourth time because he's gone off his regimen or something has happened, he doesn't say or think to himself, 'You dirty diabetic, you.' But members of the helping profession whose tolerance has disappeared look at the alcoholic and think, 'Dirty alcoholic, why can't you quit?' "

The lesson, of course, is that all too few health care professionals accept the fact that the illness of alcoholism is often characterized by relapses. And clearly, as Weisman's real-life illustration shows, alcoholic relapse frustrates the physician more severely than the relapses of many diseases with less favorable prognoses—such as rheumatoid arthritis, duodenal ulceration, diabetic acidosis, and ulcerative colitis.

"These diseases do not engender hostility, yet alcoholism does," argues Dr. Ephraim T. Lisansky, professor of medicine and associate professor of psychiatry at the University of Maryland School of Medicine. "These are also diseases of unknown etiology, yet their recurrence is not interpreted by the physician as a rejection of his authority."

Apparently, the ubiquitous attitude among health care professionals is that alcoholism is a self-inflicted condition. Even the National Council on Alcoholism flatly asserts that only about one in three hundred physicians is capable of diagnosing the disease accurately.

It is generally unrecognized among physicians, for example, that acute alcoholic patients with "dry mouth" are *over*hydrated rather then *de*hydrated, as is commonly believed. "Yet you're still taught in medical school," one recovered alcoholic physician told me, "that when a drunk comes in you plug in a bottle and run water through him, and he needs that like he needs a hole in the head."

No less commonplace and far more dangerous is the generally

accepted medical practice of substituting other drugs for alcohol in patients seeking treatment for their illness. As one physician puts it, the patient merely smells better, but he isn't receiving any treatment for his basic disease. Nor is it much of a medical accomplishment to switch an alcoholic from his liquid tranquilizer to a solid tranquilizer.

Maryland's Dr. Max Weisman makes the point vehemently, going so far as to say that doctors are actually dangerous to alcoholics. "In my practice they are," he says, "because many of them have contributed to the deaths of alcoholics by feeding them tranquilizers without any control of their alcohol intake, and I know some patients have died of double addictions because the doctor has given them a pocketful of Librium capsules without proper instructions."

I realize today, not without alarm, that my personal experience closely parallels the cases cited by Dr. Weisman. Not once, but at least half a dozen times, I was automatically fed tranquilizers within minutes after admission to hospital emergency rooms in a state of deep intoxication. At no point was my blood alcohol level checked, nor at any time was I told what I had received and for what purpose.

Personal witness aside, if more substantial affirmation be needed, an incredibly high 90-plus percent of 13,050 physicians (respondents in the study referred to earlier) reported *routinely* prescribing chlordiazepoxide (Librium), phenothiazines (Thorazine, Mellaril, Stelazine), diazepam (Valium), and antidepressants (such as Benzedrine, Methedrine, Dexedrine, and Ritalin) in the treatment of alcoholism.

Given such statistics, one can only conclude, as does Dr. Richard Bates, chairman of the Michigan State Medical Society committee on alcoholism and drug dependency, that, apart from the danger involved, "Writing prescriptions at ten to fifteen dollars a head doesn't take much medical expertise."

Yet medical expertise is precisely what is needed, and, for the most part, precisely what is lacking in the treatment of alcoholism in America today. To cite still another example of far-reaching ignorance, few health care professionals seem to be aware that withdrawal from alcohol can be *fatal*—to a much greater extent, in fact, than withdrawal from such drugs as heroin.

I recall, in this connection, an emotion-charged meeting with Dr. Robert G. O'Briant, who heads the alcoholism treatment facility at Garden Hospital Jerd Sullivan Rehabilitation Center in San Francisco. A new patient had been admitted that morning. The thirty-five-year-old man had been a daily drinker since the age of sixteen, O'Briant told me, and it was the first day in nineteen years during which he had not consumed alcohol. "God only knows what's going to happen to him," the doctor muttered.

Commenting on the patient's appearance, as well as on the fact that he had never lost a job, wrecked a car, or been jail, I responded naïvely, "He sounds like a guy who hasn't really hit the traditional bottom. You know, he's been functional, he's never had DTs, and the rest."

Dr. O'Briant straightened me out quickly, charging that I was apparently as ignorant of the withdrawal phenomenon as most M.D.s.

"This guy is a prime candidate to have DTs and severe withdrawal," he said. "Much more so than the guy down on Fourth and Market, the skid row guy. The skid row guy hasn't got money. He has to bum, he gets picked up, and then he's in the can for seventy-two hours. He gets breaks in his drinking," O'Briant added, "and this guy never had the opportunity to have a break. He's been drinking every single day for nineteen years, and more than a quart a day in the last couple of years. So withdrawal will be much more severe in this guy than in the skid row guy, believe me."

We talked further that day about alcoholic withdrawal seizures; O'Briant allowed that an inordinate number of physicians were wholly unaware of the phenomenon, let alone its predictability in certain patients during the first seventy-two hours of detoxification. He spoke at length, too, of mortality rates, and of needless deaths resulting from his profession's ignorance of the condition.

As if by design, Dr. O'Briant's nurse hurried into the office late that afternoon. "We're having a seizure," she said urgently. As he rushed toward the ward, O'Briant nodded silently to me in answer to a question that I had not yet put into words.

Yes, it was the thirty-five-year-old "virgin alcoholic," I later learned; and yes, he was fine. He was fine, of course, because Dr. Bob O'Briant and his staff knew and were ready. Remembering that somewhat eerie afternoon, I find myself wondering about numberless other patients of doctors who, to this day, do not know.

Yet by the nature of his calling, the physician is among those to whom we often ascribe magical, and even mystical powers. The Bible admonishes us to "Honor a physician with the honor due unto him," and through the ages various philosophers and authors have urged that we do the same.

Viewing the evidence, however, one is inclined to agree with John Donne, who took a considerably less deferential view toward doctors when he wrote, in 1624, "I observe the physician with the same diligence as he the disease."

Observed with diligence by all those in America directly or indirectly affected by the disease of alcoholism, the physician and those other health care professionals surrounding him would be hard put to it to seek honor, deny their ignorance, defend their dedication, or even hide their embarrassment. It is becoming increasingly difficult in twentieth-century America to ignore such travesties as these:

• Probably fewer than 10 percent of the nation's alcoholic people are receiving the treatment they need.

• Less than half the nation's hospitals will admit patients with a primary diagnosis of alcoholism.

• Most communities continue to jail acutely intoxicated people without referring them to treatment for overdose of a drug.

• The vast majority of health professionals remain unwilling to accept their proper responsibility for the treatment of alcoholic people.

These, then, are some of the sordid realities facing alcoholics and their families seeking aid and comfort from America's

132 /   D R I N K I N G

health care practitioners. If shock value alone were the *raison d'être* of this book, it surely would suffice to stand back judgmentally and simply rest my case.

Admittedly, the temptation dies hard. There were times, during those early months of sobriety, when I would have settled for nothing less than vengeful retribution against those numerous medics who had refused to treat me because my alcoholism had relapsed ("He's a loser," one such physician told my family. "I wash my hands of him."); who had blithely filled my veins with liquid Valium even while my blood alcohol level approached near lethal peaks; who had reinforced my denial because my symptoms paralleled their own; and who, like "Doc Holiday," worked at "getting me mad" so that I would leave their wards against medical advice, thus relieving them of legal, if not moral, responsibility.

I am thankful that, for me, the time of such emotional foolhardiness is past. It would serve a far more constructive purpose, certainly, to examine the reasons behind the negative attitudes and destructive practices of America's health care professionals. Perhaps, in fact, there is something to be said in their defense.

By any bench mark, the overriding reason for the medical profession's backwardness in this area is the fact that the average American physician invests upwards of eight or ten years in studying for his career, but seldom receives more than token exposure to the critical health problem of alcoholism.

When he was in medical school, if the truth be known, today's average doctor learned more about such exotic (and, in America, nonexistent) diseases as *tsutsugamushi* (an acute infectious disease, sometimes called "Japanese river fever," or "scrub typhus") than he did about alcoholism. By the same token, he knows far more about the effects and role of triglycerides, cholesterol, and nicotine upon body systems than that of alcohol.

In point of fact, current lecture time in medical school related to alcoholism and its associated disorders totals no more than one or two hours, prompting one hospital chief of medicine to coin the comically yet accurately descriptive phrase, "Four-two-three syndrome."

"You go to medical school for *four* years," he scoffs, "and get *two* hours' exposure to alcoholism, which is America's number-*three* killer.''

The same point is made by Michigan's Dr. Richard Bates, who estimates that the majority of medical schools devote only one hour to alcoholism during the entire four-year curriculum. And numerous studies bear out Bates' charge, including a recent survey of American Medical Association student members. The study polled ninety-two medical schools and five schools of osteopathy, revealing that many students—even at advanced levels of training—remain fundamentally ignorant of many aspects of alcoholism.

''The only formal training I had in medical school on alcoholism was one hour by the toxicologist,'' says Dr. Charles Juff, a recovered alcoholic physician who now practices in California. ''We·talked mainly about hangovers. It was a sort of a joking, fun-type hour.''

''That,'' adds Juff, ''plus despising the winos that they brought into the county hospital emergency room when you were on duty. They're derelict-type winos, and you're working them up, and they're just a pain in the ass, because you don't know what to do with them. They keep coming back, and you build up a resentment, and that's pretty much the sum total of what you know about alcoholism when you get out of medical school.''

Given the fact that the average young medical student is confronted with frustrating alcohol-related problems similar to those encountered by Juff, it is hardly surprising that negative attitudes toward alcoholic patients develop in the very earliest stages of clinical training.

Given the additional fact that two hundred hours of training are needed merely to produce a competent paramedical alcoholism aide (according to many physicians, including Dr. Frank L. Iber, who is professor of medicine at Tufts University School of Medicine), the one or two hours' training given to most budding M.D.s is nothing less than ludicrous.

Even if today's average doctor was among those fortunate enough to receive more than token education about alcoholism, the chances are overwhelming that he learned about the sequelae, or secondary effects, of alcoholism, but not how to diagnose and treat the primary illness.

As one physician explains it, here is the way that learning process is expressed in practice today:

If a patient presents himself at an emergency room without any specific complaint—other than being alcoholic—he is turned away without any question of treatment for his primary illness. "If the same alcoholic's ticket of admission to the hospital is 'esophageal bleeder,' " the doctor continues, "he is admitted, treated, and then discharged when the acute symptomatology has subsided, rather than having an active treatment plan for his disease process formulated."

This is analogous, the doctor adds, to giving a chronically feverish patient aspirin, "thus relieving the presenting symptomatology, without further exploration for the possible diagnosis and then treatment of the underlying disease process."

"As a result," declare Drs. LeClair Bissell and Susan M. Deakins at the Smithers Alcoholism Center in New York City's Roosevelt Hospital, "patients enter and leave the hospital through a revolving door—detoxification and treatment of medical complications of alcoholism, discharge after warnings and scoldings only to drink again, readmission, discharge to drink, and so on. Failure to recover," they add, "is then blamed on the patient, who is described as not motivated. Rarely is alcoholism defined as the primary problem underlying these repeated admissions, and the medical staff takes refuge in treating its late sequelae."

Still another reason for physicians' reluctance to treat alcoholics is what many doctors describe as their own feelings of "omnipotence and omniscience," self-images that are reinforced by such societal attitudes of deification as "my son the doctor," to put it crudely.

As one physician says, "The lack of educational experience in the disease process of alcoholism challenges the physician's feelings of being all-powerful. Naturally, this creates anxiety. And the anxiety is usually manifested by irritability, and at times even out-and-out anger and hostility toward the alcoholic patient."

Mount Zion's Jack Gordon adds bluntly, "If you can't do something for a patient, your chances of running out there to try to help him diminish. If you've got something that's going to work like magic, that's different. If somebody's choking with asthma and you've got some Adrenalin, and you know it's going to work in one minute, man, you practically leap at the chance. But if a guy's out there drunk in the middle of the street, you'll drag your feet and hope a cop or somebody will come by first."

Adds Gordon, "I guess everybody likes to do something successfully, and very few people like to fail. You hang your head and you get defeated. And you begin to feel guilty about taking money for the work."

Other physicians with whom I have talked are more outspoken than Gordon, who is by no means taciturn. One such person who treats "public inebriates," in Seattle, agrees that most doctors lack education and merely treat alcoholism's symptoms. But he goes further, charging, "Yet they won't send the patient elsewhere, because they're afraid of losing the patient. Physicians hate to lose patients, especially paying ones."

Clearly, there are myriad reasons explaining the reluctance of physicians to make the diagnosis of alcoholism; some of the reasons are conscious and, not surprisingly, some are more or less *unconscious.* University of Maryland Medical School's Dr. Ephraim Lisansky summed it up to a group of his colleagues at a gathering of the New York State Medical Society during its General Session on Alcoholism in 1973.

Among the conscious reasons for avoiding the diagnosis, Lisansky said, are:

Lack of knowledge about alcoholism; feelings of uncertainty about what alcoholism is; vagueness about the limits of heavy drinking; the discovery that many patients want a definition of alcoholism for the purpose of refuting it for their own specific situations; a confusion over whether alcoholism is an illness or a "symptom of something else"; a lack of understanding about the complex interrelationships between physical and emotional problems; unfortunate experiences with alcoholics who have resisted treatment; and lack of knowledge of current resources in the management of alcoholics and their families.

Equally important, Lisansky pointed out, are the more or less unconscious reasons, which may include:

Anger at the alcoholic, who is felt to be willful, uncooperative, and unmodifiable; the presence in the physician's family of alcoholics, which may be either a positive or negative influence; fears of losing the patient if he is told he is an alcoholic; doubts about whether alcoholism is really an illness or a sign of misbehavior; fear of legal reprisals; and misgivings about the physician's own drinking pattern.

Dr. Lisansky's last point is an especially telling one; by any standard, it would be difficult to overestimate the personal and societal impact of alcoholism among physicians themselves. "Alcoholism is an epidemic among doctors," cautions NIAAA's former director, Dr. Chafetz. "And," he adds, emphasizing the obvious, "most alcoholic doctors are incapable of giving their patients the best possible care because of the dulling effects alcohol has on the reflexes and the mind."

The astonishing fact is that more than 18 percent of America's 356,000 physicians suffer from alcoholism—*three times* the percentage of alcoholics found in the general population.

The estimate is based on a lengthy study by researchers from Harvard and Tufts universities on the drinking habits of physicians. "In a group of medical students, 7.7 percent were found to be alcoholics," says Donald Godwin, chief of the occupational program branch of NIAAA. "Thirty years later, after the same group had been well established in medical practice, the study revealed that 18 percent were alcoholics."

Still other studies have shown that 17 percent of all hospitalized physicians are alcoholics, and that 39 percent of all physician suicides involve alcoholism or heavy drinking. In fact, physicians have the highest rate of alcoholism of any profession in America, says Dr. William Quinn, member of a committee investigating alcoholism for the American Medical Association.

Moreover, each year the medical profession loses about six hundred doctors—equivalent to the annual output of six medical schools—from excessive use of alcohol, self-administration of narcotics, and suicide. Two-thirds of this loss is attributable to alcohol, asserts Dr. Ray L. Casterline, president of the U.S. Federation of State Medical Records.

In this regard, it has been argued that physicians become alcoholics because of the pressures inherent in medicine. After all, what about the hourly crises in the day-to-day world of a doctor, not to mention those life-and-death decisions he makes?

"Bah," snorts Dr. Richard Bates of the Michigan State Medical Society. "Not more than 40 percent of physicians ever make a 'life-and-death decision.' When they do, they don't make it alone. The biggest decision I make some days is to recommend one aspirin or two."

What should not be overlooked, of course, is that alcoholic physicians are in no way different from alcoholic house painters, secretaries, or bus drivers. They are certainly no different in that they are afflicted with a progressive and incurable yet treatable illness and exhibit the same symptoms as all other alcoholics—including the denial and stigmatization that are nurtured by their peers and by society itself.

One such alcoholic physician resides on the West Coast, not far from my home. Like "Doc Holiday," he is a recovering alcoholic and a member of AA; for purposes of identification, I'll simply call him Richard West.

Following a tour of military service in Vietnam, West decided to set up private practice in Laguna Beach. He was married, had three young daughters, and, admittedly, didn't fully know what he was doing.

"It was tough financially to get the practice going," he remembers. "I was working hard, felt inadequate, and I can see now that a lot of alcoholics have that feeling. I always felt that I was the dumb G.P.

"Doctors feel that the internists are the super-cool and brainy guys," West adds, smiling at that memory. "The internists depend on G.P.s for referrals, but they sort of treat you like dumb shit country cousins. That got to me a little bit, because I always had sort of an inferiority complex all my life anyway. The doctors were very aloof, and I could never get any of them to join me for lunch or get chummy. So I started drinking, and soon I was doing it more and more."

Initially, West was covered by two other doctors; they alternated calls, and he was "pretty rigid about not drinking when I was on call—at *first*." But soon, West remembers, "it got so that I started drinking a little bit at noon, a 'to get through the afternoon' sort of thing. It got to the point where at evening time I was drinking close to three-quarters of a quart of vodka, trying to get that feeling gone.''

Eventually, the alcohol stopped working for the young physician. ''One night I realized, when I walked out to get another drink, that I had gone through a quart of vodka, and that feeling was still there. I was soused without getting rid of the feeling, and that's what really upset me. I started adding pills, since the alcohol alone wouldn't do it.''

Not long afterward, Dr. West was named chief of medicine at the hospital. That in itself was bewildering, he notes, since it was ''unheard of'' for a general practitioner to be honored with such a position.

''But I did pretty well as for getting along with people,'' he explains. ''In fact, I had always been a hyper-achiever. Anyway, one night I showed up to chair a meeting, and I was loaded. I was either just asking for it, or crying for help.''

Several days later, a group of West's ''good friend'' doctors got together and asked him what the problem was. One of the doctors was a recovered alcoholic, West adds, ''and he knew what the problem was. They recommended that I go to treatment at a private place. I went through that, but I was pretty hostile the whole time. I didn't think booze was my problem, I thought drugs were. You know, the old typical rationale; I figured, 'Man, if I get over this drug business, when I get out I can have a couple of drinks.' ''

I asked West if that rationale was based on the idea that alcohol is *not* a drug. ''I know of it as a drug,'' he answered, ''but I didn't choose to think of it that way. I separated the 'drug' drugs from alcohol.''

When he left the private facility after four weeks, West limited himself to two drinks a night. ''Because everybody—including my wife, her psychiatrist, and her brother—thought, 'You can't take *everything* away from him, so it's okay if he has a couple of drinks.' Those two drinks kept getting larger and larger, and pretty soon I was drinking six ounces of vodka on the rocks times two, twelve ounces a day.''

West went back to the private facility for a short time, then to

Alcoholics Anonymous. During those last months, he had overdosed on alcohol, in combination with other drugs, and almost died. He had also fallen down and broken his shoulder.

"By this time my practice was going to hell," he says. "I was still functioning pretty well as far as my patients were concerned, but the office was a chaotic scene. The bills hadn't gone out, and I was in debt. When I broke my shoulder and went into the hospital, I started really getting involved in AA and realized that I couldn't drink anything if I was going to get well. This was in 1973," West concludes calmly, "and I haven't found it necessary to take a drink or use any other chemical since."

Today, says West, he lives one day at a time. That's hard for him, he concedes, but he feels he's "getting there," and that it's hard to change forty-four years of habit overnight. "Yet I feel good about the future, and I don't have nearly so many dreads as I used to have. I'm not driven the way I used to be, and I'm content with my lot. I look forward to AA meetings, and I'm growing a lot mentally, spiritually, and every other way. I just plain feel good."

If there is anything unusual about West's long-standing denial of his own alcoholism, perhaps it is that it is *not* unusual. The fact that 18 percent of America's physicians are alcoholic is verifiable in more ways than one; the shocker, however, is not the high incidence of alcoholism among doctors, but the fact that so few recognize their own alcoholism and often become disabled or die from the illness.

Proving this, during the past several years the Alcoholism Rehabilitation Center at Long Beach Naval Hospital has conducted a two-week study course for civilian and military physicians. The physicians attend lectures, visit with recovering alcoholic patients, go to AA meetings, and, in short, learn more about alcoholism in ten days than during all their years of med school and residential training.

"The first thing they have to do," says Dr. Joe Pursch, "is to confront their *own* drinking patterns. Very often, the doctors stay, signing themselves in as patients. As a matter of fact,"

Pursch says seriously, ''one out of every six doctors who have been through this facility—ostensibly to observe—has decided to sign in as a patient.

''During the first week,'' explains Pursch, ''they become aware of the nature of their own illness. But most of all, they become aware that there is a *hope*. Because many of them had known that they were alcoholic for some time, but they shared other, lay people's pessimism about the 'hopelessness' of the illness. Today, as a result,'' Pursch told me in February 1975, ''there are something like forty-one recovered alcoholic physicians in the Navy alone.''

One such physician is Dr. George Pohle, an internal medicine specialist. It occurred to Pohle some years ago, as he was asking his alcoholic patients about their drinking patterns, that he was answering most of the questions ''yes'' right along with them.

In April 1974, when he was forty years old, Pohle came to Long Beach as an observer. ''I immediately identified with the stories and symptoms,'' he says today, ''but I still wasn't able to accept the fact that I was an alcoholic. I initially came to Long Beach for two weeks, then extended for a third week, and then at the last possible moment, I finally surrendered and said, *'Okay,* take me, admit me.' I spent another six weeks,'' Dr. Pohle adds, ''and I've been sober one day at a time every since May 9, 1974.''

As noted, physicians like ''Holiday,'' Juff, Pohle, and ''West'' are exceptions in medical circles in terms of their acceptance of alcoholism as a ''respectable'' illness. Pohle, for example, recalls an incident that starkly illustrates the continuing stigma that remains so widespread in American health care facilities today.

Pohle had received a call from a man who runs a halfway house for alcoholics. ''He wanted to know if I could admit a fellow into the hospital for detoxification,'' Pohle says, ''and I said 'Sure.' I called the emergency room and said, 'Joe Brown is arriving. Admit him and I'll come by a little later and see him,' which I did.

''I didn't get to the hospital until two hours later,'' Pohle adds, ''and Joe Brown was sitting in the emergency room with the manager of the halfway house, patiently waiting for me to come. I said to the doctor, 'Why didn't you admit him?' And he said, 'Christ he's just a *drunk*. He doesn't need to be in the hospital.'

"The point is, of course," Pohle says with quiet understatement, "that a lot of doctors do a lot of drinking and have a lot of guilt feeling about their own drinking. So it's hard to point the finger at somebody else and say 'You're an alcoholic' if that person isn't in the gutter."

Added to this is the commonplace practice, among health care professionals, of "covering up" for each other. Consider, in this connection, the fact that the health care industry is one of America's ten largest employers; a five-hundred-bed hospital with some two thousand employees, for example, could well be regarded as a medium-sized industrial firm. "While health workers are busy helping others, what are we doing about our own problems?" asks Roosevelt Hospital's Dr. LeClair Bissell. "Where, within a major hospital, is an alcoholism program for the physician, nurse, social worker, or technician?"

Up until recently, the lack of legal procedures for ill alcoholic doctors—plus medical societies' reluctance to confront and discipline alcoholic members whose abilities have been demonstrably impaired—has not only permitted the conspiracy of silence to persist, but may have encouraged it to a large extent by allowing the sick doctors to feel "secure."

"When the medical society has no provision for the policy," says Dr. Herbert Modlin, chairman of the American Medical Association's council on mental health, "charges about a doctor's inability to practice encounter very subtle opposition. They are concerned about the problem, but when an individual is named, the feeling is apt to be, 'Good old Joe? Why, he's a past president,' and Good Old Joe is allowed to go ahead killing patients."

All too often, when older physicians finally do seek help for their alcoholism, they have suffered a great deal of physical deterioration, including brain damage. "One doctor in particular had to stay here for three months before he even knew what was going on," says a staff physician at Long Beach Naval Hospital.

"He's had a lot of brain damage, and he's not clear now. A lot of doctors fall into the same category," the physician adds, "and as a matter of fact, three doctors died here in Long Beach in the last three weeks because of alcoholism."

For those three deceased physicians, as well as the rest of us, the bottom line is that death from alcoholism is *needless* death. Unquestionably, alcoholism is a terminal illness if untreated; yet, as the medical profession is slowly coming to realize, it is among the most treatable of all serious illnesses.

Nevertheless, for all intents and purposes alcoholism remains a hidden medical problem of pandemic proportions in America today. Rarely in day-to-day life does the physician view the alcoholic as a person with an illness that has certain physiological, psychological, and social concomitants; far more typical, instead, is the diagnosis of a particular physical or systemic disorder in a person who *also* happens to be an alcoholic.

The glaring irony in this situation is that all alcoholics sooner or later develop complications which bring them face to face with medical professionals. As I can personally attest, once again, every alcoholic who does not die a violent death trudges repeatedly through the waiting rooms and hallways of America's health care delivery system—with his gastritis, pancreatitis, ulcers, headaches, and broken bones.

Granted, the alcoholic usually presents himself to the emergency room orderly or neighborhood G.P. in what the psychiatrists call "an internally unmotivated state." At that point, as any recovering alcoholic knows, he generally is in search of immediate relief from alcoholism's secondary physical symptoms, from external social pressures such as the threat of job loss or family disruption, and, not uncommonly, from feelings of severe emotional discomfort.

Notwithstanding his "internally unmotivated state" (a phrase that friends of mine call "the shibboleth of the shrink"), the alcoholic's concern with symptomatic relief rather than long-term treatment of the disease hardly precludes the treating person from turning the crisis into a productive therapeutic alliance. It is precisely at that critical juncture, in fact, that doctors, nurses, and other members of the "helping professions" have a uniquely valuable opportunity to start alcoholic persons toward recovery during the *early* stages of their illness.

It was recently brought to my attention, in this connection, that the Chinese word for "crisis" is separated into two symbols: one means "Danger," the other "Opportunity."

This point has been hammered home time after time during recent years by numerous physicians, notably by Dr. Marvin A. Block, a private practitioner in Buffalo, New York, who for ten years was chairman of the AMA's committee on alcoholism. Dr. Block concedes that alcohol is so commonplace in our society— and excessive drinking so prevalently acceptable as a social activity—that it is difficult for anyone to determine whether or not the ordinary individual who drinks is an early alcoholic or problem drinker.

Block strongly believes, however, that his fellow physicians can play a key role in detecting early signs of alcoholism. The challenge for most doctors is that this preliminary yet all-important procedure must be a self-taught practice. Block reiterates, "In most medical schools, instruction about alcoholism is so inadequate that the average medical student taking a medical history dwells very little on the drinking patterns of the patients he sees."

Dr. Block advises his colleagues to take medical histories in a "thorough but nonjudgmental way." The early signs of alcoholism must be identified so that "the information elicited is in no way different from other information in a history," he cautions, "and carried out in exactly the same objective way with no change of expression or suggestion of criticism."

Truly useful and effective health professionals would begin, as Dr. Block urges, with a high index of suspicion as to the possibility of alcoholism in *every* patient. Beyond that, the enlightened physician's duties would include treatment of alcoholism as a chronic illness often characterized by periodic relapses; an obligation to the patient extending much further than the treatment of physical complications; referral of the patient to appropriate agencies and organizations, such as Alcoholics Anonymous, for long-term care and support for which the physician is not available; and, finally, referral of the spouses and children of alcoholic patients to counseling as appropriate, and to such organizations as Alanon and Alateen.

A giant stride has finally been taken by the prestigious American College of Physicians, whose Board of Regents not long ago approved and published the following "Statement on Alcoholism":

Alcoholism is one of the major problems of our time with both social and health implications. The American College of Physicians strongly supports the efforts being made to curb excessive use of alcohol and urges all members of the College and other physicians to participate actively in educational programs regarding its hazards and in treatment programs for persons with this illness. . . .

The treatment of advanced alcoholism is unsatisfactory; but this fact does not relieve the physician of responsibility. He treats many chronic illnesses for which no completely satisfactory treatment is available. If the alcoholic patient is regarded as a patient in need of help and if individualized treatment is applied, many can be rendered asymptomatic and others greatly helped.

Clearly, this is an important, positive, and long overdue pronouncement. And, on a somewhat lesser scale, there have been numerous other calls for action—especially regarding the urgent need for adequate alcoholism education in medical schools— from the American Medical Society on Alcoholism (AMSA), which is the medical component of the National Council on Alcoholism; from the NIAAA; and from various state medical societies.

A recent resolution by the Medical Society of New Jersey, as one case in point, not only called for liberalization of the admission policies for alcoholics in hospitals across America, but also strongly urged physicians "to abstain from using terms of other pathological conditions in place of the diagnosis of alcoholism, when alcoholism is the primary manifested illness."

In much the same fashion, physicians within the military finally have begun to take a hard look at alcoholism among their professional associates. Not long ago, in a sharp departure from the past practice of condoning the "cover-up" of alcoholic physicians in the armed forces, the Navy's Vice Admiral and Surgeon General D. L. Custis sent a no-nonsense directive to commanding officers of all naval hospitals and dispensaries.

"In the past we have sometimes tended to ignore alcoholism among our colleagues," Custis told the COs, "but we must now face the fact that this disorder is a potentially fatal illness and that its incidence among members of the healing professions is startlingly high. It is essential for both the individual and the organization," Custis urged, "that our Medical Department personnel with alcohol problems be promptly identified and treated."

In his unusually forthright communiqué, Surgeon General Custis conceded that confronting an alcoholic colleague with the facts about his or her alcoholism "is an unpleasant task" which requires a high degree of clinical objectivity and courage.

"Many of us have mixed feelings about alcoholism," he admitted. "We may question the effectiveness of treatment, and we hesitate to harm an associate's career. Confrontation, however, is the most vital initial step in treatment. We must not stand idle when we see a colleague impaired by alcoholism. His career is already seriously jeopardized by the disease. By confrontation and rehabilitation, we must reverse the predictably downward trend of this disorder."

Unfortunately, although not surprisingly, the response to such urgings has been generally perfunctory and often misdirected, in the opinion of psychiatrist Dr. John S. Tamerin, former research director of Silver Hill Foundation and now medical director of the Center for Alcohol and Health Services in Greenwich, Connecticut. Acknowledging with one-handed applause the fact that substantial government funds have been appropriated toward the understanding and treatment of alcoholism, Tamerin stops just short of outright hostility when he describes a sudden "resurgence of interest" in alcoholism among psychiatrists and behavioral scientists.

"Unfortunately," Tamerin charges, "much of this recent work reflects a disquieting trend towards perceiving the alcoholic as an experimental animal with a habit disorder, rather than a human being who drinks because of serious psychological problems. Consequently, the literature is now replete with studies of innovative approaches to manipulating, training, or shocking the alcoholic into an aversion to alcohol, or at least an aversion to the state of intoxication—without bothering to ask why these human beings continue to drink despite all the adverse consequences their drinking has already heaped upon them.

"If we thoughtfully consider the human being who drinks," Tamerin adds bitterly, "it seems rather far-fetched to assume that an alcoholic who has been medicated to vomit while drinking warm vodka in an experimental setting on a few occasions will develop an equal aversion to a cold martini when he returns to the loneliness and desperation, or the chaos and tension of a fragmented life, perceived by him as overwhelming, meaningless, or hopeless. Where such treatment does work, it is usually because the guilt-ridden individual has been primed to change even if it means accepting a painful and humiliating treatment in order to do so.

"It is time for psychiatrists and psychoanalysts to accept their responsibility for formulating and developing meaningful treatment approaches for alcoholism," Tamerin urges. "However, in accepting such a mandate, it is imperative that doctors take a fresh look at the human being who drinks to excess—a view uncluttered by the traditional bias against the alcoholic."

If real progress is to be made in achieving an effective and lasting therapeutic alliance between alcoholic patients and healing professionals, a great many steps must be taken. For preliminary treatment of alcoholic persons who are acutely intoxicated or in DTs, to tackle the most visible challenge, physicians such as Tamerin, Block, and others already mentioned recommend that at least three primary objectives be established. First, they urge, alcoholic patients should be admitted by all general hospitals. Second, all hospitals should be equipped with whatever modern drugs and other facilities are needed for the treatment of patients who are intoxicated or suffering from delirium tremens. And, third, suitable advanced training and orientation in the care of alcoholics should be provided for staff physicians, nurses, attendants, and administrative personnel.

As for long-term therapy and rehabilitation, obviously much more is required. Just for openers, NIAAA's "Standards of Comprehensive Services for Alcoholic Persons and Their Families" calls for a planned continuum of care—"from initial response to acute needs, through long-term follow-up." As NIAAA puts it, in the rather typical jargon of government agencies, such continutity of services helps to "ensure that the client, entering the system at any point, may progress through a treatment sequence designed to respond efficiently to needs as perceived by the individual."

Glossy brochures and sometimes incomprehensible terminology aside, as for achieving NIAAA's idyllic "continuum of care" for alcoholics, the hard fact remains that America is starting not only from scratch, but virtually from belowground.

When it comes to adding the subject of alcoholism to medical school curricula, as a beginning point, most of today's faculty members admittedly find it difficult, if not impossible, to teach about a subject with which they are neither faintly familiar nor even remotely involved.

In addition—and far more important for the alcoholic man or woman seeking treatment now—one can hardly ignore the all-important matter of health insurance; to be sure, the presence or absence of health insurance frequently spells the difference between seeking and avoiding help in the first place.

The reality today? Hardly a handful of insurance companies do provide coverage for alcoholism in America today; even among that handful, moreover, some provide coverage solely for the acute or detoxification phase.

Unquestionably, some progress is being made. For example, legislation enacted by Congress in 1974 prohibits hospitals receiving federal assistance—directly or indirectly—from discriminating against or denying admission to alcoholic patients with medical problems solely because of their alcoholism. The same legislation provides federal financial support (a mere $13 million, unfortunately) to those states enacting the Uniform Alcoholism and Intoxification Treatment Act, the law that removes public drunkenness from the criminal code and places it in the health domain, where it has always belonged.

Finally, the legislation guarantees the confidentiality of medical records of patients under treatment for alcoholism, safeguarding those records ''from the prying eyes of others,'' as one disgruntled physician puts it.

In addition, the National Institute on Alcohol Abuse and Alcoholism has undertaken various efforts to expand the alcoholism education of doctors; at this writing, a number of medical schools are being encouraged to integrate alcoholism studies in their curricula through training grants awarded by NIAAA. Moreover, for the first time, various medical organizations and state legislatures are beginning to acknowledge the problem of alcoholism and, in some instances, even trying to do something about it.

The Michigan State Medical Society, for example, has prepared a proposal which would educate physicians about their own alcoholism and provide a referral service for them. Similarly, the AMA has drafted a model law dealing with sick physicians incapacitated by alcohol or other drugs. Also encouraging is the fact that nine states (Connecticut, Illinois, Louisiana, Minnesota, Mississippi, New Jersey, Washington, Wisconsin, and Massachusetts) have enacted legislation requiring either that benefits for alcoholism treatment be included in all group health policies, or that the coverage be offered to policyholders as an option.

Health professionals who have begun to wonder about their own direction concerning the treatment of alcoholics might do well to ponder suggestions made in an Alcoholics Anonymous pamphlet entitled *If You Are a Professional*. The pamphlet notes that Alcoholics Anonymous has had more than thirty-five years of trial-and-error experience, face to face with literally hundreds of thousands of drunks. ''This mass of intensive first-hand experience, with all kinds of problem drinkers, in all phases of both illness and recovery, is unparalleled as far as we know,'' the pamphlet states. ''AA is glad to share it freely with any professional person—or any alcoholic—who wants it.''

The pamphlet suggests that going to AA meetings is the best possible way to get a feeling of the form and dynamics of Alcoholics Anonymous, urging professionals to try several meetings, since no two are exactly alike. "Then, if you have any questions," the pamphlet goes on, "you might have a cup of coffee with two or three of us after the meeting. By far the best way to refer an alcoholic to AA is to *take* him or her to an AA office or meeting. Establishing direct telephone contact between the alcoholic and AA while the client or patient is with you can also be effective. Some professionals who regularly make use of AA services began by getting to know several AA members personally and by attending AA meetings."

In the final analysis, perhaps the best advice to medical professionals comes from "Doc Holiday," the recovered alcoholic physician described earlier in these pages.

"I feel that medicine is going to have to play a very important role in alcoholism," he told me during that Christmas season in Atlanta. "In our health care–oriented society, every alcoholic who doesn't die does end up at one time or another in front of a health care person. So we have to educate the doctors, nurses, and technicians in such a way that they *recognize* the alcoholic, that they feel comfortable confronting him about his disease, and that they treat him for *alcoholism* and not something else.

"And this is where Alcoholics Anonymous comes in more than anybody else," Holiday said. "Once doctors learn to recognize alcoholism and be comfortable with it, they can confront the patient and tell him, 'You don't need me, because I can't help you. I've been screwing you over for two hundred years now, and you really need something like fellowships. You need AA, you need an alcoholism center for a while."

Doc Holiday added, "We have to teach doctors to be less technical and more humane, less comprehending and more understanding, less prescribing and more *pro*scribing—*pro*scribing alcohol, *pro*scribing all sedative mood-changing chemicals, and not *pre*scribing more and more junk. We have to make people more independent and self-reliant rather than dependent on continued medical care."

Doc Holiday gazed for a moment at the crowds of Christmas shoppers far below his office. He finally turned to me and said, with deep conviction, "Every time I deal with one of my alcoholic patients in such a way that he no longer needs me, I'm a success. Every time they keep needing me, I can blow smoke up my ass and tell myself how smart I am. But," he added softly, "I'm not really enabling that person to become an independent adult who can love me or anybody else, especially himself or herself. Instead, he has to keep *respecting* me, and *needing* me, and *fearing* me. And that's not serving."

8

The Funny Drunk
and Other Works of Fiction

The night that I visited the Nugget, Bertha sashayed to stage center at the tail end of her act, and let fly a barrage of what can only be described as mammoth manure. She was billed as one of "the world's most talented performing elephants."

Mellowed by the effects of a seven-dollar-per-person cocktail show minimum in the form of four drinks served back to back, the Reno audience accepted Bertha's midnight offering with howls of delight.

Next among the roster of headliners, preceding Juliet Prowse, was guest star Foster Brooks, the silver-bearded comedian and raconteur known far and wide as America's "lovable lush." Resisting allusions to pink elephants and the like, Brooks adhered to his regular routine of "intoxicating humor," rewarding the audience with the familiar barrage.

With much staggering and stuttering ("F-F-F-Frank likes to f-f-f-fish . . ."), Brooks regaled us with tales of mentally defective relatives, martini-fueled adultery, deceased ex-wives ("The first died from eating poisoned mushrooms, the second from a fractured skull. She wouldn't eat her mushrooms."), birth control ("I'm gonna buy a condominium." "I don't care, I take the pill anyway . . ."), a one-armed fisherman, and on and on.

At one point, he feigned a drunken and lengthy memory lapse

during which he couldn't remember his own name. He then sang "Happy Birthday" to himself, grinning triumphantly when he came to the "dear *Brooks*" part. From time to time, he struggled futilely with words, inevitably choosing more easily pronounceable substitutes.

Perplexed by the goings on and wondering what the cheering was all about, a withered and very elderly lady at my table finally stage-whispered to her hilarious son, "What's wrong with him?" And the son replied impatiently, "For God's sake, Mom, he's playing a drunk."

The seven-dollar-a-pot coffee was good that night, and I certainly bear no personal malice toward Foster Brooks. For some five years now, sixty-three-year-old Brooks has made a comfortable living by playing that funny drunk, entertaining television and night-club audiences in the tradition of W. C. Fields, Jackie Gleason, Red Skelton, and many others known for their "lovable lush" characterizations. To this day, of course, Dean Martin's ever-present cocktail glass remains as familiar as his theme song, and Johnny Carson's snidely humorous asides about Ed MacMahon's "drinking problem" are as much a trademark as the "Heee—ere's Johnny" opening on that durable nighttime variety show. In short, hardly a day goes by when America's TV viewers and radio listeners are not subjected to at least one comic portrayal of a stumbling, bumbling inebriate—all in the name of good, clean fun.

In fairness, few among us have not occasionally snickered at the twisty-tongued performance of a hiccuping Foster Brooks or the wide-eyed antics of a Flip Wilson doing his drunken bartender sketch; as depicted by a talented and inventive comedian, television's so-called "funny drunk" can indeed evoke laughter.

On the other hand, considering that most Americans are adversely affected by both drunks and drunkenness—directly or indirectly, in degree ranging from chronic dismay to acute disaster—it does seem astonishing that we applaud, let alone condone, such portrayals.

Certainly, from that standpoint, it would be inconceivable for television viewers to tolerate comic portrayals of, say, a fat lady having a massive heart attack, a child in the teeth-rattling throes of a convulsive seizure, or, just for laughs, the eye-rolling prelude to a diabetic coma.

Bad taste? Unquestionably. In the long run, however, the comic drunk is far less a question of bad taste than perpetuation of what amounts to a killer myth: the alcoholic or "drunk" is clearly a weak-willed and ludicrous individual and, hence, alcoholism is merely a matter of weak-willed ludicrosity. As a friend of mine puts it, "You don't hear people 'confessing' that they have ulcer disease, do you?"

The point is, of course, that the funny drunk is simply not funny. Yet "funniness" and the whole idea of "fun" are primary threads from which have been woven the whole cloth equating alcohol with good times, good fellowship, and, most misleadingly, the good life.

My pilgrimage to "the world's biggest little city" began in San Jose, California. In the Hughes Airwest waiting room, a colorful poster (lettered in an ad man's version of a child's crayoned scrawl) informed me that "the airline's planes go to a zillion places," that "the stewardesses are real nice," and that "Dad likes it when they have the free wine."

Good old Dad was featured prominently on the poster. Depicted in cartoon style and obviously soused, Dad was drinking the free wine with relish: his tongue lolled from his mouth and his eyes were crossed. His succinct message to air travelers was *"Yum!"*

Aboard the tiny F-27 prop-jet, the message was somewhat more sophisticated; no sooner were we airborne than a woman's voice announced that "cocktails are available at the Happy Hour price of one dollar."

It was a short flight, providing barely enough time for the stewardess to take and fill those "Happy Hour" orders. Leafing through *Time* magazine as we began our descent, I noted a full-page advertisement for twelve-year-old Johnnie Walker Black Label Scotch. It showed an ice-filled glass and proclaimed, "The road to success is paved with rocks," and urged me to "Let us smooth them for you."

Onward and downward, I eventually made my way to the

Nugget itself, where I was swallowed up not only by the regulars, but by a swarming, bacchanalian army of conventioneers. Their embossed name tags let it be known that they were members of the all-male "T/K Golf Safari," and I soon learned that: 1) T/K is a manufacturing company located in Illinois; 2) 240 T/K golfers come to the Nugget every year for a four-day funfest; 3) most of those 240 T/K golfers (about 238, it seemed) were raucously drunk; 4) the Nugget's myriad bars, temporarily named "The 19th Hole," "The 20th Hole," and so on, were running out of booze; and 5) if I was not careful, I would stumble over a passed-out T/Ker or pass out myself from the fumes.

In all, it was a memorable evening, capsuled in my mind by an especially vivid flash of a T/Ker swaying precariously backwards on a bar stool, a man so intoxicated that he could neither hear, speak, nor move from his perch at The 19th Hole; he had been drinking crème de menthe, I surmised, for his lips, teeth, tongue, and shirtfront were bright green.

Admittedly, I am biased, but the fact remains that perhaps thirty of those 240 T/K Golf Safari carousers are, at least statistically, alcoholics. Apart from that bit of unassailable reality, I wonder how many of the entire group faced their shaving mirrors the next morning saying—and believing—that they had truly "had fun."

Had they asked themselves that question, chances are that a considerable number of those hung-over golfers would have responded affirmatively. And that is not the least bit surprising. For the fact is that most of us have been conditioned, literally since childhood, to automatically associate the "romance" of alcohol and the drinking of alcoholic beverages with a wide variety of positive and enjoyable activities, emotions, attitudes, capabilities, and types of behavior.

One need not be a sociologist to become aware that the purveyors of beer, wine, and hard liquor have long been selling not products, but promises. If we purchase this or that brand, the mass media advertisements assure us, we will achieve or experience heightened status, increased happiness, a more enjoyable sex life, an unsullied reputation, freedom from fear, unbreakable bonds of camaraderie, the reality of truly belonging, social prominence, and, implicitly, more fun than a barrel of monkeys.

In a manner of speaking, we have, of course, fallen victim to the fine art of seduction—as expertly and effectively practiced by America's $30-billion-a-year alcoholic beverage industry. And, in deference to that industry, our capitulation has resulted not only from the continuing onslaught of what Vance Packard two decades ago dubbed "hidden persuasion," but also from our own willingness and even eagerness to *be* seduced.

The aftermath of such seduction has been detailed many times over during my travels. One "on target" interview that illustrated this seduction took place in a sun-soaked Malibu, California, apartment within shouting distance of my own front porch. The almost classical victim of media seduction in this case was a petite and charming young woman whose voice still echoed the twangy drawl and dryness of Oklahoma City, where she was born and raised.

Her name is Gretchen; she is the mother of two children, divorced, and a recovering alcoholic who had her last drink on the evening of March 19, 1973. For the better part of a day, Gretchen shared the cause-effect chronology of her brief courtship and whirlwind seduction by advertising wizards who thoroughly convinced her that their various elixirs would provide "a whole special way of life."

Describing her first experience with alcohol at a wedding rehearsal when she was sixteen years old, Gretchen recalled, "I drank because it was going to be fun. And it really *was* glamorous, like something out of the movies. You know, even when I had sipped drinks at home with my parents, it was always the pretty occasions. It was always the Pink Ladies at Christmas, and the fancy cocktail shaker. Daddy wore furry white gloves with silver bells on them, and when he shook that shaker, the bells jingled. We had little red glasses, and I can still see them. God, it was all so special."

The next time Gretchen remembers drinking was yet another celebration. By then she was married, she said. "The words 'Let's celebrate' meant 'Get out the bottle.' It was martinis, and

I loved it. I loved the glass, and the napkin and the olive. I loved the idea of sitting down before dinner, and I became attracted to that and obsessed with that almost from that moment on. I loved 'cocktail hour' almost immediately,'' she added, ''and that's the only way I knew you celebrated. I didn't know that you marked any occasion—a happy occasion, or a sad one as it turned out later—with anything *but* booze.''

The young couple moved about, ending up in Hollywood for a time. ''I was into budget cooking,'' recalled Gretchen. ''I could just barely afford hot dogs and fried potato patties, but I would put candles on the table and get wine. I didn't know one thing about wine, and bought a huge bottle of that cheap wine—oh, like that Thunderbird and things like that. I didn't know that Thunderbird wasn't *okay*. Had I known, I wouldn't have drunk it. But I soon did learn, and eventually got into the whole 'brand' thing. Anyway, I thought that wine made the dinner, you know, *elegant.''*

As her husband became increasingly successful in his profession, Gretchen began to acquire more and more equipment for those cocktail hours and ''elegant'' dinners.

''I did the whole thing, the pitcher and ice bucket and silver tray and all that, and the equipment increased as my drinking increased. I loved everything that went *with* the drinking. And I eventually went from paper napkins to linen napkins, with four sets of napkins for four different kinds of occasions. I used to play the same record over and over in the apartment,'' she remembered, ''so that when people came in, it would be a certain musical mood and set the whole mood of the party. I even had a certain napkin that went with the decor of the apartment, although no one noticed, I'm sure. Then, when I discovered the 'brand' thing from the ads, I began pouring cheap booze into good booze bottles, so that people would think we were drinking Smirnoff or whatever. I always kept an empty Jack Daniels bottle around, for instance, so I could fill it up with a cheap bourbon—because I believed the ads, and the ads said that Jack Daniels or Smirnoff or Chivas Regal was the *best*.''

As the afternoon waned, we talked about those ads at length.

At one point, I asked, "What was it those ads were really selling?"

"Exactly what I *bought*," Gretchen replied unhesitatingly. "They were selling and, of course, are still selling the glamour and the fun, and the whole aura of that. I wanted that. It wasn't that I necessarily wanted to be that sophisticated, but it was a *way of life* that I wanted. All those pictures, that's what I wanted. The walks in the park and the balmy evenings and the moonlight. They're selling a life style," Gretchen added, "and I tried to live that life style. I really got caught up with that. But then I got caught up with the addiction that I had no idea was there."

The word "seduction" came up repeatedly during our conversation, and Gretchen said, "In terms of wanting to be 'seduced,' I can think of what for me was the perfect example. I never did like the taste of Scotch. But when I started to drink, it seemed clear to me that those people in that life style—the life style that I by now had been conditioned to want—drank Scotch. So I learned to drink Scotch. I might have preferred to drink beer," she added thoughtfully, "but I never even tried it. Also, people said that you had to 'acquire a taste' for Scotch. And that made it seem even more special, so that's what I did. I taught myself, because it implied being a gourmet, like acquiring a taste for snails, which most people didn't like or were afraid to try. I didn't want to be like *most* people. I wanted to be like the people in those pictures.

"I saw the fireplace going and heard the music," she said, smiling. "I would have preferred every night to be in a long, flowing dress, coming down the staircase like Scarlett O'Hara with a martini glass in my hand. I loved the clinkle of ice. That's what they showed me in the TV commercials and magazine ads: gorgeous rooms, gorgeous furniture, gorgeous people—all, you know, drinking. It was prestige and it was rich and it was classy, and it was a world I wanted to be in. And in that world there was booze, and it was all so fun."

The sun had begun to set in Malibu. Gretchen poured more coffee. Just a little embarrassed at a new recollection, she said,

"I can almost see it now, those ads and what they did to me. People brushing snow off their shoulders. Coming into a house holding a glass, and, you know, it all had to do with the music and the fireplace. In those ads, they're always lying on the floor in front of the fireplace, or in a mountain cabin in front of the fireplace. I always wanted to go to a mountain cabin," she continued, "but it never occurred to me to go to a cabin and *hike*, or walk around, or look at the scenery. I wanted to go to a mountain cabin and be in front of the fireplace with a drink and the music going and the whole romance of it."

I was invited to stay for dinner that evening, and we talked for a while about what drinking before dinner "used to be like" for each of us.

"If you were drinking before dinner," Gretchen remembered, "that seemed to put you in a different *class*. You know what I used to call them, the other people? I used to call them 'Joe Lunchpail.' Joe Lunchpail was the guy who came home and read the paper and had dinner. And I wasn't going to be Joe Lunchpail. I was going to sit down with a drink before dinner even if I was making less money than Joe Lunchpail—that part never occurred to me. It had nothing to do with the reality of dollars and cents.

"I was starving," she added, "and going to work on the streetcar. But I'd come home and sit down with the cocktail and then have dinner. That made me better than Joe Lunchpail. I mean, what did he know? The way to live was to have cocktails before dinner; that's what you had to do to be somebody."

In addition to my tape recorder, I had also brought with me that day the October 1973 "40th Anniversary Celebration" issue of *Esquire* magazine. I had been saving that dog-eared 564-page tome for almost two years, struck not so much by its awesome bulk as its unusual fold-out cover illustration. Depicted are thirty-nine famous writers, living and dead, whose works are represented in the anniversary issue; illustrated, for example, are Ernest Hemingway, John Updike, William Faulkner, F. Scott Fitzgerald, Dorothy Parker, Vladimir Nabokov, Tennessee Williams, Sinclair Lewis, and John Dos Passos. The writers (marked with numerals and identified in a margin) are bunched together in what seems to be a unique party; all but a few hold cocktails raised to their lips or in salute, while a red-jacketed waiter hovers at the ready in the foreground with a tray containing a fresh supply of cocktails.

I've long wondered about the point or, for that matter, the *raison d'être* of that cover illustration. Was its purpose to subliminally perpetuate the long discredited myth that the drinking of alcohol somehow nourishes creativity? If so, *Esquire* couldn't have made a worse choice of writers. A considerable number of the writers are reputed to be afflicted with alcoholism, and a somewhat lesser number—including several Nobel laureates and Pulitzer Prize winners—long ago died alcohol-related deaths.

Perhaps, on the other hand, the selection of that particular cover illustration simply had to do with selling booze. For, by my count, there are forty-eight liquor, liqueur, wine, and beer ads in that single record-breaking issue of *Esquire,* and, predictably, their themes cover the full spectrum from camaraderie and celebration to status and sexuality.

At any rate, the ads *in toto* were no less classic in their use of symbolic seductiveness than was Gretchen's retrospective description of her actual seduction by similar albeit earlier-day ads. I leafed through the magazine with her; here is Gretchen's spontaneous reaction to some of those advertisements.

J & B SCOTCH

ILLUSTRATION: Young woman wearing ''women's lib'' symbol is leaning on the edge of a pool table, cue stick in one hand, drink in the other; bottle and another (man's) drink are in the foreground.

HEADLINE: ''Scotch and the single girl''

COPY: None.

GRETCHEN: This is the kind of life I lived. I had several friends who had pool tables, just like what this girl is doing, and the dart board and the game room and the whole thing. And all the time we used to go and play pool, and that was quote ''fun.'' I'd get so drunk, but that looked like fun to me. That looked to me like how you played pool. If you said to me, ''You want to come over and play pool?'' then click-click in my mind went, ''Oh, come over and play pool, gorgeous dress, lean over the table, and hold a drink.'' And I never played pool in my life without a drink.

JOHNNIE WALKER BLACK LABEL 12-YEAR-OLD SCOTCH

ILLUSTRATION: Unopened bottle in the sky, nestled in clouds at the end of a multicolored rainbow.

HEADLINE: None.

COPY: None.

GRETCHEN: That's so sick. Oh, that is so sick. Everything that Scotch ever did to me was the complete opposite of a rainbow. And the ad tries to say to me now, ''That's glorious and wonderful, and everything's going to be marvelous.'' Rainbow time. It says to me, ''Everything's just clouds and beautiful and everything.''

BENEDICTINE LIQUEUR

ILLUSTRATION: Paris sunset with Eiffel Tower in background; photo inset of luxurious room where formally attired couple are holding liqueur glasses and having an animated conversation.

HEADLINE: ''La Grande Liqueur Française''

COPY: ''After coffee enjoy Benedictine. The spectacular way to end a dinner and begin an evening.''

GRETCHEN: Now you've got to say she is a *lady*. She's sitting there with the pearls, her hair is groomed—she looks just gorgeous. And that gorgeous man is paying a lot of attention to her. Both with cocktail glasses. It wouldn't occur to me to see her without one. This here, the silver tray with the bottle on it and two glasses—I continued to do that all the time. Until I started using the kitchen glass in the cupboard. That's the way I saw it, because I related to pictures like this. So that's what I did, and that's the way I wanted it in my home. And if you had said to me, ''Let's go to Paris,'' that's what I would have thought of Paris.

''Spectacular way to end a dinner and begin an evening''? Boy, at the end it was pretty spectacular. It was pretty spectacular to walk down the road in a bathrobe and begin an evening careening off walls and falling down and having people say, "Well, you'd better go home now." You know, crashing into bed, trying to find the bed . . .

SEAGRAM'S SEVEN CROWN WHISKEY

ILLUSTRATION: Photo of young couple on country road, arms linked, smiling at each other, carrying a picnic basket.

HEADLINE: "The Seven 'n Cider"

COPY: " 'You tired?' 'Just a little.' 'Want to stop?' 'Okay.' 'There. That's a nice spot. By the big pile of leaves.' So while she unpacked an autumn kind of picnic, he put together an autumn kind of drink . . ."

GRETCHEN: Now, I had this whole picture image. And I always wanted to go on a picnic and I wanted to do just what they're doing. I wanted to have a basket that looked just like that and sit down. I would have loved that. Just perfect. I would have wanted to wear the same clothes, have him, be by the leaves, and the whole thing.

OLD GRAND-DAD KENTUCKY STRAIGHT BOURBON

ILLUSTRATION: Small plaster bust of "old gentleman," flanked by glass of bourbon on the rocks.

HEADLINE: "If you're calling the shots, we're the shot you're calling for."

COPY: "Old Grand-Dad. The good stuff."

GRETCHEN: That would have impressed me. "If you're calling the shots, we're the shot you're calling for." So that would have made me think, "Well, I'd better order that." That's all status.

JIM BEAM KENTUCKY STRAIGHT WHISKEY

ILLUSTRATION: Actors Fredric March and Mike Connors seated side by side, each smiling and holding a drink thrust forward.

HEADLINE: "Generation after generation, Jim Beam"

COPY: "Back in 1946 when Fredric March was starring in *The Best Years of Our Lives,* Mike Connors was starring on the basketball court at UCLA. They're of different generations,

these two, but each is a craftsman. The Beams, too, are crafts-
men . . .''

GRETCHEN: I loved to read about people who drank, and I
loved to see that. And if I read an article about anybody famous,
I'd just scan it; I wanted to read, ''Before dinner, Fredric March
sits down and has cocktails.'' It didn't have to say he got
drunk—but ''before dinner he has cocktails,'' and I would think
(snapping her fingers), ''That's living, *right?*'' You know he's
not a square. I used to think of people as square who didn't
drink.

DEWAR'S SCOTCH

ILLUSTRATION: Photo of man wearing business suit and tie.

HEADLINE: ''Dewar's Profiles''

COPY: ''Ellis E. Reid. HOME: Chicago. AGE: 38. PROFESSION:
Attorney. HOBBIES: Art, travel, good restaurants. LAST BOOK
READ: *The Exorcist.* LAST ACCOMPLISHMENT: Elected President
Cook County Bar Association (second term). Started scholarship
fund for minority law students. Directs a lawyer's reference plan
for the poor. QUOTE: 'The Law must be available to all. For study,
for protection, for justice. Working for those goals has made being
an attorney more rewarding than I had ever hoped.' PROFILE:
Dedicated. A strong spirit. A leader that finds no job too small to do
himself. Concerned for others. Willing to take action in their
behalf—even at a sacrifice. SCOTCH: Dewar's White Label.''

GRETCHEN: I would have always been impressed, especially
the part about the attorney and good restaurants. It was a whole
status thing. He drank Dewar's and so did I, so that put me in
that category, too.

CHIVAS REGAL SCOTCH

ILLUSTRATION: Chivas Regal bottle fashioned out of stacks of
coins.

HEADLINE: ''The Rich Man's Scotch''

COPY: ''(And yet, Chivas Regal doesn't cost that much more
than regular Scotch.)''

GRETCHEN: Well, oh, of course. I believed that. If I had had a
bottle of Chivas Regal, I would have put it in the front of the

liquor cabinet. I would have put it ahead of Dewar's or anything, just because it cost more. I might not have even preferred
that Scotch. I believed *all* of that.

Needless to say, the equation of alcohol drinking with good
times, fellowship, and status—or what Gretchen calls "all of
that"—epitomizes advertising that does exactly what it is supposed to do: sell. It is one thing, however, to sell the "sizzle"
and not the steak; it is quite another thing to create or even perpetuate myths which, for many persons, are potentially destructive. Untold millions of Americans still believe, and during the
foreseeable future will continue to believe, "all of that."

"Consider the promotional value of all the myths, the folklore, the fallacies that have built up in our society through the
years," says Fred Klein, executive vice-president of Chicago-
based Grey-North advertising agency. "Such as 'Alcoholics are
skid row bums.' Does that mean you may consume limitless
quantities of alcohol with no bad effect if you live on Riverside
Drive?" Adds Klein, whose agency since 1971 has developed
the public service alcoholism-education posters and broadcast
ads for the National Institute on Alcohol Abuse and Alcoholism,
"We're trying to rock a pretty big boat."

To find out quickly just how big that boat is, one need only
riffle through the pages of the *Liquor Handbook,* published annually by Gavin-Jobson Associates and considered the industry's
marketing "bible." According to the 1975 edition of that publication, Americans consumed a record 152.6 million cases of distilled spirits—the "hard stuff"—in 1974 alone. That averaged
out to 983.7 fifths per 100 Americans and brought a whopping
$13 billion or $35.6 million per day to liquor producers' coffers.

Add to that the $2.6 billion spent on wine and $13.8 billion
spent on beer by Americans in 1974, and the staggering total
comes to $29 billion—or almost $80 million a *day.*

Given such astronomical sales figures, one can appreciate distillers' concern about possible threats to future revenues and
profits. Speaking for the industry, editor Clark Gavin and research director Bernard Appel spelled it out this way in their
foreword to the latest edition of the *Liquor Handbook:* "Last

year, apparent consumption of distilled spirits held up well against the background of a limping national economy and a record rate of inflation. But the fact remains that the price-profit squeeze has tightened, and this has happened just as annual rates of sales increase have lessened.

"In the first years of the Seventies," Gavin and Appel caution, "rates of gain each year have been only about half what they averaged in the 1964–1969 period. What are the prospects for raising the annual 'plus' and can this be done on a better profit-per-case basis?"

As alcoholic beverage industry executives well know, the answer to that question will once again be determined in large measure by the scope, impact, and "effectiveness" of their ad campaigns in the mass media. Although ad budget expenditures are perhaps the most closely guarded secret among America's breweries, wineries, and distilleries, authoritative estimates range from $500 million to $1 billion annually.

Granted, there is quite a spread between those two numbers, yet either figure is hardly chicken feed. In any case, advertising—more than anything else—remains the industry's primary sales lever—just as it is for the low-product-cost cosmetic and pharmaceutical industries.

As Gavin and Appel sum it up for the marketing VPs and VIPs who dedicatedly peruse their publication, "Whatever the destinies of any one distilled-spirit product type, future sales progress for the industry as a whole will still be tied to this motive power as it expresses itself in the continuing entertainment boom (on and off-premise), accelerating diversification, extension of the occasions market, development of special markets, the formation of new 'fashion' and 'status' concepts, and the very marked catalytic effects the still dominant youth market will have on consumer choices."

A flock of trade ads in that same edition of the *Liquor Handbook* make the point in rather more down-to-earth fashion. The *Ladies' Home Journal,* for example, attempts to solicit liquor ad dollars by showing a photo of a woman's hand holding a cocktail glass, exclaiming to potential *Ladies' Home Journal* advertisers, "No matter how you pour it, 52% of your market is now women!'' The *Journal* goes on to note that more than half of all liquor-store shoppers today are women—a jump from 44 percent in 1968. ''Why not offer a drink to our 16 million readers?'' the *Ladies' Home Journal* urges. ''They won't turn you down.''

Family Circle magazine, similarly, woos liquor advertisers by showing an elegantly clad woman holding a silver tray containing four cocktail glasses; the backdrop is a liquor- and stemware-laden home bar. ''How can you reach 17,226,000 American women who buy liquor but never see your ad?'' asks *Family Circle,* which claims to be ''the world's largest selling woman's magazine.''

Palm Springs Life magazine, in turn, exhorts liquor firms to ''influence the affluent,'' while the Detroit *News* claims it's ''ahead of Detroit's other paper by 295,022 cocktails a day.''

Clearly, as with just about all else in American society, it comes down in the final analysis to basic economics and that dollars-and-cents ''bottom line.'' It costs amazingly little—pennies, actually—to distill and bottle a fifth of, say, Smirnoff Vodka. Whatever the exact production expenditure, however, it assuredly costs far less to make the clear liquid than it does to billboard the notion that Smirnoff will leave you ''breathless,'' that Smirnoff invented the Bloody Mary, or that Smirnoff and apple juice or cranberry juice are the greatest things to come down the pike since sliced bread.

The point, of course, is that the booze-beer-and-wine business is not only very big business, but extremely profitable business. Just one dramatic example of that profitability can be seen by spotlighting the sales and pre-tax revenues of giant, industry-dominating E. and J. Gallo Winery, which produces some 28 percent of all wine sold in America—including close to 50 percent of the wine that retails for less than three dollars per half gallon.

According to a recent study by *Forbes* magazine, the Gallos (who started with nothing forty years ago) are now one of America's richest families—with a fortune estimated at about $500 million.

''The E. and J. Gallo Winery alone probably earned about $40 million before taxes last year [1974] on revenues of around

$335 million," says *Forbes*. "Then," the magazine's October 1, 1975, cover article continues, "you must add the profits and sales of tne business' other family-owned segments—the 5,000 acres of vineyard, 2,000 acres of apple orchards, one of the West's biggest bottling plants, one of California's largest trucking companies and several big wine distributors. All told, the family's annual pre-tax profits appear to approach $48 million on revenues of $475 million."

Yet even Gallo's 1974 revenues pale when compared to those of Seagram distillers ($1.84 billion), National Distillers ($1.43 billion), Heublein ($1.31 billion), or Hiram Walker ($889.7 million). So it assuredly does come down to economics—as it did in the 1600s when frontier traders used alcohol as a medium of exchange in their bartering with native Americans, as it did during the Whiskey Rebellion in 1794, and as it did during the years of Prohibition, when some of America's greatest fortunes were amassed.

Far more important, and impossible to ignore, it also comes down to people. "I hadn't the faintest idea that alcohol was a drug, not until I came to AA," a young recovering alcoholic in Miami Beach told me. "I find it ludicrous to advertise a drug, period—much less in such a provocative fashion. My young daughters watch television and flip through magazines, just as all kids do, and they see alcohol synonymized—if there is such a word—with glamour, festive occasions, and being 'in.' They certainly don't see alcohol related to scummy, crummy, embarrassing, horrible situations. And I think that's ludicrous.

"It's just like advertising poison," the young man continued angrily. "It *is* an addictive drug, and alcoholism is an illness to which a lot of people are susceptible. I was, and still am. All right, some people can drink alcohol and have an enjoyable time. Some people can take a walk in the woods and make that 'loaf of bread, jug of wine, and thou' scene. But other people are going to have that jug of wine and think they're going for a walk in the woods, and they're going for a whole different walk. They're going to walk right to skid row, whether it's in an alley or their own bedroom or whatever.

"You don't see ads for heroin," he added flatly. "You sure don't see pictures of people in tuxedos sitting around a mahogany table, laughing and chatting, with needles and syringes in front of them. From where I sit, those booze ads *kill* people."

Although the young Miamian's point is well taken, I suspect that not even the staunchest WCTUer would agree that liquor ads, *per se,* are lethal. One could argue that particular proposition endlessly; more to the point, however, is the net effect and end result of such ads.

For Gretchen, the young woman who had been so captivated by the liquor industry's pictures and promises, the net effect and end result was utter disaster and near death. Like the young man in Miami, she eventually sought help and achieved sobriety in Alcoholics Anonymous. For more than seven years before that day, though, her illness had progressed and her life had spiraled rapidly downward. The story of those years is uniquely her story and her story alone; yet Gretchen's story is not unlike countless other stories I have heard and countless others yet to be told.

"The drinking progressed until, as I say, it was no longer fun," Gretchen recounted. "I got to the long-dress stage sometimes, and would swish in with the cocktail, but I came to the point where I could barely get into the dress. I still always called it 'cocktails before lunch' and 'cocktails before dinner,' but the cocktails were with blue Levi's and a red sweater and tennis shoes, and 'cocktails before lunch' got earlier and earlier.

"It went from there," she continued, "to drinking practically the whole time I was awake. And the cocktail hour before lunch was a very shaky hand trying to hold the glass and get the drink down. It wasn't very romantic any more, to say the least. I wasn't using glasses or ice or a napkin, and a lot of times I would drink out of a paper cup or the bottle. I'd be down on my hands and knees pouring a drink in the hallway out of an extra supply in the hallway closet. I *had* to put it down on the floor, because I was shaking so hard I couldn't hold the cup and hold the bottle all at the same time."

The glamorous after-dinner liqueurs turned into brandy slugged into a half-filled coffee cup, Gretchen remembered. "I'd jump up from the table and wait for everybody to disappear just for a split second so I could grab that bottle of brandy immediately, even while I was still chewing the food. And at four or four-thirty, when I'd start the 'cocktails before dinner,' I'd take one sip and I'd be loaded, because I was still loaded from noon.

"Glamorous in my glamorous home, where I thought it was so nice to have cocktails?" Gretchen questioned, smiling wryly. "Well, a lot of time I wasn't in my home having cocktails. I was in my bathrobe walking down the street, knocking on people's doors to see if I could find somebody to drink with me. Or just simply to get out of the house because I couldn't stand the pressure of not being able to drink as much as I wanted to when I wanted to."

During the last year of her drinking, Gretchen phone-ordered from a nearby liquor store every other day "just like a robot," asking them to send two quarts of Beach Boy Vodka, two quarts of King George Scotch, and a carton of cigarettes—along with a pound of coffee or quart of milk "to make it look okay."

She was separated from her husband and essentially friendless then, in 1972, barely able to get her children off to school. There were no more parties, yet her last bill from the liquor store came to $353 for a single month. She was also buying liquor at the grocery store when she could brave the check-out line, "because I didn't want the liquor store to think I was buying too much booze."

In short, it was hardly glamorous or sophisticated in those last days before she finally conceded to herself that she was power-less over alcohol and that her life was in fact unmanageable. "It wasn't any more good times or fun or celebrating or status or associated with anything. It was alcoholism. I would pass out every night and 'come to' every morning with my lips swollen and my eyes puffed up and actually black underneath," she added. "And my hair was coming out by the handfuls, just by the handfuls. It would be all over the floor in the bathroom, and I don't mean just wispy hairs. I mean piles.

"I had bruises all over me," Gretchen continued relentlessly. "Some of them I remembered, some of them I didn't. And I couldn't sleep, so I had big bags under my eyes. *Glamour?* Jack, I was the least glamorous person you've ever seen."

One would hardly expect booze-beer-and-wine sellers to allocate space in their "promise-them-anything" ads for cautionary footnotes or, for that matter, photo insets of late-stage alcoholics who have reached that "least glamorous" state. Nor would one seriously expect liquor advertisers to highlight the fact that alcoholism is America's number-one health problem and number-three killer illness. On the other hand, one would expect something, if only recognition that all is not "wine and roses" from sea to shining sea.

Fortunately, the pressure to do something is mounting; as facts about alcohol's deleterious effects and alcoholism itself have become more widely known, the licensed beverage industry has been finding it increasingly difficult to maintain a head-in-the-sand posture. "Until only very recently," one former Seagram executive told me, "the industry's attitude has generally been one of avoidance. In other words, 'If we ignore it, maybe it will go away.' "

It has not "gone away"; on the contrary, as we have seen, alcoholism's toll has risen in almost catastrophic degree. Ironically, the $25-plus billion annual cost of alcoholism to Americans is well on its way to exceeding annual revenues from the sale of alcohol to Americans. Consequently, as might be expected, industry associations are gradually beginning to respond or, at the very least, "take a position."

Among those positions, at the childish extreme, is an approach which literally "pooh-poohs" the entire problem and, indeed, the idea that a problem in fact exists. Editors of the *Liquor Handbook,* for example, insist that the "barrage of publicity on use of alcohol has misled the general public, according to the well-established principle in a TV age that the 'seriousness' of a situation rises in direct proportion to the amount of money spent in talking about it."

The more prevalent approach (one, in my opinion, that is only slightly less childish) argues that alcoholism and "alcohol abuse" will diminish and eventually disappear if Americans, God love 'em, will only learn to drink "sensibly," "responsibly," and "in moderation."

This approach is used, for example, in the on-again-off-again (and generally seasonal) campaigns of the Licensed Beverage Industries, Inc.—campaigns which seek to place the burden of responsibility on people who *buy* alcoholic beverages. "Best thing to mix with liquor is common sense," said a typical LBI ad, which ran in such national publications as *Time* and *Newsweek*.

Let us backtrack, momentarily, to a seminar for journalists held in the White House on July 10, 1974. That day, former NIAAA director Dr. Morris Chafetz defined so-called heavy drinkers as those whose alcohol consumption exceeded "Anstie's limit." Anstie's limit, it was explained, is "not more than one and a half ounces of absolute alcohol (approximately three ounces of whiskey, one-half bottle of wine, or four glasses of beer) taken only with meals or food, and with all hard liquor in well-diluted form."

According to British physician Francis Anstie—who made his calculations more than a hundred years ago in pre–Civil War days—that is the amount of alcohol "that an adult man could drink daily without being adversely affected in general health."

In the months following that 1974 press conference, many alcoholism authorities sharply criticized Dr. Chafetz for dredging up and actually endorsing Anstie's outmoded concept, a concept that has little to do with the reality of alcohol as an addictive drug or the actuality of alcoholism as a pandemic illness in bicentennial America. One critic noted that Anstie's daily limit, multiplied by 365, would come to 68 pints of whiskey, 182 pints of wine, or 365 quarts of beer in a year.

Another critic, in a letter to the editor of the Washington *Post,* charged that the impact of NIAAA's latest "Report on Alcoholism" was "diluted by Dr. Morris Chafetz's continued insistence that 'moderation' and 'social responsibility in the use of beverage alcohol' are the solutions to the problem."

The letter writer was Mrs. Eleanor Edelstein, a staff member of the Washington Area Council on Alcoholism and Drug Abuse. "Dr. Chafetz persists in referring to something he calls 'responsible drinking,' " Mrs. Edelstein wrote, "and, unfortunately, few reporters examine this thesis carefully and discover that the logical conclusion of Dr. Chafetz's argument is that in-dividuals who have problems with alcohol are, therefore, irre-sponsible.

"As a recovered alcoholic," Mrs. Edelstein went on, "I have learned that my own problems with alcohol were not the result of stupidity, lack of moral fibre, or bad luck. It turned out that my body and my psyche could not handle any amount of alco-hol, and I am tired of Dr. Chafetz telling me that, because I can-not drink three ounces of whiskey, a half bottle of wine, or four glasses of beer a day, I am irresponsible and somehow socially inferior. When it comes to irresponsibility, in fact," Mrs. Edel-stein's letter concluded, "I find that Dr. Chafetz's attitude and remarks take first prize."

Criticism of Chafetz and/or the NIAAA aside, the licensed beverage industry quickly seized on the whole idea of "Anstie's limit"; it provided a ready-made and colorful ribbon for their al-ready neatly packaged proposition that "customer responsi-bility" is the ultimate and definitive solution for alcoholism, so-called alcohol abuse, and, for that matter, *all* alcohol-related problems.

In the heart of Kentucky sour-mash bourbon country not long ago, where I had been guest speaker at the opening banquet of the Fifth Annual Kentucky School of Alcohol Studies, I unex-pectedly heard that same proposition straight from "the horse's mouth." Early one morning, two friends drove me from Louis-ville to the Old Fitzgerald Distillery in nearby Shively.

As a writer, I managed to arrange a special tour through Old Fitzgerald's sprawling 126-year-old facility. My friends and I prowled among the giant mash vats and through the deathly quiet aging warehouses; from steel catwalks, we watched the au-tomated bottling, labeling, and packaging process. In all, we were treated with warm hospitality and, when the tour ended, were personally greeted by Old Fitzgerald's president, Mr. Burnside.

The four of us chatted briefly, and I mentioned casually that my friends and I were attending the School of Alcohol Studies that week. Mr. Burnside nodded with apparent approval; his expression seemed to indicate that he thought it was a "good thing." Then there was a long pause.

Finally, Mr. Burnside broke the silence. "Well, you know," he said seriously, "the answer is moderation. Anything in more than moderation is bad for you. Food, work, play, anything. *Moderation.*"

We nodded quietly and again thanked Mr. Burnside for his hospitality. He waved goodbye as we stepped through the front door. His last words, as I recall them, were, "Well, good heavens, even too much *milk* will make you sick."

It's difficult to take issue with that last statement; indeed, there's little point in attempting to do so. Although Burnside's opinion parallels that of other industry executives, his words were his own and he hardly presented himself that morning as a "spokesman."

He had no need to do so, for the industry apparently has as many official and unofficial spokesmen as it needs, not to mention public relations teams, registered lobbyists, numerous publications, associations, councils, and peripatetic executives who travel far and wide to "carry the message."

One such executive is Chris W. Carriuolo, corporate group vice-president of Heublein, Inc., which distills Smirnoff Vodka and numerous other alcoholic beverages. When Carriuolo was recently buttonholed by the press during a conference of the Distilled Spirits Council of the United States (DISCUS), he quickly ticked off half a dozen industry shibboleths, many of which were printed verbatim in local newspapers.

Among Carriuolo's seemingly authoritative pronouncements that day, for example, was the notion that today's generation is learning to "live safely" with alcohol, which is becoming part of its life style.

He asserted, moreover, that the energy crisis was a cloud with a silver lining, predicting that it will serve to re-popularize the neighborhood pub and home entertainment; during a week-long power outage in Fairfield County, Connecticut, Carriuolo noted with pleasure, alcoholic beverage consumption increased by 50 percent.

Still another healthy trend, in Carriuolo's view, is his personal forecast that there will be a greater proportion of women drinking than before, "and not just in urban areas, but also suburban and probably even rural areas."

Carriuolo also stressed proudly that "75 percent of all the drinks which have been developed in the last 20 years have been ours—the Moscow Mule, Bloody Mary, Vodka Martini, the Screwdriver." Then the Heublein executive fired his parting shot: "With these drinking trends evident in the new generation, the drug culture seems to be giving way to alcoholic beverages."

One would imagine that DISCUS members—gathered together that day in Scottsdale, Arizona—gave Carriuolo a round of applause for his last statement. For one thing, it was printed word for word in the local newspaper that carried the interview. For another, Carriuolo's seemingly innocuous final statement effectively managed to: 1) Equate the drinking of alcohol with the "good life"; 2) declassify alcohol as a drug; and 3) overtly encourage young people in Scottsdale to switch from "real drugs" to booze, at the same time assuring them and their parents that such a switch would be not only desirable, but praiseworthy.

In addition to quotable executives like Chris Carriuolo, the licensed beverage industry also utilizes the talents of professional letter writers to "carry the message." Consider, for example, Mr. Allen Bell of Denver's Beverage Analyst Group. A couple of summers ago, Mr. Bell took strong issue with something that had been printed in the Denver *Post*. Mr. Bell's vitriolic and lengthy letter to the editor, which the *Post* printed in its entirety, begins this way: "I would like to respond to the comments of one Gerald Barnes in which he quotes Judge Robert H. Close: 'Why should we pay for the care of drunks? The liquor industry should fund the treatment of alcoholics.' "

Mr. Bell goes on to note that "the liquor industry is already paying not only for the treatment of alcoholics, but also for a healthy portion of other costs of social welfare and the operation of the federal and state governments."

Bell pursues that point for several paragraphs, then gets to the primary thrust of his letter. Because that letter succinctly sums up the licensed beverage industry's views on alcoholism and, more particularly, alcoholic beverage advertising as it relates to alcoholism, it speaks volumes to me, as it will, I suspect, to anyone concerned about alcoholism in America.

Let me tell Mr. Barnes one startling fact: The consumption of hard liquor has dropped every year since repeal on a per capita basis. What this means is that fewer people are drinking more.

This of course is nothing for the industry to crow about, and neither is obesity, gluttony or any other excess to which people are prone.

Another observable fact which may have escaped Mr. Barnes' notice in his claim that alcohol is responsible for half of the deaths caused on the highways is that since the speed limit has been reduced to 55 miles per hour, deaths on the highway have dropped noticeably.

The alcohol beverage industry persuades no one, least of all adolescents, "to take up habitual drinking." He's 160 degrees off course when he states that our periodicals "display alluring, often sexy, full-page liquor advertisements." Let me refer to the credo of the liquor industry as stated by the Distilled Spirits Council of the United States:

• Distilled spirits shall not be advertised by radio or television; on the comic pages of newspapers, magazines or other publications; in publications owned or sponsored by wholesale or retail liquor dealers or their associations, without approval of the president who shall act only after consultation with the executive committee or the board; in publications devoted primarily to religious topics; in publications of schools, colleges or universities or their student bodies, or in programs of athletic contests in which students are exclusive participants (it is permissible to advertise in publications other than athletic programs sponsored wholly by an alumni group or organization of an educational institution); or in motion picture theaters.

• No ad shall contain an illustration of a woman unless it is dignified, modest and in good taste, and it shall not show her in provocative dress or situation.

• Agents shall not be employed to secure advertising "plugs" on radio, television, in moving pictures or on the legitimate stage.

• No billboard or other device shall be maintained near a military reservation if directed especially to military personnel.

• No ad shall contain the name of, or make reference to Santa Claus or any biblical character.

• No ad shall depict a child or immature person, portray objects suggestive of a child, nor appeal especially to children or immature persons.

- All ads shall be modest, dignified and in good taste.

This code is not simply window dressing. It is a hard and fast set of restraints that are scrupulously adhered to. The fact is, many distillers go even further than this. They actually spend money in their advertising telling people not to drink to excess. And also, much to their credit, they never publicize the fact that many medical researchers have stated that alcohol in moderation is quite beneficial, particularly to older people.

As a final observation, if the use of alcoholic beverages is a dire problem which is growing at a pace implied by Mr. Barnes, then everyone in the world, starting with pre-biblical times, would be a confirmed alcoholic.

Does it not follow, as Mr. Barnes charges, that if the industry is attempting to make drinking "sophisticated" that excessive drinking would be looked down upon, as is gluttony or any other form of excess?

Denver   ALLEN BELL
Beverage Analyst Group

Though it's unlikely that I'll ever meet Allen Bell in person, I've thought of his Denver *Post* letter and the "credo" of DISCUS often during my travels. Bell, Carriuolo, and those Licensed Beverage Industries "responsible drinking ads" come to mind, in fact, every time a billboard urges me to "Try Black Velvet on your neighbor," to "Get something started with Wolfschmidt," or to "Put a little cherry in your life" with Kijafa.

The hypocritical ambivalence of it all was brought sharply back into focus, most recently, as I watched the filming of a wine commercial on a beach just north of Malibu. The sand had been carefully raked, and a volleyball net had been stretched taut; actors and technicians milled about while prop men readied a portable barbecue, positioned a gingham-covered picnic table laden with exotic foods, and, finally, spotlighted the wine bottle and filled the gleaming stemware.

The director called for action and the "son and daughter" began their volleyball game; on cue "Mom and Dad" clinked

glasses and gazed at each other with looks, presumably, of un-
dying love. The camera panned from the surf to the volleyball
game and across the sand to the table, finally dollying in on the
wine bottle and then zooming in for a closeup of Mr. and Mrs.
America about to begin another "good life" afternoon.

There was nothing revelatory or spectacular about that particular commercial, yet it was fascinating to watch all the same. I
remember thinking that millions of Americans would soon see
that sixty-second sales pitch on their TV screens one evening
and probably for many evenings thereafter.

They'll watch wheeling gulls, hear lilting music above the
surf sounds, and see the togetherness of those four beautiful people living their outdoorsy good life. What is more, a great many
of those TV viewers will eventually plunk down several dollars
for a sampling of the commercial's prettily packaged promises.

And that, in short, is the hard reality of alcoholic beverage advertising and alcoholic beverage promotion in America today.
The suggestive message is neither covert nor even subtle; more
and more these days, instead, intentional blatancy seems to be
the name of the game.

"Aren't there rules, as there are for other drug advertising?" I was asked by a student at the Kentucky School of Alcohol Studies. "What about all those state laws and regulations?"

In an attempt to answer those questions, as well as to assuage
my own curiosity, I sent DISCUS $7.50 for their latest edition
of a red-white-and-blue volume entitled *Summary of State Laws
and Regulations Relating to Distilled Spirits*. For several hours,
I slogged through a ninety-two-page morass of the state-by-state
variables (such as advertising, container sizes, credit, days and
hours when sales are prohibited, fair trade, legal age, licensing,
markup formulas, and price posting); the result for me, was a
boggled mind and a headache reminiscent of earlier-day "terminal" hangovers.

Suffice it to say that I found a crazy-quilt pattern and al-
together frivolous maze of totally illogical regulations. Not long
ago, those same rules and regulations were aptly described, by
an NIAAA writer, as "a consistent inconsistency between wet

versus dry; by the bottle versus by the glass; on-premise versus off-premise; window shades up, to prevent public ridicule, versus window shades down, to remove all temptation.''

No less illogical and frivolous (and, at times, almost absurd) are the so-called ''advertising guidelines'' of the National Association of Broadcasters (NAB) Code Authority. Some verbatim samples:

• *Quietus on quaffing.* Subscribers and advertising agencies are reminded that the on-camera consumption of beer is unacceptable.

Also barred are such visual techniques as lip-smacking, swallowing, wiping foam from the mouth, tilting mugs, cans or glasses—all giving a distinct impression that beer has just been drunk.

• *Wine cocktail products advertising.* Acceptable: ''Zappy wine cocktails have a unique taste.'' Unacceptable: ''Zappy *Manhattan* wine cocktails have a unique taste.''

The word ''Manhattan'' is associated with hard liquor and would be at odds with the Guidelines even when part of a product name. (References in advertising to mixed drinks which contain hard liquor—''Screwdriver,'' or ''Bloody Mary,'' etc.—are tantamount to the advertising of hard liquor and are unacceptable.)

• *Reference to liquor is banned in lounge and restaurant ads.* Advertisements for businesses which sell liquor in addition to other products or services are acceptable under the Radio Code provided there are no references to hard liquor. In restaurant and lounge ads, then, copy such as ''. . . and martinis are just \$X at XX,'' ''Expertly mixed drinks at XX,'' or ''You'll always find your favorite mixed drinks at XX,'' would be at odds with Radio Code II-C-I and Section 4 of the Guidelines. Other terms that would be unacceptable include (but are not limited to) ''highball,'' ''spirits,'' ''cocktail,'' etc.

The only situation in which use of the word ''cocktail'' would be acceptable is when it is part of the actual name of the establishment and is mentioned to fulfill sponsor identification requirements. For example, ''XX Cocktail Lounge and Restaurant offers the finest food and beverages'' would be acceptable under the Code.

Leafing once again through DISCUS' summary of laws and regulations and the NAB's ''Advertising Guidelines,'' I'm struck, first, by their ''wonderlandish'' quality of unreality. It occurs to me, moreover, that the ''consistent inconsistency'' of those often inane rules and regulations is an anachronism harking back to Prohibition days, when legislators and physicians wrangled endlessly about "liquor as medicine."

Perhaps the "wets" and "drys" will someday lock horns again. Perhaps, more likely, a battle will be waged between the liquor industry and those who would ban all liquor advertising; those who would require cautionary health notices on alcoholic beverage labels; those who would make alcoholic beverage advertising a non-deductible business expense for tax purposes (a step which would strike at all liquor advertising, while also raising tax revenues by at least $250 million annually); or those who advocate use of the Federal Communications Commission's "fairness doctrine" (which enabled opponents of cigarette advertising to obtain equal radio and TV time in promoting their cause).

If some of my recovering alcoholic friends were to get their way, that fairness doctrine would express itself in harshly dramatic "before and after" fashion.

"I'd like to see *that* picture, which is pure fiction," says Gretchen, pointing to a full-page magazine ad for J & B Scotch, "with a picture of me—at the end of my drinking—right next to it. That same gorgeous lady with her hair sticking up, with no makeup and no fingernail polish, wearing a rumpled sweat shirt over whitish-yellowish skin, with a flushed red face and eyes like melted holes in the snow.

"And that would be a sitting-still picture," Gretchen adds. "If you put that picture in motion and had that gorgeous woman get up and sashay over to a gorgeous-looking man at the bar . . . Well, when I got up in those last months, I was bouncing off walls and staggering just to fall into bed to pass out, so I could get up and drink again. And throwing a blanket over me and having the nightgown on wrong side out. That's what I'd like to see in those ads—the reality instead of the fiction.

"And I'd change the headline. Maybe I'd use that Rod McKuen line, 'Holidays gone wrong . . .' "

9

Holier than Thou

None come too early,
None return too late

—Inscription above the main entrance doorway
of Guest House, a rehabilitation facility
in Rochester, Minnesota, for alcoholic
Catholic priests and brothers

The Reverend Monsignor Thomas Murray is a dead ringer for
Friar Tuck, save for the fact that Robin Hood's twinkly-eyed
confidant never wore a bright blue jump suit with a gleaming
floor-to-ceiling zipper. So when fifty-one-year-old Father Murray
hitched up the legs of his jump suit and sat cross-legged on a bed at
Guest House, I found it difficult to suppress a smile.

"Hardly the uniform for a Roman Catholic priest," he conceded, "but I'll tell you, it's the most comfortable thing I've
ever worn."

Father Murray is a recovering alcoholic, sober some four
months when I met with him in Rochester, Minnesota, during
the summer of 1975. Earlier that afternoon, he volunteered to
show me around Guest House. He whisked me across punc-
tiliously groomed lawns and through oak-paneled rooms, pointing out an indoor pool and sauna, a fruit-juice-packed refriger-
ator, group therapy and meeting rooms, the chapel, and, finally,
an art therapy room.

"This morning they introduced us to armatures and plas-
ticene," Father Murray told me, grinning impishly. "I had
never put my hands on sculpting material, never in my entire
life. And it was the strangest feeling. I actually felt that I was

doing something sinful. The act of Creation,'' he confided in a whisper as he kneaded his fingers together.

When we returned to Father Murray's book-strewn room, he unabashedly described his alcoholism as ''the classic pattern at work,'' ticking off such familiar symptoms as loss of control, driving under the influence, hiding bottles, and, during the last couple of years, morning drinking. ''I won't even go into all that, because it's so typical,'' he said. ''You've been there. Fortunately, I escaped any drunk-driving arrests, and, believe me, that was just a happy circumstance.''

I asked Father Murray about the ''bottom,'' or turning point, that had brought him, first, to Hazelden Foundation in northern Minnesota and, two months later, to Guest House.

''It was during Lent, I remember very well,'' he said. ''I was in my bishop's office. And, oh, I *knew* it was going pretty bad, because I was carrying the vodka in my briefcase, tippling in the car, in the office—you know, the whole picture. Anyway, the bishop looked at me, and the bishop said''—Murray paused, melodramatically lowering his voice—'' 'Thomas, are you having some problems with drinking?'

'' 'I think I am,' I said, 'but I'm not sure how far it's gone. Give me ten days, or two weeks.'

''So, again following the classic pattern, I went on the wagon for two weeks. Then—and this is very appropriate for a priest—'' Murray smiled. ''I fell on Good Friday.

''Well, that did it. The same day, I called a friend of mine who's an abbot. I knew he was a recovering alcoholic. His name is John, and I said to him, 'John, I'm in trouble. What do I do?' He told me,'' Murray concluded. ''He told me what he had done and how he had got sober. Anyway, here I am. I'm going home in a few days.''

As if on cue, someone knocked at the door. It was one of Guest House's senior counselors. ''Sorry to interrupt,'' he said to me, ''but you have about ten minutes, and I thought you might want to wash up or something. The Fathers are really looking forward to your talk.''

''My talk?''

''No one told you?'' he said in disbelief, winking at Murray.

"You're kidding. Well, why not just play it by ear? You're an alcoholic, I'm an alcoholic, Father Tom here's an alcoholic, We're all alcoholics. Besides, it's just a small informal meeting."

As he left the room, the counselor added casually, "There'll only be about thirty or forty priests."

I looked at my watch. That play-it-by-ear talk was so imminent that my butterflies barely had time to take flight. "Forty priests," I muttered. "Christ." Flustered, I added quickly, "No offense, Father. But *forty* priests? What can I say to forty priests?"

"We *are* human." Murray smiled wryly, shrugging his shoulders. "Tell your story. Share your feelings. If you have to, say what you just said: 'Forty priests, Christ.' "

He pondered for a moment, then suggested, "And here's something. What would be your reaction as a layman toward seeking some kind of spiritual help from a minister that you knew was an alcoholic, a recovering alcoholic? Would you have any misgivings? Would there be another, kind of subconscious feeling of, 'Well, he's a bit flawed'? That notion?"

Some three dozen priests had already gathered when I walked into the basement auditorium. They were wearing street clothes and were seated in a semicircular grouping of metal chairs. A card table and chair had been set up for me at the front of the auditorium. I was, to put it mildly, extremely nervous.

That's the way I began, as I recall. I told them that I was nervous as hell talking to a roomful of priests, probably because my involvement with religion during the drinking days had been limited to occasional bleary-eyed scrutiny of Mogen David wine labels.

They chuckled at that, for which I was thankful, and I went on seriously, "My name is Jack. I'm an alcoholic, and I assume that you all are alcoholics, too, which means we have much in common. You're also priests, which means you're supposed to know about miracles. For me, after twenty-seven years of obsessive boozing, *sobriety* is a miracle. And I'd like to talk about that tonight . . ."

I did talk about that, and Lord knows what else; I simply told my story to a group of fellow alcoholics. At the end, considerably more at ease, I asked the group if they'd share their experiences with *me*. Remembering Thomas Murray's suggestion, I asked if any of the Fathers and Brothers were concerned about the attitudes of parishioners once they returned to jobs and ministries in the "outside world."

A young priest raised his hand immediately. "You know," he said, "the astronauts aren't the only ones who have re-entry problems. In a month or so, I'm going to be standing in the pulpit of my old parish. And the way I feel right now, I'm going to be wondering what they're wondering. They'll know about my alcoholism, and the recovery process, because it's important that they do know. But still, it's the whole horrible idea of a drunken priest. For a while, I had this fear of some parishioner stage-whispering, mid-sermon, 'You think he's really sober? He looks sort of loaded to me . . .' "

The room exploded with laughter, and the floodgates opened. For the next two hours, then, we talked about re-entry and the super-stigma of alcoholism in a cleric. As the evening ended, an elderly Jesuit talked about a personal battle to overcome his conviction that he had somehow "failed God."

As it turned out on that "night of the thirty-five priests," I learned more about my own attitudes toward alcoholic clergy than about recovering alcoholic clerics themselves. Intellectually, of course, I know that alcoholism is no respecter of occupation, ethnic background, sex, or what have you; trumpeted over and over in these very pages is the assertion that no grouping of persons is more or less susceptible to the illness. Yet intellect, repetition, and my own alcoholism notwithstanding, it belatedly occurred to me that I—like most people—did perceive alcoholic men and women of the cloth in somewhat altered perspective.

Most of us do ascribe magical and mystical powers to persons with certain callings—"healers" and "holy men" are but two cases in point. Moreover, we seem to reserve the loftiest elevations to those uniformed individuals who "officially" serve

God, placing them upon pedestals which stand far above the landscape of human frailty.

In terms of reflex reaction, our shock at the odor of whiskey fumes wafting through the confessional curtain is matched in degree only by the unthinkable spectacle of a drunken brain surgeon—scalpel in hand—staggering toward his anesthetized patient on the operating table.

In that regard, when recovering alcoholic clerics express concern about "re-entry"—or, as Father Murray puts it, the notion that a recovering alcoholic priest may appear a "bit flawed"—that concern is rooted in the reality of cultural experience.

"Not long ago," Father Murray told me by way of example, "a group of little old ladies came up on a bird-watching trip. The grounds are quite rustic, and we are sort of isolated, so there are many unusual species of birds here. Anyway, they were local ladies, and I showed them around. Very strange. A very strange experience.

"I was very open," Murray continued. "I mentioned that I was an alcoholic. I said we had just had a magnificent lecture on alcoholic liver and central nervous system damage, and how alcohol completely wrecks our bodies. All they did was smile. Two of them were trained nurses, and they didn't ask me one single question about alcoholism. Not one," Murray said with mild irritation.

"We keep a lot of candy around here, and they'd say, 'I see all this candy.' And I'd say, 'Yes, alcoholics like to eat candy, and so do other drug-dependent people—they eat candy all day long.' So the ladies kind of tittered, hee-hee. They didn't know how to frame the questions, but mostly they couldn't even use that word. And although I kept trying to create these little openings—because I really want experience in talking to people about alcoholism—they avoided the subject completely.

"Here were these women who were mature. I think they just didn't know the words or really how to say them. I am, after all, a priest."

Not surprisingly, such lay attitudes often serve to augment the denial systems—so sharply symptomatic of alcoholism—that are already manifest in the alcoholic cleric.

That point is straightforwardly made in a Guest House brochure, one of several given to newly admitted patients. "No one stands higher in the esteem of his fellow man than the priest," says the caption opposite a stark photo of a despairing alcoholic clergyman. "Yet when he falls from the pedestal on which society has placed him—when he succumbs to a human disability such as alcoholism—no one feels so alone, so unworthy of help and forgiveness.

"Members of a parish often tend to consider a priest a special kind of person not subject to the ills and weaknesses of the flesh. In trying to live up to this high regard, and indeed in living up to their vows, some priests falter," the brochure continues, stressing that the problem is truly a sensitive and difficult one, and that treatment of alcoholism among priests has unusual aspects.

When a priest "falters," for example, his problem can be compounded in several ways. A priest's life style may allow him to hide his illness until it reaches disastrous proportions. As one priest told a Guest House counselor, "I cannot describe the terrors I endured. I was afraid to live each day, I was afraid to die, and I was even more afraid that I would go on living in this hell."

Additionally, even when a priest concedes to himself that he is in fact alcoholic, there remains a strong reluctance to tell a superior or confrere. "I didn't want to see anyone I ever knew," another priest said during a group session. "I wanted oblivion."

Finally, and perhaps most painfully, the priest hesitates to "undo the trust" that others have placed in him, be the "others" parishioners, superiors, or, as the Jesuit Brother expressed it to me that night, "God Himself." In the last days of his active alcoholism, one former Guest House patient says, "My mind was troubled and my body tormented. I felt the despair of Dante's Inferno."

Guest House is to Dante's Inferno what sobriety is to drunkenness. Founded in 1956 with its first facility at Lake Orion, Michigan (the Rochester, Minnesota, sanatorium was opened in 1969), Guest House is a lay-operated, non-profit organization devoted exclusively to the treatment, therapy, and rehabilitation of Catholic priests and brothers suffering from the disease of alcoholism. It is financed by contributions, or what administrators call "free-will offerings," and its board of volunteer officers and directors include Chairman John Naughton, vice-president and general manager, Ford Division, Ford Motor Company; President Norbert T. Madison, partner, Haskins & Sells; Vice-President Robert F. Sage, president of the Sage Foundation; Treasurer Edward M. Herstein, director, Defense Special Projects, General Motors Corporation; and Secretary Richard F. Van Dresser, partner, Touche Ross & Company.

At this writing, there have been more than 1,500 admissions to the Guest House sanatoriums, and the lasting recovery rate stands impressively at 74 percent. Put another way, more than 1,100 priests—whose lives were being seriously threatened by alcoholism—have returned to active ministries and sober, productive lives.

Considering that clergymen are reputed to be "the toughest alcoholics to treat," those figures are all the more impressive. One could endlessly debate (as some ivory-tower academicians do) the relative merits of "peer group" versus "mixed group" treatment for alcoholism, yet it is a well-established fact that Guest House's peer group environment is indeed efficacious for alcoholic Catholic priests and brothers.

"The denial systems and rationalization and all the things you and I have had to go through—as alcoholic laymen—are far more intense with these fellows," one of the counselors told me. "These trained logicians can make two and two add up to five, kind of, and then prove it to you. So we concentrate on encouraging them to share feelings, as opposed to intellectual and philosophical concepts. For example, we want these guys to tell us, first person singular, how they feel about God, not how they know about God.

"Okay, you've got two highly trained theologians—two trained philosophers with Ph.D.s coming out of their ears," he explains. "At Guest House, the one Ph.D. says to the other, 'You're full of it, Charlie—get off that intellectual crap.'

"It just wouldn't work that way in a lay treatment group, because the laymen are agog at this priest's philosophical insights. It takes one to know one. In other words, it takes one priest with the same intellectual prowess as that other priest to say, 'You're full of crap, Charlie.' And to say it in such a way that he's not insulting the guy's dignity or integrity, but calling the shot as he sees it.''

In that regard, a primary goal at Guest House is to help the alcoholic priest first restore and then sustain his sense of self-worth, particularly as it relates to the dignity of the priesthood.

''We are so inculcated with this in our training—almost excessively so when we are becoming priests—that when we lose it, the effect can be devastating,'' says one Guest House patient. ''I don't like to use the word 'failure,' but my addictive drinking gave me a feeling of failure in almost a tangible sense. The big book of Alcoholics Anonymous describes alcohol, or alcoholism, as 'cunning, baffling, and powerful,' and I can really relate to that in terms of my loss of self-esteem. I lost it in some cunning, baffling, and powerful way.

''I really have felt wounded by my experiences as a priest alcoholic,'' the young Jesuit adds. ''And if this wound had festered, it might have had a deleterious effect on my priesthood and my ministry—in spite of my *physical* sobriety.''

The day-to-day process of regaining self-esteem (or, as that young Brother expressed it, ''learning to put the collar back on'') is sometimes punctuated by dramatic breakthroughs at the two Guest House facilities. A long-time Rochester staffer shared several such experiences with me.

''I remember one patient, who was just a beautiful priest,'' he said. ''But he was spiritually arid—just totally despairing. We were talking about what his concept of God was, and he just couldn't talk about it.

''So at the next counseling session, he sat down just where you're sitting and said, 'I'd like to do something.' And I said, 'Sure, Father.' He wanted to go to chapel. We went in and we genuflected, and then I sat down. He was just standing there in front of the altar, quietly and for a long time. Then he suddenly raised his arms. And he screamed, 'You son of a bitch!'

''He *had* to say that,'' the Guest House staff member added quietly. "He broke down in tears then, and I had to share my tears with him. I mean, I really felt for the guy. We came back here and sat down, and he said, 'Okay, let me tell you how I feel about God.' "

Describing a somewhat similar experience, another Guest House counselor told me, "We encourage our men to stimulate the basic senses, because, unfortunately, intellectual prudes are all brain and no soma. I want them to do things like walking in the grass barefooted, and I ask them things like, 'When's the last time you took a look at the Big Dipper?'

"Anyway," the counselor said, "there was this Franciscan, and I asked him if he had ever seen a pine tree. 'Oh, hell, yes, I've seen a lot of pine trees.' 'Have you ever tasted a pine needle, Father?' I asked. And he said he hadn't. 'Go taste one,' I told him. So he took a chair and sat on the end of the bluff. He just sat out there in the middle of nowhere, being aware of nothing but the outdoors.

"And damned if a deer didn't come walking up. The doggoned deer came right up to him, Jack, so close he could have touched him. Some other priests were watching out the window, and saw the whole thing. Later, the Franciscan said to me, 'I sat there, not mesmerized, but just so peaceful and serene, that that animal came walking right up to me, and then he calmly turned and walked away.'

"And the feeling the priest got from that," the counselor concluded, "was 'My God, if an animal can trust me, why in hell can't I trust myself? What's so *bad* about me?' Then he was able to talk at gut level, for the first time, really, about his personal concepts of spirituality, and redemption, what the validity of his ministry is, and so on. So the breakthrough was a dumb deer walking up to him and giving that guy the feeling of 'Hey, I guess I ain't so bad after all.' Or as that author said, 'I ain't much, baby, but I'm all I've got.' "

To be sure, dramatic "breakthroughs" at Guest House and other facilities for alcoholic clergy are hardly everyday occurrences. On the contrary, the daily regimen is quite predictable, combining psychotherapy, group therapy, regularly scheduled

Alcoholics Anonymous meetings, as well as various forms of recreation (including, during my visit, Yoga instruction and sand sculpture).

As one visiting priest-alumnus explained it to me, "We see alcoholism as a disease affecting the body, mind, and spirit. And we treat the whole man. Guest House does spend a lot of time on recreation, but in the literal sense of the word—to *re-create*."

By way of elaboration, another counselor added, "I have yet to meet a priest, Jack, who knows how to *recreate*. If I ask him, 'Father, are you recreating pretty well?' he says, 'I have trouble taking one day off a week.' I say, 'Father, I'm not talking about taking one day off a week—even God rested on the seventh day. I'm asking if you take time every day to recreate, to just sit on your can and do nothing, or to relax. How do you rejuvenate yourself?'

"In other words," the counselor concluded, "priests are notorious workaholics. They're typically either working their fannies off or doing not a damned thing."

Over and over during my stay in Rochester, I was reminded that Alcoholics Anonymous—its principles and fellowship—is the hallmark of Guest House's program. "And that's simply because it's the proven instrument," I was told by a senior counselor who is himself a member of AA. "It's the best after-care available, it's the cheapest medicine available for the recovering alcoholic, and besides—it *works*," he stressed. "So at Guest House we have a total discussion of what AA is and does, didactically. The priests attend three meetings a week while they're in treatment, and they're encouraged to remain involved once they return home."

In talking with the priest-patients, I wondered aloud if the simple spirituality of AA's program—expressed in terms of a "higher Power" or "God as you understand him"—conflicted in any way with the priests' theological training and beliefs. The Fathers agreed, almost to a man, that there was no conflict whatsoever; most, in fact, were surprised to see how easily AA's concept of spirituality meshed with their own beliefs.

"I had to be *sold* AA," one sixty-year-old priest admitted. "My attitudes were rather snobbish, to tell you the truth. They

really were. There's something about AA I can't quite concep-
tualize—something about the pattern of attendance at meetings,
and the continual reminder of my powerlessness over alcohol by
this group of peers from all walks of life. AA *is* a peer group—
in the sense that, above everything else, we're all human and
we're all alcoholics.

"For me today," he added, "one of the big attractions of AA
is that it's non-hierarchal, it's not structured. I have an abhor-
rence of structured societies. I guess I only belong to one, and
that's the Church, and sometimes I feel a little tenuous there.
But"—he laughed—"I try to overlook the church structure."

During a rap session, another priest said that he was delighted
by his smooth transition from the spirituality of organized religion to the spirituality of Alcoholics Anonymous. "Actually,"
he said, "it was not so much transition as it was enhancement of
my own concepts about spirituality, especially with the 'love
brother' trends today. What I mean is that it ties in with this
idea: 'If you can't love the brother whom you can see, how can
you love Me, your God, whom you *cannot* see?'

"Since Vatican II and the mid-sixties," the Father added,
"this element of brother touching brother is extremely strong in
the Church, particularly among young priests or those who have
accepted what we generally lump into the concept called 'renewal.' So AA's brotherhood aspect is particularly apt today. In
any event, it's certainly apt for *me*."

I wondered also during that visit to Guest House exactly how
an alcoholic priest got from "there to here." Stepping again into
a hypothetical situation—as a forty-year-old Los Angeles priest
in the tremulous middle stages of alcoholism—I asked what my
route to recovery might be. In various Catholic dioceses across
the United States, I learned, so-called intervention committees
exist; there is such a cardinal-sanctioned committee, for example, in the Los Angeles archdiocese.

"Let's say that one of your parishioners calls the chancery office and says, 'Hey, Father Jack fell off the altar Sunday,' " I
was told. "Okay, this committee would then get in touch with
you and say, 'Father Jack, it looks like drinking maybe is a
problem,' and you would deal with that committee."

Assuming that "Father Jack" agrees to accept treatment for alcoholism, the committee would suggest Guest House or one of several other alcoholism treatment facilities. If I, Father Jack, were to choose Guest House (assuming there was "room at the inn," as one priest puts it), the facility's administrators would then only require the approbation of my "boss," the bishop. And, Guest House officials say, if an intervention committee does in fact exist within a particular Catholic diocese, permission from its bishop is generally not withheld.

If, on the other hand, my bishop is reluctant to send me for treatment, an attempt is made to persuade him; he is told in so many words that it's his responsibility to force me to accept treatment, since my alcoholism is no less life-threatening than leukemia or coronary occlusion. In short, my bishop would possibly require some down-to-earth education by his intervention committeee about the realities of alcoholism as an illness and about the effectiveness of coercion, or "tough love," in arresting its progression.

Assuming permission is granted, Guest House would then try to obtain as much documentation as possible:

Father Jack fell off the altar at 10:30 mass on March 16, 1975.

Father Jack was arrested for drunken driving on Saturday night, April 5, 1975.

Father Jack was hospitalized following a fall as a result of drunkenness on May 2, 1975.

"I won't necessarily confront the man with the documentation," a senior counselor noted, "but I've got to know why the bishop thinks Father Jack is an alcoholic. Hell, if the bishop doesn't know, how in hell am I going to work with a guy that first of all, even if he's honest, is still deluged with the deceit and delusion we call the denial system? Father Jack is trying to be honest, but he can't be because of the illness. Alcoholics lie, but they're not liars."

In any case, getting back to my role as an alcoholic priest filled with denial, I would be admitted to Guest House and, within a very short time, be told something to this effect:

"Father Jack, I know that you're here because the bishop wants you here. I think the most stupid thing I could ask you right now is 'Father, are you an alcoholic?' I'd better tell you what the disease is before you tell me whether you think you're an alcoholic or not.

"But Father Jack, this is fact: Somebody in your diocese feels that you have alcoholism. I'm not going to ask you to accept that opinion, because, in a sense, you're here first of all to find out. So that's my number-one job, to tell you what the disease is and to help you work through the dynamics of understanding the disease. And then perhaps we can go ahead and work."

The overall approach, at least within many Catholic dioceses, is not unlike the shape-up-or-ship-out industrial alcoholism programs; put simplistically, deteriorating job performance brings about confrontation, while the threat of job loss provides a strong motivational lever for acceptance of treatment. As with industrial alcoholism programs, moreover, if the package is to be meaningful and effective, it must be sold to and bought by the "big boss," or bishop.

It would appear, from all the foregoing, that organized religion (and the Catholic Church, particularly) is a model of enlightenment when it comes to acceptance of alcoholism as a respectable illness that is treatable and worth treating. The truth is that Guest House is a very unique facility within the over-all structure of the Catholic Church; against the backdrop of organized religion as a whole, additionally, it stands as a rather solitary and almost forlorn beacon.

Certainly, in any investigation of attitudes toward alcoholism and alcoholic clergy, one can hardly ignore the twelve-million-member Baptist Church or, for that matter, the Episcopal Church. Frankly, I had no idea what I would find when I began to explore; the more deeply I dug, of course, the clearer became the picture. And over all, in my view, it is a far from pretty one.

On one occasion during my travels, I was introduced to a sixty-five-year-old retired Episcopal priest called Father Jim. We met in his home and, as a noisy cuckoo clock sounded the quarter hours, he traced his experiences as an alcoholic clergyman within the structure of the Episcopal Church in the United States.

Father Jim was all but a teetotaler while attending college and theological seminary; he didn't begin to use alcohol until several years after his ordination in 1933. He was a "goer and doer," and within a short time was elected dean of a cathedral parish; Father Jim, at thirty-two, was the youngest dean in the Episcopal Church and received considerable adulation as a result. "It's interesting as I look back," he says, "that that's when I began to drink. Maybe it was due to what I've heard described as the 'success neurosis,' because I had to succeed and I had to be somebody."

The young priest quickly did become somebody, traveling extensively during World War II as his bishop's representative. He lived in a "dry" state and generally attended conferences in "wet" states, invariably returning home with liquor-filled suitcases.

The next step up the clerical ladder was election to what Father Jim describes as a "Gold Coast parish" on the north shore of Chicago, where drinking was not only accepted, but encouraged. "I had an honorary membership in one of the swanky country clubs and was actually urged to spend lots of time in the cocktail lounge there making converts.

"Well, it's an old story that the drinking progressed, until it was out of control," he said. "I knew I was in trouble, and so did my parish, and so did my bishop in Chicago. So in typical alcoholic fashion, I started to make the geographical changes."

Within a relatively few years, Father Jim had done most of the things that practicing alcoholics are prone to do. He had climbed on the wagon and fallen off time and again; he had moved from parish to parish, always just short of being fired. He went to psychologists, psychiatrists, doctors, and hospitals; he had to remain in one hospital for eight weeks and, when he was discharged, was given a three-page typewritten report for his vestry. "But nowhere did they say anything about my being an alcoholic," Father Jim recalls. "Just that they thought I drank too much, and that it might be a good idea if I cut down."

And so it went, alcoholism's progression and Father Jim's denial moving along in tandem. Finally, still another psychiatrist threw up his hands in dismay, telling Father Jim that he just couldn't help him.

"I realized he was going to cut me off, and where did I go from there? And then this psychiatrist said to me, 'Have you ever tried Alcoholics Anonymous?' I said, 'Well, no, I can't say that I have. I've got an AA group that meets in my parish hall, and they come once a month and hand me a check for the rent of the hall, but I've never identified with that bunch of drunks.' "

That night, at the age of forty-five, Father Jim was taken to his first AA meeting. "I walked in and looked around at the people who were there," he remembers, "and I knew for the first time that I was home free. *Everybody* was there. The mink coat crowd, black men, Mexican fruit pickers. People of all classes, races, nationalities. I sat and felt that the load was finally off my back."

After the meeting, a friend asked Father Jim about his first impression of Alcoholics Anonymous. He replied that years and years earlier, in seminary, he had learned about the beginning history of the Church as an underground movement. "Because it *was* that type of movement," the Father said, "a person could walk in and lay his cards on the table and find acceptance. You know, no matter what he had been or what he was, here was a group that understood and loved him for what he was—a child of God. This is what I felt about AA. It was for men and women of all classes—all sorts and conditions of men, as we say in the Church. And that was the beginning of my life of sobriety right there. It was 1954."

Father Jim went home on the bus that night. "And when my wife met me at the bus station, she said—as she's said many times since—'I knew that you had found something. Just by the spring in your step, or the glint in your eye, or *something*. You were a different man.' "

I probably said something congratulatory at that point, for Father Jim, after all, had been sober for more than two decades. I expected he would tell me, next, how everything had got "better and better'' after that. As the cuckoo clock sounded once more, I sat back in anticipation.

Things did get better in terms of Father Jim's release from the physical and emotional prison of alcoholism, but life soon became anything but a bed of roses.

"Not long after that first AA meeting, I made an appointment with my bishop and told him I had discovered that I was an alcoholic,'' the priest said. "Well, like so many people, this bishop just didn't understand what alcoholism was, and took a very dim view of alcoholics. And so he insisted that I sign a statement—a pledge, so to speak—that I would never take another drink. And that if I did take another drink, I would ask to be deposed from the priesthood.''

Father Jim paused reflectively, then added, "The ministry of the church was the only thing that I had ever turned my hand to, really, so he was threatening to take away my professional future in return for this pledge. So I told him,'' the priest continued, " 'I'm sorry, Bishop, I can't promise you that. I can't promise you that I won't take a drink tomorrow. I have to do this one day at a time. I feel in my heart right now that I will not drink, but I can't promise that. And I don't want to sign something that would jeopardize not only my whole professional future, but my family's security.'

"Well, that was it. He was adamant—either do it his way or not at all. And that's the last I ever saw or heard from him. The upshot was that I was forced to resign. I was left high and dry without a job; I didn't know what to do or where to go. We had to put our household goods in storage, and my wife had to live in a convent and I had to live in a monastery. For a long time after that,'' Father Jim added, "my wife and I lived out of suitcases, sleeping on bare floors in empty vicarages, with just enough to keep body and soul together. It was, to say the least, a rather tenuous kind of existence. And the biggest difficulty I faced was getting another start. The whole point was—and, to a certain degree, still is—who wants to hire somebody known as a drunk? Who wants to hire an alcoholic priest, of all things?''

Father Jim did eventually find a job, in a run-down parish that had fallen on hard times—''a dog that nobody else would take,'' as he puts it sardonically today. In any case, he did eventually find acceptance, other jobs, and, ultimately, a great deal of respect. Before his retirement in 1974, he had served as priest and rector of a large West Coast parish for more than fourteen years.

As I gathered up my papers and recording equipment late that afternoon, the priest's brother-in-law walked in and asked guilelessly if I would like a cold beer before I left. Smiling quickly at Father Jim, I replied, "No thanks, I don't drink alcohol. I'm an alcoholic."

"Oh, that's a coincidence. My brother-in-law Jim here is one, too."

"Yes, I know," I said, trying to keep a straight face. "We're taking over the world."

Father Jim and I shared a laugh when we were alone once again. Then I asked him if there was anything he'd like to add, and he told me to switch on my tape recorder for just another minute.

"You know," he said, "the thing that almost caused me to lose my faith was this bishop who was willing to take away my priesthood if I wasn't willing to sign a pledge. He forced me to resign and never had another thought for me or my family's welfare from that time on. He's dead in his grave now; perhaps he knows better.

"But I began to wonder," Father Jim recalled, "what in hell is this I've been preaching? I preached and I believed—for twenty-some years before I became an alcoholic—that the Church was the redemptive society, that its business was to reconcile people, it had a ministry of healing, it believed in forgiveness. Yet when the chips were down, how did they handle a person who needed healing and forgiveness, reconciliation, redemption?

"I went to bed at night saying that AA prayer—'God grant me the serenity to accept the things I cannot change, courage to change the things I can, and wisdom to know the difference.' I just about lost my faith; I thought, well, when the chips are down, what does it mean?

"I finally realized," Father Jim concluded, "that that bishop was simply ignorant. He didn't *know* about alcoholism. He likened it to cutting down his smoking during Lent. You know, *willpower*. And this is pretty much the story that still exists in the Episcopal Church, and it's true in the United States, not just the Church.''

There are thousands of people who need what the Church could offer and who are not getting it. The most woeful examples, it seems to me, are America's all but invisible alcoholic nuns. As alcoholics, members of the religious community—and ''women, believe it or not,'' as one recovering alcoholic Sister phrases it—nuns endure a sort of triple stigma and, in turn, develop an armor of denial that can be virtually impenetrable.

''The sense of guilt and shame is just terrific for an alcoholic Sister, since, in many instances, she has spent years projecting and internalizing an image of herself which is above reproach,'' says Sister Therese Golden, an Adrian Dominican sister and a counselor at Lutheran General Hospital in Park Ridge, Illinois. ''The frightening discrepancy between this image and the reality of her alcoholism is extremely hard to reconcile.''

At a 1974 national symposium on the role of Christian churches in the recovery of the alcoholic, Sister Therese described from personal experience the tendency within the sisterhood to minimize the occurrence of alcoholism among nuns. She described, as but one example, the reaction of a sister superior from New York who had recently been asked about the subject. ''Oh, we don't have a problem with alcoholism in this order,'' the nun had assured Sister Therese. ''It's against our rules.''

When I told that story to another recovering alcoholic nun on the East Coast, she smiled and said in response, ''Well, the Lord must love us rule-breakers, because He sure seems to have made a lot of us. If there's *shame,*'' the Sister added seriously, ''it's not in alcoholism itself, but in the failure to recognize that alcoholism is a treatable human condition, and that any person who drinks is at least a potential alcoholic.''

That same point was made to me by Dr. Robert Varley, the former Episcopal bishop of Nebraska, who is now a family counselor. ''I ran into a former nun who was rather high up in one of the larger orders,'' he says, ''and while she won't put anything down on paper, she admits that alcoholism is a frighteningly real problem in convents. But what they do is to put all the alcoholic nuns in a retreat house somewhere out of sight, and no one ever gets any data on them.''

Bob Varley himself became something of a *cause célèbre* in 1975 when wire-service stories across the country blared out the news, ''The Episcopal House of Bishops has accepted the resignation of the Rt. Rev. Robert P. Varley of Nebraska, believed to be the first bishop of the church to publicly admit that he received treatment for alcoholism and drug addiction.'' One Associated Press headline read, ''BISHOP QUITS, WAS ALCOHOLIC.''

As Bob Varley himself is the first to point out these days, he's *still* an alcoholic. However, he no longer drinks, and, consequently, his alcoholism has been arrested. We spoke for several hours one mid-October morning, and fifty-three-year-old Varley shared not only his personal story, but his views concerning alcoholism among the clergy; what he considers prevalently negative attitudes among the Church hierarchy toward alcoholism; and, finally, some revealing exemplifications of such attitudes as directed toward Varley himself.

Varley's first exposure to mood-altering chemicals took place almost thirty years ago, when he was given Demerol for a kidney-stone episode. Subsequently, he developed migraine headaches. ''As my work and pressure increased, the migraines increased also, psychosomatically, I think,'' he says thoughtfully, ''to the point where I was actually giving the medication to myself intramuscularly. Over the years, that medication included Demerol, Tuenol, Seconal, sodium amytal, sodium pentothal—you name it.''

Shortly after the priest was named bishop of a large diocese in 1971, he developed a high blood pressure problem. Still more drugs were used to treat the condition. Instead of conducting a ''chemical inventory,'' as Varley phrases it, doctors ''juggled the medication around,'' adding Valium, Librium, reserpine, Endoril, and several other mood-altering drugs.

''I was a moderate drinker and had no problems with it,''

Varley says, "but with the introduction of Valium, Librium, and reserpine, the need for alcohol increased. The combination of mood-altering alcohol and the other mood-altering chemicals made me irascible and detached. It certainly inhibited my work program and dulled my thought capacity. It made me just a bear to live with and to work with," he adds flatly.

Several members of Varley's clergy eventually confronted him with the situation as they saw it. Bishop Varley accepted treatment at Hazelden Foundation, primarily to "prove them wrong," he says today with candor. "But after a few days at Hazelden, I realized I *was* a dependent person, and that I did indeed have a problem."

I had learned earlier that bishops such as Varley have but one superior—the presiding bishop headquartered in New York City. I had been told, moreover, that although a priest can easily be disciplined or fired by his bishop (because, as Father Jim had said, "the bishop has the authority and the clout"), bishops themselves are "untouchable."

In any case, when Bishop Varley accepted treatment at Hazelden and conceded that he did in fact have alcoholism, his own superior was most supportive. "He came to see me," Varley says, "and his attitude was 'Hey, this is neat. You're the first bishop to ever say you had a problem.' And we know," Varley adds, "that a number of other bishops have it, but are unwilling to accept help."

Bob Varley insists that his resignation as bishop of Nebraska was a matter of personal choice. He explains, however, that the revelation of his alcoholism seemed to "embarrass" people, and that in itself was a phenomenon with which he had already become familiar.

"I was born in Philadelphia and brought to the Midwest some ideas which, I'm afraid, were far too liberal for this climate. I espoused the ordination of women, and because my doctorate is in the field of human behavior, I work with the homophile community and advocate that they be accepted as persons. I even sought their ordination."

In short, Robert Varley was a controversial figure in the Church even before his public announcement that he was an alcoholic. "My going away for treatment became the occasion around which this type of hostility solidified," he says. "And when I came back, it was obvious that I faced a pretty strong batch of guys who were, you know, 'anti-Varley,' so to speak. As a result, I just decided that I would go back to the work I enjoyed most before I became a bishop. And that is in the field of marriage, family counseling, and sexual support systems. I've now added to it, with the help of Hazelden, the dimension of chemical counseling."

At one point, I asked Varley how the hostility he describes was actually expressed. He told me that while he was in treatment, one of his prominent clergymen described the bishop's alcoholism as "moral depravity" in a sermon. The irony in that particular expression is that Varley's father suffered from alcoholism. "I always thought he was a depraved individual," the former bishop said.

"It gets back to what you said earlier." Bob Varley told me. "It's the whole association of alcoholism with 'weak will,' 'immorality,' and so on. I'm often told these days, 'You look *good,*' or, 'You sure don't *look* like an alcoholic.' And I'm tempted to say, 'What did you expect, two heads?'

"When I went on vacation before I resigned, they sneaked an audit on me, quite sure I had absconded with funds. It turned out that they owed me $16.32"—Varley laughed—"because I had forgotten to put it on my expense account."

Bob Varley talks freely today of his own belated enlightenment, conceding that he had long perceived alcohol as "something in a brown paper bag" and the alcoholic as "someone sleeping in a doorway." Based on his personal experience, of course, his views have changed drastically. On the other hand, he strongly believes that the Church itself has a long way to go.

"As you know," Varley emphasizes, "there's a tremendously strong denial factor among alcoholic clergy. It's my understanding, based on several studies, that alcoholism has risen among the clergy almost 200 percent in this decade, yet those accepting treatment are minimal compared to the need.

"I think there are two factors here," he adds. "First, I think that clergymen let religiosity get in the road; in other words, the acceptance of their own alcoholism threatens their image as clergymen, so they simply *don't* accept their alcoholism. And they call on religion in almost a magical sense for a cure. You know, 'the pledge' and things like that. But what they lack is the second element, and that's spirituality," Varley continues. "I believe that going through treatment made my spiritual life a heck of a lot richer than some of the exercises I found in religion. To be frank, I had to get rid of an awful lot of stuff before God could get through."

Among the more astute, intelligent, and perceptive church leadership, as Varley phrases it, there have been some attitudinal changes. He believes, however, that among the vast majority of those within the structure of the Church, "the attitude swings from extremely naïve to extremely judgmental."

The Church is prepared to pass mighty resolutions concerning chemical dependency, Varley stresses, but lacks the ability to deal with an individual who is chemically dependent.

"In our church, for example," Varley told me, "we've been called Whiskeypalians for years because of our liberal attitude toward alcohol. Yet we have absolutely no mechanism within the entire Episcopalian structure to deal with an alcoholic person, particularly among our own clergy.

"We put them in a closet," he adds ruefully. "Our homophile friends have their closet queens, and we have our closet curates."

I remember thinking that Dr. Varley had effectively said it all with those last few heartfelt words; his poignant image of America's "closet curates" seemed, if nothing else, a made-to-order chapter ending.

But there is more to be said. The Church's dereliction toward its alcoholic clergy is, unquestionably, grievous in its own right; the greater misfortune is that the Church is not only missing a unique opportunity to practice what is preached within its own rectories, but, more important, to walk as it talks among countless followers *beyond* those cloistered walls. For few families within America's myriad congregations, parishes, and communicant groups have not, at one time or another, been adversely affected by the ravages of alcoholism.

It is well known that clergymen are those to whom most people first turn for solace and guidance in times of crisis; and, of course, untreated alcoholism is invariably characterized by crisis upon crisis. In my own crisis-scarred experience, I "came to" several times in hospital wards where the first face I saw was that of either a chaplain or a sister/nurse.

In short, nun and priest are regularly brought together with parishioner and lay person at hours of the day and times of the year unrelated to Christmas, communion, mass, or meditation. To be dramatically specific, we need only visualize such commonplace realities as . . .

A priest intoning last rites at the floodlit scene of a drunk-driving disaster . . .

A guilt-tormented husband, bewildered by family-directed violence during an alcoholic blackout, baring his soul in confessional . . .

A physically and emotionally battered victim of that same senseless violence, desperately seeking answers within the quietude of the family's church . . .

Rather less dramatic but no less a reality in the life of America's clerics are those daily phone calls, letters, and rectory confrontations:

"What should I do, Father? Charlie was expelled from school, for drinking again . . ."

"Father, he spends his whole paycheck on liquor—*all* of it now. No money left for food, rent overdue . . ."

"She's gone again, Father. The kids were home alone, the place was a shambles. For God's sake, what can I do . . . ?"

Life would assuredly be easier for alcoholism's victims if answers to such pleas were forthcoming. Yet on the whole, clergymen are as ignorant of alcoholism's whys and wherefores as are physicians, lawyers, or other professionals with privileged family and community relationships.

There is, however, one critical difference: Unlike the doctor or lawyer, the clergyman needs no special invitation to call upon a family; moreover, his services and ministrations are available without charge. Given this unique position of the shepherd—as well as the ubiquity of alcohol-related crises among his flock—it is clearly imperative for clerics to finally learn the facts about alcoholism.

"There exists today an abundance of informative literature on the subject, and a good pastor will read, mark, and inwardly digest it," urges the Reverend James T. Golder of El Granada, California. "He will learn to *recognize* the symptoms of alcohol addiction. He will also learn the Do's and Don'ts in ministering to problem drinkers and their families."

Moreover, stresses Golder, a recovering alcoholic, the "good pastor" will become familiar with alcoholism resources in the community: with information centers, clinics, treatment and rehabilitation centers, and with physicians who accept alcoholics as patients. He'll also know what hospitals in the community will admit patients with an alcoholism diagnosis.

Golder believes that if a pastor is to carry on a successful ministry in this field, it is also essential that he become familiar with "the principles and dynamics of the most successful approach to the problem of alcoholism—Alcoholics Anonymous."

Father Golder adds adamantly, "A priest going to AA meetings should remember that he is there to *learn,* not to expound his pet theories. To put it bluntly, let him keep his mouth shut and listen. He may be surprised at how much he learns about alcoholism and the alcoholic in a short space of time. What is more, he may become acquainted with recovered alcoholics on a first-name basis, on whom he may call for help in his ministry to alcoholics. It is a wise priest," Golder concludes, "who has a list of men and women, members of AA, on whom he can call for assistance when the need is acute."

Needless to say, when recovering alcoholic priests like James Golder return to their parishes following treatment, they usually find that a new dimension has been added to their pastoral ministries. Apart from the fact that they can quickly empathize with suffering alcoholics and suffering family members, they have become able to provide the kind of "how to" comfort and advice that is all too rare in most structured religious bodies today.

"I think I've been a far more effective priest because of my illness," says Golder. "In all modesty, I was a successful priest before I acknowledged my alcoholism, but I've been a far more effective and helpful pastor to people in trouble since I acknowledged my problem and got on top of it.

"I think I'm more tolerant and understanding," he adds. "I can love the 'unlovable' as I never could before, because I've been through hell and back, and now I can identify with the poor joker who's still suffering."

Another recovering alcoholic priest—one who shares Golder's feelings and beliefs—makes it a point always to wear clerical garb when he attends Alcoholics Anonymous meetings. "I always appear at the meetings as a priest. I think it's an important example to a hell of a lot of guys who are trying to make it. They look at me and say, 'Well, if that "sky pilot" can make it—if he's got the problem—what the hell am I crying about?' "

Clearly, in short, America's clergy and nuns can provide an enormous service to those suffering from alcoholism—merely by virtue of knowledge alone. Moreover, the recovering alcoholic cleric and nun can even more effectively carry the message in day-to-day confrontations with those touched directly or indirectly by the illness. As a Guest House counselor sums it up, "The clergyman probably sees the patient before anyone else. We know that. And if he has knowledge about alcoholism—book-learned or pain-learned, as the case may be—he then has another arrow in his quiver of armamentarium for helping people."

Helping people in that very special way is a way of life for many recovering alcoholics. Certainly it has become so for the Reverend James T. Golder, who has long urged fellow clergymen to become knowledgeable about alcoholism. He has been urging the Episcopal Church hierarchy itself to follow that same path—by first taking an official stand on alcoholism and then, ideally, adopting and funding a Church-wide alcoholism program.

For years, the priest's carefully prepared suggestions were received with little more than stony silence by the powers that be, even though Golder himself served on the Episcopal Church's executive committee as a member of its now defunct Advisory Committee on Alcoholism.

"Through the years," says Father Golder, who is now retired, "the proposals were blue-penciled. And for years my wife kept telling me and alcoholic clergymen friends, 'You guys are fools if you're going to wait for the Episcopal Church to do it. *You guys* are going to have to do it.' "

In 1968, having "had it" with blue-penciled proposals, James Golder finally heeded his wife's advice. He published a letter in *The Living Church,* the Episcopal weekly, inviting correspondence from other recovered alcoholic clergymen.

"Lo and behold," Golder says, "I received twenty-two replies right off the bat. Five of the twenty-two were able to meet with me in San Francisco, the idea being to talk over the whole situation and see what might be done about it. We sat in my office for two and a half days and just brainstormed the whole problem. And it was then that RACA was born, on October 24, 1968."

RACA (a word with biblical connotations—Matthew 5:22—associated with "fool") is an acronym for Recovered Alcoholic Clergy Association. "We don't mind being called 'Fools for Christ,' " says Father Golder, who has served as executive director of RACA since its inception. "We were fools when we drank as we did, offending people and sometimes causing harm which we lived to regret. With restoration of health has come a new sense of direction and purpose in life, and a willingness to be fools, if need be, in the service of the Church and society."

RACA's threefold purpose is mutual self-help, fellowship, and "pastoral concern" for clerics with a drinking problem. Membership is open to bishops, priests, deacons, members of religious orders, and bona fide theological students who have overcome a drinking problem. Members must be willing to reveal their identity to other RACA members but, as Golder puts it, "outside RACA's membership, strict anonymity is maintained."

At this writing, RACA has some 130 members in fifty-five dioceses in the United States and in Canada, and the organization is beginning to swing some weight within the Episcopal Church. For example, although RACA rigorously guards its organizational independence, it has been working cooperatively with the Right Reverend David E. Richards, a non-alcoholic bishop who heads the Episcopal Church's high-level Office of Pastoral Development, which was created by the Episcopal House of Bishops. That close relationship has enabled RACA to organize several open conferences for bishops and other clergy, to draft a proposed (but not yet adopted) policy statement on alcoholism for the Episcopal Church, and to publish a set of guidelines designed to assist bishops who must deal pastorally with clergymen "who have given evidence of a drinking problem."

Not long ago, in this regard, Bishop Richards told the House of Bishops that there are upwards of 750 Episcopal clergymen and members of their families who are having trouble with alcohol. With due respect to Bishop Richards, Father Golder maintains that that estimate is quite conservative.

"We have approximately twelve thousand members of the clergy in the Episcopal Church at present," he says, "and if you take the standard accepted figure of one out of every fifteen drinkers, you come up with about 760 or so. And remember, that *doesn't* include members of their families. So I'd say that Bishop Richards' figure, shocking though it may be to some people, does not reveal the true extent of the problem within the family of the Episcopal Church. Obviously, we'd like to get more of these sick clergymen into RACA, but some bishops still take such a negative attitude about this problem that the afflicted ones don't dare come out into the open with their problem.

"On the positive side, however," Golder adds, "RACA is getting more and more requests from bishops and others for help. Part of this increase is due to the recent establishment of RACA's 'Hot Line,' which has been circulated through the Church."

RACA's Hot Line began with four phone numbers of RACA members in widely separated parts of America. The approach has proved so successful that RACA has now expanded it to include ten phone numbers.

While the Recovered Alcoholic Clergy Association operates on an austere budget ("Our request for a grant from Trinity Parish in New York was turned down recently," Golder told me, making clear that such turndowns are the rule rather than the exception), the organization's activities and successes far outweigh its financial limitations and low publicity profile.

"There is a tremendous difference between *spirituality,* as expressed through people, and *religion,* as expressed by institutions," concludes another member of RACA. "Spirituality can indeed move mountains; religion, on the other hand, can move only slowly."

The old concepts date back to antiquity. The most deeply rooted one, by far, depicts the alcoholic as a sinner and moral degenerate who can redeem himself only by drawing upon his God-given willpower to abstain. This mildewed concept prompted many brethren of the cloth, no doubt, to support the nineteenth-century temperance movement and, later, national Prohibition—the noble experiment that failed because it penalized the majority of citizens who could drink without ill effect in order to deter the minority who could not.

Returning to the reality of the 1970s, churches today remain sharply divided over the very use of beverage alcohol. Year after year, the Southern Baptist Convention, for example, has excoriated Demon Rum. In 1972, as but one case in point, retired SBC president R. G. Lee vehemently depicted beverage alcohol as "sewage in the drinking fountain . . . a rattlesnake in the nursery . . . a rapist in the girls' dormitory!"

On the other side of the coin, the United Methodist Church in 1968 repealed its prohibition of alcohol consumption by clergy and laity, quoting biblical passages to support moderate drinking, and citing studies to illustrate the requirement of abstinence to eliminate "intemperate drinking." The Trappist and Benedictine monks, in turn, both produce renowned wines and brandies, while Christian Brothers' wide variety of vintages is reputed to have paid for St. Mary's College in Moraga, California.

More significant is the fact that America's religious institutions are gradually beginning to recognize alcoholism as a disease; some, moreover, are coming to believe that they should somehow play a role in treating that disease.

As long ago as 1958, for example, the General Board of the

Protestant National Council of Churches declared, "The churches share a pastoral concern for alcoholics, problem drinkers, and their families. We recognize that once drinking has passed a certain point it becomes alcoholism, an affliction which cannot be met effectively by the unaided efforts of the victims. Alcoholics are persons in need of diagnosis, understanding, guidance, and treatment. They are especially in need of pastoral care and the divine love which the church can bring them."

A similar position had previously been taken by the General Assembly of the Presbyterian Church. In recent years, moreover, the General Board of Christian Social Concerns of the Methodist Church officially recognized that alcoholism is a disease requiring competent help, and that the Church's fellowship should be numbered among the resources available for prevention and rehabilitation. This was a major breakthrough for a church whose traditional policy was one of total abstinence.

More recently, exhaustive publicity was given to the so-called "mass wine controversy" in the Catholic Church, whereby the Vatican finally and reluctantly granted permission for alcoholic priests to use grape juice instead of wine when celebrating mass. The departure from tradition was granted in a letter, dated May 1974, from Franjo Cardinal Seper to John Cardinal Krol of Philadelphia.

Still, the old attitudes die hard. Following publication of Cardinal Seper's letter, a Vatican spokesman was asked if there are many alcoholic priests in the United States. "There is no hard figure available," he replied to reporters. "An estimate is that less than 10 percent of the country's 57,000 priests are alcoholics."

The revealing phrase in that reply is, of course, "less than." By my reckoning, 10 percent of 57,000 is 5,700; 5,700 suffering alcoholics, regardless of vocation, constitute an army of human beings. Implicit in the Vatican spokesman's phraseology seems to be the view that 5,700 alcoholics are "no big deal"—or at least nothing to get excited about.

So it does come down, once more, to a question of attitude. Obviously, the attitude of RACA members differs sharply from

that of the Episcopal House of Bishops, just as the attitude of
Guest House counselors is a world apart from that of the Holy
See. In any case, whatever a church hierarchy may stipulate,
most important to the alcoholic seeking treatment are the attitudes of the local pastor and his congregation.

For the most part in America today, organized religion still
remains very much out of touch with the reality of alcoholism—
not only among its own clergy, but among those whom the
clergy ostensibly serve.

The Reverend William B. Van Wyck, a RACA supporter,
describes the experience of one alcoholic rector: "How we
roared at his blue jokes! We did not know that in their early
stages alcoholics are a charming lot.

"But the problem surfaced as the years went by," Father Van
Wyck adds. "We found ourselves angered by the rector's behav-
ing out of character. We were disappointed and embittered when
we sought strength and found fragility. In the course of vestry
meetings surreptitiously called to discuss The Problem, the solution was inevitable: by fair means or foul, to get rid of the clerical blight and to bring in a new and, we hoped, unalcoholic
man.

"From that moment, the journey to the bishop's office was
rapid and direct," Van Wyck says. "Perhaps, years afterward,
the rumor will be circulated of the former rector's death in a
hotel room in an eastern city or his end in a vicious brawl in a
midwestern city or his working as a janitor in a slum hotel on the
West Coast. These three finales are true, having taken place
within the last year.

"Who takes care of the caretakers?" Father Van Wyck concludes irresistibly. "To date, the Church has been mute—or has
dumped the ailing upon the haphazard kindnesses of community
professionals. Except in the service of our Lord, clergy are not
expendable. I beg of the Church to reverse this stand, to take a
few hours and a few dollars from the urban crisis to do what can
be done to bring ailing caretakers back to life, health, and use-
fulness."

10

The American Alcoholic:
What, Why, Who?

It's only a short walk to the studios of KDKA Radio from Pittsburgh's once gold-hued and now grime-tarnished Hilton Hotel.
At fifteen minutes before midnight on a snowy February night in
1974, I made that walk in what may have been record time.
Gateway Mall was deserted, and I imagined stealthy footsteps
crunching on the pathway behind me.

In my bone-tiredness during the first leg of a seventeen-city
publicity tour for my novel *The Morning After,* I was chilled and
irritable. Why in hell had I foolishly consented to do a live radio
interview at *midnight?* Who ever heard of the Jack Wheeler
Show? And who, besides nodding drunks and hyped-up insom-
niacs, would bother tuning to a talk show at that ungodly hour?

It turns out that a great many people listen to the Jack Wheeler
Show during the small hours between midnight and dawn; they
not only listen, but actually phone the studio from cities
hundreds and even thousands of miles from Pittsburgh. KDKA's
50,000-watt clear-channel signal "zaps into homes from Talla-
hassee to Tulsa," Wheeler told me affably.

Unlike most interviewers, Wheeler had actually *read* my
novel. His questions were incisive, probing, and sometimes cal-
culatedly unkind, enabling me to talk less about myself than
about the illness of alcoholism. I had been set up with my own

microphone, headset, and Thermos of coffee. As we talked, I could see the engineer fiddling with dials and, at one point, motioning to Wheeler when the phone buttons all lit up simultaneously.

"They love it," my host announced perfunctorily during a commercial break. "Let's take some calls."

We began to take calls at about 12:30 A.M., and I quickly became enamored with the whole idea of call-in talk shows. There *were* people out there. Indeed, the phone buttons rarely went dark; by 2 A.M. I was as wide-awake as those night people in Radio Land. I had become turned on and then hooked, so that when it was over, at 3 A.M., I wanted more.

During the days that followed, I was to get more—late-night and early-morning radio and TV talk shows in New York, Cleveland, Chicago, Detroit, San Diego, San Francisco, Denver, Boston, and on and on. I was primed, pinned down, and, not infrequently, pleasantly surprised by such hosts as Arlene Francis, Bob Kennedy, Dennis Wholey, Fred Griffith, Dorothy Fuldheim, Marie Torre, Thelma Tierney, Marcia Rose, Larry Angel, and Barbara Howar. And, looking back, I was able to get a strong feeling about the kinds of things the folks "out there" know and don't know about alcoholism.

Some callers were downright hostile, to be sure, going so far as to characterize my alcoholism as not only immoral, but reflective of my lack of religious training, weak will, and, of course, strong oral drive.

For the most part, however, those scores of callers in more than a dozen cities wanted to know about alcoholism. The upshot, for me, was that the on-the-air questions were far more revelatory than my occasionally faltering answers. Here, in fact, is the way those call-in sessions generally went:

"Mr. Weiner, my son drinks a lot of beer, sometimes more than a case a day. He says it's only beer, and it's true that he never drinks hard liquor. So he can't be an alcoholic, I know, but still . . ."

"Jack, do you think that a person who gets drunk once a week, just on Saturday night, can be an alcoholic?"

"What about wine? My doctor said I should drink a glass of

sweet wine before dinner. My husband says it changes me, and
maybe it does a little, because it loosens me up and my stomach
feels better, but we've begun to argue . . .''

"I caught part of your show on the car radio, and I have this
friend. Well, what I really want to ask you, how can you *tell* if a
person is an alcoholic?''

"Jack, I'm a salesman, so I have to drink, because a big part
of my job is entertaining customers. Wouldn't you go along with
the idea that in certain social situations, or let's say certain business situations, that drinking is sort of essential?''

"Mr. Weiner, you said that alcoholism is an incurable illness.
So how come you're cured? Isn't that double-talk?''

"You talked about cirrhosis of the liver. I drink every day
after work, and all right, sometimes quite a bit. You know, I get
a little high. Not alcoholic or anything like that. But anyway, I
eat a lot, too. My liver's fine, I think, so isn't it true that if you
just eat . . . ?''

If memory serves, and if my tapes of those myriad question-
and-answer sessions can be considered a representative if admittedly unscientific sampling, it would be safe to say that it all
boiled down to barely half a dozen basic questions:

What, actually, is alcohol? How does it work? What does it
do? What *doesn't* it do? Who is the alcoholic? How can you tell?

To begin at the beginning, my own initial experience with
alcohol took place when I was fourteen and "drank *at*" someone
or something, angrily downing perhaps half a fifth of my father's
best bonded bourbon. The orange and black Old Grand-Dad
label remains sharp in my consciousness, together with a retrospective awareness that the fiery amber liquid was "100 proof"
and, hence, the most costly brand among my parents' meager
supply.

Little did I realize, during that first encounter and its woeful
aftermath, that I would drink alcoholically for another twenty-
seven years. Depending on the state of my financial resources,
my personal inclination, and, finally, the ferocity of my need, I
was to drink my way through virtually entire brand rosters of
straight and blended whiskeys, bourbons, brandies and cognacs,

cordials and liqueurs, gins, vodkas, tequilas, rums, and wines—
dry, carbonated, fortified, and otherwise.

In the midst of one especially needful period, I became briefly
familiar with Mennen After Shave lotion, later to be followed by
an innovative mixture of Scope mouthwash and Aramis cologne;
to the cognoscenti among my alcoholic brethren, those two last
potions were known as Green Lizard and Harum Scarum, re-
spectively. I recommend them to no one.

Morbid nostalgia aside, it was only during sobriety that I was
to become somewhat knowledgeable about the whys and wherefores of my long-time companion John Barleycorn.

Point one, by way of response to the lady with the beer-drink-
ing son, is the fact that alcohol is alcohol is alcohol: a 16-ounce
can of beer containing 4½ percent alcohol by volume provides
as *much* alcohol as a 1½-ounce "shot" of 100-proof whiskey
or vodka; so does a 3½-ounce glass of sweet wine containing
20 percent alcohol, or a 5-ounce glass of table wine containing
14 percent alcohol. The all too commonplace notion that "two
beers never hurt anyone" is easily disproved not only by those
facts, I told that same lady, but also by the considerably more
empirical truth that alcoholics in Germany are almost *exclusively*
beer drinkers.

Point two is the fact that "drinking alcohol," in liquor, beer,
wine, or what have you, is otherwise known as ethanol or ethyl
alcohol; it is quite different from isopropyl or rubbing alcohol,
and methyl or wood alcohol, both of which are *not* for drinking.
Separated from its flavorings, colorings, and congeners, ethyl
alcohol is a volatile, colorless, and water-miscible compound
with the surprisingly simple chemical formula C_2H_5OH. Which
is to say that alcohol is composed, molecularly, of the very stuff
of life itself—carbon, hydrogen, and oxygen.

It follows, going on to point three, that the production of
alcohol is literally child's play, requiring merely the cooperation
of Mother Nature and Father Time—in the form of mild warmth,
and the action of airborne yeast spores on mashes of such fer-
mentables as grain, fruit, berries, potatoes, and even weeds. Artificial distillation of these products increases their "proof," or
alcoholic strength. In America, "proof" is an arbitrary labeling
term which, when halved, indicates the product's alcohol con-

tent by volume; 100-proof whiskey, for example, contains 50 percent ethyl alcohol, and most distilled spirits—such as whiskey, vodka, and rum—range from 80 to 90 proof.

It is a certainty, using paleontology and recorded history as guides, that man learned to brew beer long before he learned to bake bread. Noah carried grapevine cuttings aboard the ark, and is duly credited with bringing wine to the Hebrews. Moreover, as every Sunday-school scholar knows, the Bible itself is rife with references to alcoholic beverages.

Since the beginnings of written history, in short, there is voluminous evidence from the Egyptians, ancient Hebrews, Greeks, Romans, and Chinese that alcoholic beverages and their effects were well known within those cultures. Today's use of the word "bacchanal," for example, derives from the ever-grinning (and perhaps ever-intoxicated) Greco-Roman god Bacchus, credited with introducing wine to *his* countrymen. That introduction, in turn, eventually prompted one anonymous thirteenth-century bacchanalian to describe alcohol's pleasurable effects in these heady superlatives:

It sloweth age, it strengtheneth youth, it helpeth digestion, it abandoneth melancholie, it relisheth the heart, it lighteneth the mind, it quickeneth the spirit, it keepeth and preserveth the head from whirling, the eyes from dazzling, the tongue from lisping, the mouth from snaffing, the teeth from chattering, and the throat from rattling; it keepeth the stomach from wambling, the heart from swelling, the hands from shivering, the sinews from shrinking, the veins from crumbling, the bones from aching, and the marrow from soaking.

On the other side of the coin, the oldest temperance tract on record was written in Egypt some three thousand years ago; entitled "Wisdom of Ani," it admonished tipplers in these somber terms:

Take not upon thyself to drink a jug of beer. Thou speakest, and an unintelligible utterance issueth from thy mouth. If thou fallest down and thy limbs break, there is none to hold out a hand to thee. Thy companions in drink stand up and say, "Away with this sot." And thou art like a little child.

Somewhere between these two extremes can be found point four—that alcohol in one form or another was probably the first mood-altering tranquilizer known to human beings; that alcohol has a long and distinguished record as a medicinal drug; and that, if alcohol were discovered tomorrow, it doubtless would bring nothing less than Nobel laurels to its discoverers.

Alcohol is indeed a powerful (albeit potentially addictive) drug. By virtue of its proven pharmacological action and seemingly magical ability to tranquilize, sedate, and anesthetize, its "rediscovery" would garner not only awards, but also headlines—as was the case with insulin, penicillin, and Salk vaccine. The critical difference between these latter-day "wonder drugs" and alcohol, however, is that alcohol's effects—along with the mechanisms by which it induces those effects within the human body—are all but unknown among those who produce the drug, sell it, and consume it.

Few high school students, for example, are *un*aware that insulin is used to treat diabetes; that penicillin effectively combats a variety of infections; or that Dr. Salk's vaccine has all but eradicated the crippling illness called poliomyelitis. In contrast, those same high school students—along with their parents, most distillers, brewmasters, liquor distributors, bartenders, physicians, and imbibers—haven't the faintest idea of alcohol's "what, how, and why."

In sum, considering our long experience with alcohol, it is astonishing how many drinkers are ignorant of the way their favorite alcoholic potions affect them, for better or for worse. And, of course, the same applies to non-drinking relatives and friends who, more often than not, find the drinker's behavior wholly incomprehensible.

How, then, *does* alcohol work in the body? And what are its effects?

Going back again in time to my own momentous introduction to ardent spirits, I have since learned that the ethyl alcohol in that 100-proof Old Grand-Dad was absorbed directly and immediately into my bloodstream through my stomach walls and intestines. Unlike other "food," alcohol does not have to be digested, and literally rushes into the bloodstream; the bloodstream, in turn, swiftly transports the alcohol to the liver, the heart, and, most important, the brain.

Within minutes after I had belted down that bourbon, the alcohol had reached every tissue and organ in my body; I lost perhaps 5 percent in urine, perspiration, and exhaled air, while the remaining 95 percent was metabolized by my body processes (the oxidizing action of my liver, in particular) at a fairly constant rate. I weighed perhaps 140 pounds at the time, and now know that in a 150-pound man, alcohol is metabolized, or "burned," at the rate of about three-quarters of an ounce per hour.

Of course, it all seems elementary in retrospect: When a person drinks faster than his body's ability to metabolize the alcohol, the drug accumulates, resulting in higher and higher blood alcohol levels. Obviously, the more a person drinks beyond the amount his body can metabolize in a given period, the more intoxicated he or she becomes.

For those, including myself, who have wondered why they have sometimes got "loaded" more quickly on some occasions than on others, the speed with which alcohol enters the bloodstream and exerts its effects on the brain and body depends on several things:

• *How fast you drink.* If you "nurse" your drink, at the rate of about one drink an hour, the alcohol will not "jolt" your brain; it won't have an opportunity to build up in your blood, and chances are you'll feel little unpleasant effect. Gulping that drink, on the other hand, will cause immediate intoxicating effects.

• *What you drink.* Wine and beer are absorbed somewhat less rapidly than distilled spirits, not only because they contain less alcohol by volume, but also because they contain small amounts of non-alcoholic substances that slow down the absorption process. (It is worth repeating, however, that a 16-ounce can of beer contains the same amount of alcohol as a 1½-ounce shot of 100-proof whiskey.) Diluting an alcoholic beverage with another liquid, such as water or milk, also helps slow down absorption. Mixing with carbonated beverages such as club soda, tonic, or ginger ale, on the other hand, *increases* the rate of absorption.

• *How much you weigh.* The same amount of alcohol can

have a considerably greater effect on a 120-pound person than on a 180-pound person, since alcohol is quickly and uniformly distributed throughout the entire circulatory system. So the heavier person will have smaller concentrations throughout his bloodstream than the lighter-weight person.

• *Whether your stomach is empty or full.* Eating, especially before drinking as well as during drinking, will slow down the rate of absorption into your bloodstream.

• *Your drinking history and body chemistry.* Each person has a uniquely individual physiological makeup, which may affect his or her reactions to alcohol. Within certain persons, for example, the stomach empties more quickly than is normal, and alcohol seems to be absorbed more rapidly. Emptying time may also be slowed down or speeded up by fear, anger, or stress, as well as the condition of the stomach tissues. In persons with a long history of drinking, a *tolerance* to alcohol develops, so that over a period of months or years larger amounts are required to produce the same effects produced early in drinking. Conversely, persons with serious drinking problems find that the curve of tolerance reverses itself, so that even very small amounts of alcohol cause notable effects.

The short-term effects of alcohol, familiar to just about everyone, range in degree from a mild euphoria commonly described by the words "buzz," "high," or, perhaps most accurately, "feeling good," to the comatose state characterized by such euphemisms as "out of this world," "stoned out of my mind," and "feeling no pain."

Be the milieu a swinging office party, airborne DC-10, spacious mansion, or skid row doorway, a person's blood alcohol level (BAL) is the prime determinant of those varying degrees of effect. And, as drinking drivers are becoming aware, blood alcohol levels have important legal implications today. All but six of the fifty states have set a BAL of 0.10 percent (one part alcohol to 1,000 parts blood) as legal presumption of intoxication; in Idaho and Utah the standard is 0.08 percent, and in Mississippi, Wisconsin, New Jersey, and Maryland the standard is 0.15 percent.

Legal considerations apart, alcohol can cause noticeable be-

havioral changes at concentrations as low as 0.03 to 0.05 percent. Even at the level of "a couple of fast cold ones," a person's thought, judgment, and restraint may be affected. Reflex
responses, reaction-time responses, and performance in such activities as automobile driving and athletics generally change for
the worse. It is especially significant that as a drinking driver's
performance is impaired, his judgment often deteriorates and,
consequently, he believes he is driving more skillfully.

In my own case, I managed on several occasions to sideswipe
my own house, rear-end and seriously damage my best friend's
parked car, and, on one memorable night, drive my 1952 Ford
through the back wall of my garage as I "skillfully" eased the
car to a stop within that well-lighted wooden structure.

To get back to the short-term effects of alcohol in more universal terms, the average drinker with a blood alcohol level of,
say, 0.05 percent generally feels loose and carefree; he or she
feels released from ordinary tensions and inhibitions. The experience can indeed be a pleasurable one and, unquestionably,
most people who drink do so mainly to achieve that "mellow"
effect. The shy and tongue-tied adolescent boy may feel courageous and articulate—sufficiently so to be able to ask that previously unapproachable girl for a dance. Similarly, miracle of
miracles, the usually restrained and painfully self-conscious
young woman may seem to suddenly "fit right in."

Clearly, the operative verb in any of these commonplace social situations is "feel." Yet, contrary to popular belief, alcohol
is neither a stimulant nor a "pick-me-up," but, rather, an out-
and-out depressant, or "downer." The "feeling" of stimulation
results from the fact that even relatively low concentrations of
alcohol in the bloodstream depress areas of the brain which normally inhibit or restrain certain types of behavior.

The first part of the brain affected is the frontal lobe of the
cerebrum, which is the seat of reasoning, conscious thinking,
memory, and self-control. And, as the frontal lobe is gradually
anesthetized by alcohol, that "magic" begins: Inhibitions disappear and tensions evaporate; Mr. Little becomes Mr. Big and
Ms. Nobody becomes Ms. Somebody.

At countless rehabilitation facilities, Alcoholics Anonymous meetings, and one-to-one interviews, it seemed to me that the recollections of those first drinks and first feelings were all but identical. Here, for example, are some verbatim interview excerpts to which, I am certain, any reader with even a modicum of drinking experience can relate:

Chicago, Illinois, a woman in her mid-thirties: "I started drinking when I was a teen-ager, because I wanted to go with the crowd and be one of them, as most of us did. But in retrospect, I thought from the very beginning that alcohol could do for me what I couldn't do for myself. I've always been a very quiet, shy person, and I found that I had less inhibitions—less hangups, I guess—after a few drinks. I felt more at ease with people. I wasn't quite so frightened, I thought, and I could communicate much easier. And so I used alcohol."

Baltimore, Maryland, a twenty-seven-year-old man: "At the high school parties, I was into some pretty heavy drinking that almost immediately gave me a feeling of success. The guy who was five-foot-eight suddenly became six-foot-two. I was able to sing, and dance, and begin to relate to people at a level that felt good to me. I learned that liquor made life a lot easier."

New York City, a seventy-one-year-old woman: "I grew up during Prohibition and everyone I knew drank. It was the thing to do. Nobody had to force me, but when I discovered it, it was sheer magic. I didn't find it easy to talk in groups of people I didn't know, and I discovered that having a few drinks solved the problem."

Washington, D.C., a fifty-year-old woman: "At age fifteen, I went trotting off to college, and I can remember the 'juke joints,' as they were called. There was dancing even at lunchtime, and everybody else was drinking beer, and—I know me—since they were drinking beer, I was also drinking. But I didn't need it to be more outgoing. I didn't need it to have fun. I was already doing those things. For many years it didn't change my mood—it *heightened* my mood. Like I always liked to dance and to go to parties, and if I was dancing, I danced more—you know—whatever was going on, I did more of that."

The common thread in each of these brief vignettes is the fact that relatively low blood alcohol levels resulted in discernible and generally pleasurable mood and behavioral changes.

That, however, is but the beginning, for as larger amounts of alcohol enter the blood, other functions of the brain become immediately involved. Specifically, at a level of 0.10 percent (one part to 1,000), hand and arm movements, walking, and speech become plainly clumsy. The drinker may trip over a bench, accidentally upend a glass, lose equilibrium, or slurringly attempt to order another "martooni."

At 0.20 percent (one part to 500), the control mechanisms of the brain's *entire* motor area are measurably impaired, along with that part of the brain which guides emotional behavior. Typically, the drinker staggers or may want to lie down; he or she may also be easily angered, may become boisterous and argumentative, or perhaps get on a crying or laughing "jag." The person, clearly, is "drunk."

Yet he or she may become drunker still. With a concentration of 0.30 percent (one part alcohol to 300 parts blood), still deeper areas of the brain are affected, especially the mechanisms that normally control understanding and response to stimuli. At this level, a person is intoxicated to the point of confusion and disorientation, suffers dulled hearing and blurred vision, loses sensibility to pain, and may lapse into a stupor.

With yet greater concentrations of alcohol in the blood (0.40 to 0.50 percent, equivalent to one part in 250 or 200), the drinker is in coma. Finally, still higher levels affect the medulla oblongata, that portion of the brain responsible for such vital functions as heartbeat, blood flow, and breathing. It is at this point that the drinker will go into shock and possibly die.

None of this is to say, by any means, that the consumption of alcohol *per se* is right, wrong, good, bad, or indifferent. To return to those radio and TV call-in shows, the point is that the average person's lack of knowledge about alcohol's workings and effects seems almost inversely proportionate to alcoholism's increasingly devastating toll in America today.

In that sense, recovering alcoholics who have "been there" are fortunate. By sharing our experiences with each other, we tend to increase our knowledge, progress toward our recovery, and, more often than not, do it all with what may appear to be a macabre sense of humor. In Minneapolis not long ago, for example, a friend remarked, "My doctor once scared the hell out of me. He said he found a trace of blood in my alcohol stream."

Merely by looking around us, we can't help but be constantly reminded of those days when *we* staggered, wept, fought, and, ineluctably, wrought havoc in our own lives and the lives of so many others around us.

It happens that I received another personal "reminder" just days before this writing. Attempting to dislodge a cigarette that had stuck to my lip, my fingers accidentally slid to its glowing end. The burning tobacco became fused between those fingers, causing me to bellow with pain and develop fast-swelling burn blisters, and, simultaneously, producing a violent reflex that caused me to fling the offending object across the room.

My mind instantly flashed to a hospital ward in New York state. It was 1965, I think, and I had "come to" following a disastrous binge. A nurse had inquired about the blisters and deep burns between my index and middle fingers. Mystified, I had shaken my head.

I now realize that I had drunk myself to that point of anesthetization—with a blood alcohol level of perhaps 0.35 percent—where I had become literally desensitized to pain. In my own bedroom, my car, or perhaps some nameless motel, cigarette after burning and forgotten cigarette had seared its way into the skin between my fingers. Fortunately, the scars and memory linger on, and serve as a reminder.

As recovering alcoholics, our recollections also include that terror-fraught phenomenon known as the "blackout," a temporary loss of memory that is not to be confused with "passing out" or being unconscious. Drinkers suffering a blackout don't remember things they did or said, or even places they went to and people with whom they spent time during the "spree."

Although a pattern of blackouts is now known to be clearly symptomatic of alcoholism, so-called social drinkers occasionally experience them as well; in that regard, the blackout could conceivably also be listed among alcohol's "short-term" effects. To observers, the drinker may have appeared to be functioning normally, a fact that is nothing less than astonishing to those who have "come to" with absolutely no recollection of their actions and whereabouts during the drinking episode. Or, the drinker may have committed violent and even murderous acts, again with absolutely no recollection of the events.

"I started drinking when I was sixteen," recalls Lloyd Bair, a man in his mid-thirties who works in a West Coast alcoholism treatment and referral center, "and I went into a blackout the first night. I remembered everything up to a point, and then all of a sudden I didn't remember any more. I vaguely remembered waking up in the middle of the night, or doing something in the middle of the night. Finally, I woke up in my bedroom at home, and of course I was scared and wondered what the hell had happened. So I called this guy and he told me what had happened. During this blackout, which I know it to be now, I'd gone completely crazy. I'd started hitting and smashing things, and of course that set my pattern for the next twelve years."

Many other recovering alcoholics with whom I talked during my travels had similar blackouts. I remember four in particular. The first "tore up" seven taverns, the second accidentally shot himself in the leg while attempting to burglarize a supermarket, the third murderously assaulted a friend, and the fourth committed vehicular homicide.

My own "record" blackout—considerably less tragic but, for me, no less frightening—began in a New York City bar on a payday night in the early 1960s. I remember cashing my check and ordering the first drink; that's *all* I remember. The next thing I knew, I was stumbling on frostbitten feet down a rutted and frozen road. My shoes were gone, a self-winding calendar watch revealed that three days had elapsed, and it took me almost an hour to determine that I was on the outskirts of Cleveland, Ohio. To this day, I have no idea of how I got there, what happened during those three "missing" days, or who acquired my shoes.

Which brings us, on a lesser scale of anguish, to that familiar condition known as the hangover—a hellish combination of fatigue, nausea, upset stomach, anxiety, and, for some, a too quickly fading state of intoxication. As every drinker or even once-a-year New Year's Eve reveler knows, there are, of course, as many alleged hangover curatives as there are cocktail recipes. The "remedies" range from such traditional standbys as black coffee and/or Alka-Seltzer to those considerably more exotic, multi-ingredient potions that contain (and sometimes combine) oysters, raw eggs, chili pepper, vitamins, A-1 Sauce, olive oil, whipping cream, *ad nauseum*.

Uncle Charlie's "surefire miracle medicine" notwithstanding, there is no known cure or palliative for the morning-after miseries, nor has science even the foggiest notion of what causes hangovers. There seems little doubt, though, that the condition is an inherent part of the "sobering up" process for some individuals. In that respect, although solid food, bed rest, and aspirin will make the discomfort somewhat more bearable, time and time alone will do the job. Because, clearly, just as the speed of alcohol absorption determines the rate at which a person becomes drunk, the speed of alcohol metabolism determines the rate at which he or she becomes sober again; in short, all one can do is to wait patiently and let the liver do its work.

Folklore dies hard, to be sure, but the fact remains that neither black coffee nor cold showers nor breaths of pure oxygen will hasten the sobering-up process. "Give a drunk black coffee and a cold shower," I've heard it said, "and you end up with something really special—a wide-awake, soaking-wet, shivering drunk."

As far as is known, it's unlikely that anyone ever died of a hangover, although a figurative death wish is not uncommon on those mornings when chirping sparrows sound like platoons of thundering jackhammers, when the day's first light seems as brain-piercingly bright as a lightning flash, or when one's tongue feels as if it had been used to clean pool-table felt. In any case, distressful as they may be, hangovers are hardly dangerous.

On the other hand, the effects of long-term alcohol consumption can be gravely dangerous. Although most people tend to scoff at the very idea of such danger, the incontrovertible fact is that frequent drinking of even moderate amounts of alcohol causes measurable damage to *every single body system*. What is more, it has been conclusively proven that frequent drinking of larger quantities of alcohol causes fatal or permanently crippling damage to the body's three primary life-support systems: the cardiovascular system (heart and blood vessels), the central nervous system (brain, spinal cord, and nerves), and the liver.

As far as the cardiovascular system is concerned, for example, doctors long believed almost axiomatically that small amounts of alcohol would be beneficial for people with heart problems. Many physicians prescribed "a little port wine after dinner," reasoning that since alcohol dilates blood vessels in the skin and thereby increases cutaneous circulation, the drug would also increase circulation in the arteries leading to the heart.

It is now known that alcohol has just the opposite effect on the heart—*decreasing* arterial circulation; elevating the level of blood lipids (fats such as cholesterol and triglycerides) and thus causing atherosclerosis, or hardening of the arteries leading to the heart; and impairing the physiology of the heart muscle in numerous other ways. Even small amounts of alcohol can adversely affect operation of the heart's left ventricle, while larger amounts can sharply depress ventricle function and cause leakage of cell components within the heart muscle wall.

Dr. Timothy Regan, a professor in the cardiology division of the College of Medicine and Dentistry of New Jersey, New Jersey Medical School, is one of numerous cardiologists who have recently determined that alcohol is not only potentially hazardous to the cardiovascular system, but directly toxic to the heart.

"On the basis of studies in three animal species and man," Regan says, "it would appear that the cumulative effect of chronic alcohol drinking can produce metabolic and morphologic abnormalities of the myocardium—or heart muscle wall—in addition to depressing ventricular function, *before* any clinical signs appear and without any evident malnutrition."

Regan goes on to note that the hearts of non-alcoholics and alcoholics alike are affected by alcohol's toxicity, and that the end result is often heart failure, heartbeat irregularities, or thromboembolism—separately or in combination.

The most commonly observed form of alcohol-related heart disease today has the difficult name alcoholic cardiomyopathy, or alcoholic myocarditis. And it is a direct result of alcohol's action on tiny particles, called mitochondria, inside the heart muscle itself. These mitochondria normally produce energy for contraction of the heart, so heart failure may come strictly as a result of mitochondrial damage—without the additional adverse impact of alcohol-related hardening of the arteries.

For imbibers who remain Doubting Thomases, perhaps most significant is the fact that alcoholic cardiomyopathy cuts across all socio-economic lines, affecting well-nourished and mal-nourished persons alike. The overriding common feature in alcoholic cardiomyopathy's incidence, reports the American Medical Association's Committee on Alcoholism and Drug Dependence, "is regular and excessive consumption of alcohol over a prolonged period of time."

The criteria for alcoholic cardiomyopathy include congestive heart failure in patients under 50; no evidence of the usual causes of heart disease; and daily intake, for about five years, of more than eight ounces of whiskey or gin, one quart of wine, or two quarts of beer. In one study at Chicago's Cook County Hospital, the same committee reports, "One patient had induction of congestive heart failure after ingesting 16 ounces of Scotch daily for 12 weeks."

One friend, now alive and well in Cleveland, nearly perished from a condition known as beriberi heart disease, in which cardiac damage and enlargement are caused by chronic beer drinking. Following his recovery, he learned that the condition had first been observed in Germany almost a hundred years ago. "They called it 'Munich beer heart,' " he says today with a grin. "It sounds sort of *macho,* don't you think? Sort of a badge of honor for the big guzzlers. But it damned near killed me, and even my G.P. didn't know what was going on."

Another friend, writer Bob Palmer, describes what Dr. Timothy Regan would probably consider a "classic" case of alcoholic cardiomyopathy. "My heart muscle began to weaken, slowly at first, then more rapidly, and one result was that my lungs gradually filled with fluid. I could barely breathe, and God, I remember how exhausted and wiped out I always felt. It got to the point," he adds, "where I had to sit up on pillows at night just to catch my breath. I was panting like a dog, and I thought it had something to do with not getting enough exercise.

"So I started taking long walks, and then jogging. I even went to Denver, thinking the altitude would help, never realizing or admitting to myself for a second that it could have a thing to do with the booze. And, of course, I was intoxicated most of the time."

At the urging of a friend, Palmer remembers, he finally visited a respiratory specialist, who immediately sent him to a cardiologist, "who diagnosed my condition as congestive heart failure within five minutes. It was a wonder I was alive. I had just turned forty, and they told me I had literally been in heart failure for months."

No less insidious and potentially disastrous are the long-term effects of alcohol on the body's central nervous system. As we have already seen, alcohol's immediate depressant action on various parts of the brain causes those manifestations of drunkenness with which we're all familiar. Far more serious, however, is the effect of heavy and prolonged drinking.

The known variety of alcohol-related neurological disorders, along with their symptoms and prognoses, could, in their own right, fill half a dozen medical textbooks. The ones most familiar to knowledgeable physicians are: *alcoholic polyneuritis,* which is an inflammation of the nerves that causes burning sensations in the hands and feet, and sometimes severe impairment of walking and balance; *Korsakoff's psychosis,* in which the patient can't remember recent events and compensates for the memory loss by "confabulation," or making up fictitious events; *Wernicke's syndrome,* characterized by myriad tiny and potentially fatal brain hemorrhages; and a veritable compendium of other degenerative conditions, each with its own lengthy name and ominous pathogenesis.

Suffice it to say that large doses of alcohol taken over long periods of time do, assuredly, cause progressive brain damage. For a time, such damage can be reversible; beyond a certain point, however, mental functions such as memory, judgment, and learning ability can deteriorate severely and *irreversibly.* A person's personality structure and actual grasp on reality may literally disintegrate to a point of no return.

There are, of course, numerous other alcohol-related neurological disorders, not the least of which is delirium tremens, or DTs. DTs can and sometimes do occur during a prolonged binge; however, the classic onset generally takes place on the third day following abrupt withdrawal of alcohol.

In DTs, the patient is disoriented and confused and experiences hallucinations during which he or she may see, hear, and actually be "attacked" by snakes, insects, other people, or inanimate objects. On occasion, there may be pleasant conversations with a relative or loved one who, it turns out, isn't actually present. Sometimes, a person in DTs may watch a highly entertaining TV program—to the point of thigh-slapping hilarity—in a room where there is no television set.

"I heard people outside my room all the time," says a health care executive and recovering alcoholic who suffered DTs numerous times during her drinking years. "Once I thought my little daughter was under the bed, and of course she wasn't, and I was like that for about ten days. That wasn't scary, though. The scary part was people coming into the room, which I remember quite vividly. There was a closet door, and I could see the closet door. The people would be talking to me," she recalls, "and all of a sudden they'd turn to vapor and go up over the crack in the door and into the closet. I was always running to the closet to see where they went, and of course I never found them. The other time, a bunch of African witch doctors were after me, and that was really scary."

In my own case, I suffered delirium tremens on several occasions, the worst being an "attack" by hordes of unfriendly sand crabs, the "best" being a dazzling display of multicolored waterfalls, soothing music that I could "touch," and a parade of lovely ladies in silken gowns.

Of those alcoholics who are arrested, tossed in drunk tanks, and allowed to endure their DTs "cold turkey" and without medical attention, at least 15 to 20 percent actually die. Moreover, the mortality rate is appreciable even with medical attention. Among a series of 10,000 cases of alcoholism admitted to the Los Angeles County Hospital, as but one case in point, the mortality rate from delirium tremens alone was a tragically high 6.6 percent—660 persons out of the 10,000.

While it is true that virtually no body tissue escapes damage from heavy and ongoing drinking, alcohol's greatest toll is on the liver. Liver disease, in fact, ranks as the foremost cause of major disability and early death in the alcoholic, occurring eight times more frequently among alcoholics than among non-alcoholics.

In the mildest form of alcohol-related liver disease, excess fat accumulates, resulting in what is called "fatty liver." If the process continues, as it so often does, fat infiltration increases and the liver becomes enlarged.

Normally, of course, a person can't feel the lower margin of the liver below the ribs on the right side. Yet the liver can easily be felt and, in medical terminology, becomes increasingly "palpable" as enlargement takes place. The phrase "belly full of liver," heard from time to time at Alcoholics Anonymous meetings and in halfway houses, is no mere figure of speech; in some cases the liver becomes so massive that it extends down as far as the crest of the pelvis, literally "hanging" over a person's waistband or belt.

Fortunately, fatty infiltration is totally reversible in the early stage of liver disease. If a person stops drinking, *period,* the impaired liver cells can readily recover, rid themselves of accumulated fat droplets, and once again function normally. But if the process continues, inflammation takes place, causing a condition known as alcoholic hepatitis, a considerably more severe form of liver damage, with a death rate as high as 30 percent.

Naturally, if alcohol consumption continues beyond this point, still greater damage occurs. Fibrous scars begin to form within the liver—dissecting, distorting, and constricting the vital organ—and causing the far more critical and irreversible condition known as cirrhosis. The complications of cirrhosis, in turn, are invariably catastrophic.

As the liver becomes increasingly scarred and incapable of carrying on its work as the body's "chemical factory," poisons tend to pile up in the bloodstream. When the level of ammonia increases abnormally, for instance, the alcoholic undergoes personality changes, becomes lethargic, and may go into a deep coma and eventually die. Jaundice may also occur, along with the excessive accumulation of hormones.

Still other complications of cirrhosis include massive gastrointestinal and esophageal hemmorrhaging, as well as swelling of the ankles or legs to a point where "ascites," or "potbellies" of fluid, develop. Until very recently, the cirrhotic patient entering a hospital with his first episode of bleeding esophageal varices has had less than a 50–50 chance of leaving the hospital alive.

Cirrhosis is a highly destructive process, usually fatal, ranking ninth among the causes of death in America, and fourth among men over the age of forty. "With the steadily increasing incidence of alcoholism in our population, death rates from cirrhosis had a parallel rise—to the point that in large urban areas, cirrhosis of the liver represents the third or fourth largest cause of death between the ages of 25 and 65," asserts Charles C. Lieber, M.D., who heads the Laboratory of Liver Disease and Nutrition at the Bronx Veterans Administration Hospital.

Although 85 to 90 percent of cirrhosis-caused deaths are associated with alcoholism, death certificates list alcoholism in only 30 percent of the cases. The point, once again, says the AMA's Committee on Alcoholism and Drug Dependence, is "the reluctance of the physician to stigmatize this disease by ascribing it to alcoholism."

The AMA, along with other professional groups, also strongly believes that some 40,000 persons in the United States today are dying of cirrhosis, and that at least another 20,000 are dying as a result of the complications of cirrhosis. At County-USC Medical Center in Los Angeles, by way of verification, a 1973 study revealed that cirrhosis of the liver had begun to top heart disease and cancer as the leading cause of death among Mexican Americans who die at the Center.

Not only at County-USC Medical Center, but across the country, cirrhosis appears to be showing up at an earlier age in patients. "We're seeing people die of cirrhosis after only five to ten years of heavy drinking," says one physician who spends much of his working time in detoxification wards. "And we never used to believe it was possible for a person to develop cirrhosis just by drinking beer. But now," he adds, *"that* old canard is going out the window."

Also going out the window is the widespread misconception—taught to generations of medical students—that poor eating habits and inadequate nutrition are the primary cause of the liver damage often associated with drinking. Major new research conducted at Mount Sinai School of Medicine by Dr. Lieber and his research associate Dr. Emanuel Rubin recently made it clear that severe liver damage can be produced by prolonged consumption of alcohol even if the person *is* receiving an adequate diet. "You can't protect yourself against alcohol damage by eating a good diet," says Dr. Rubin. "The only determinant is the total amount of alcohol you drink."

Drs. Lieber and Rubin ended the age-old debate on this controversial issue by extensive research with baboons, whose livers are essentially indistinguishable from those of human beings, and whose life spans are comparable enough to permit long-term follow-up of alcohol's effects.

The baboons—twenty-six of them—were fed a nutritious diet every day for periods as long as four years. Half of them, in addition, were given the equivalent of a fifth of liquor every day. Their alcohol intake made up half their daily calorie count, and they were never permitted to drink without eating. Nor were they permitted to stop eating.

The results? Diet notwithstanding, the alcohol-drinking baboons developed the entire spectrum of alcoholic liver disease—a fatty liver, alcoholic hepatitis, and cirrhosis. One baboon developed delirium tremens following her withdrawal from alcohol. Drs. Lieber and Rubin went further still in their research, disproving the idea that the impurities in alcoholic beverages, rather than ethyl alcohol itself, are the culprits in liver damage. They did so, simply enough, by feeding the baboons pure spirits.

In the final analysis, the damage to the baboons' livers so closely resembled human disease that Dr. Hans Poper—a distinguished liver specialist to whom Dr. Rubin gave the slides for microscopic study without identifying the patient—could not tell that it was a baboon liver.

It is now known that heavy alcohol intake over a number of years decreases bone density while increasing risk of fracture to the hip, wrist, humerus, or long bone of the upper arm, and spine. Doctors are convinced that "stumbling drunks" stumble, at least in part, because alcohol weakens their muscles. Researchers in the United States, Sweden, and elsewhere have found that the vast majority of alcoholics show definite signs of skeletal muscle damage; examined under a microscope, the muscle fibers of most alcoholics resemble in some ways those of persons affected by muscular dystrophy.

Nor is that all. "Within the past ten years it has become known that excessive consumption of alcohol can suppress the formation of red blood cells and blood platelets, which control clotting," says Dr. Yong K. Liu of the Augusta, Georgia, Veterans Administration Hospital's hematology division. "Our current studies present the first example of the suppression of white blood cell formation, in which it seems likely that alcohol itself is responsible."

Additionally, heavy and chronic alcohol consumption is known to cause impotence and, in more severe cases, to permanently destroy sexual ability in males—notwithstanding the fact that a short-term effect of alcohol is its inhibition-reducing role as a sexual stimulant. Shakespeare long ago noted in *Macbeth* that alcohol "provokes the desire, but it takes away the performance"; today, alcohol is known to have an effect on the brain, spinal cord, and genital organs which, in the words of Drs. Frederick Lemere and James Smith, does not "subserve erection."

The two psychiatrists' experience encompasses some 17,000 patients treated for alcoholism over a period of thirty-five years. They stress the importance of the malfunction of erection, they say, "because nearly all of our patients who complained of impotence still had a strong desire for sex but, much to their chagrin, were unable to perform. Unfortunately," the doctors add, "we have found no treatment for this problem."

As if this were not enough, long-term and heavy alcohol consumption is known to cause a host of other damaging effects, including gastritis, ulcers, pancreatitis, gall-bladder disease, and other gastrointestinal disorders; certain forms of cancer, especially of the mouth, pharynx, larynx, esophagus, and liver; lowered resistance to pneumonia and other infectious diseases; serious and often fatal birth defects, called the "fetal alcohol syndrome," in infants born to alcoholic mothers; surgical complications such as the increased risk of pulmonary infection, aspiration pneumonia, and respiratory depression following anesthesia; and wound-healing difficulties resulting from the malnutrition and vitamin deficiencies so often associated with alcoholism.

The skin, in particular, is a unique indicator of alcoholism and "a barometer of the systemic complications of the disease," as the AMA's special committee notes. "Before the problem is recognized by the patient," a report from the committee points out, "the early flush of the potential alcoholic becomes evident. Skin markers which develop from patterns of alcoholic behavior result from inadvertent injury to the skin, peculiar reactions to drugs, exposure to disease, and physical and emotional sequelae of detoxification. At a later stage," the report concludes, "the skin mirrors hepatic, gastrointestinal and peripheral nerve damage."

Even a hasty journey along alcohol's clinical byways can be an unsettling if not harrowing experience. Ultimately, we "dead-end" at the main thoroughfare, confronting the vexatious question we've all asked at one time or another: *Who's* the alcoholic?

The question is posed thousands of times daily across America, in much the same way it was posed to me—earnestly and almost plaintively—on the Jack Wheeler Show that snowy February morning in 1974.

Pittsburgh's bars had closed perhaps half an hour earlier; the caller's words were faintly slurred. "I caught part of your show on the car radio and, you see, I have this friend . . ." he began. "Well, what I really want to ask, how can you *tell* if a person's an alcoholic?"

Though I've never actually met that man, I feel somehow that I know him well. I, too, inquired about "a friend" on those various dire occasions when I briefly flirted with the idea of seeking help.

If that man from Pittsburgh were with me now, I'd probably tell him something of my own experiences with alcohol. I would point out, first, that I define my own alcoholism not in terms of what, when, where, or how much I drank, but, rather, in terms of what alcohol did *for* me and *to* me.

I'd tell him that there are hundreds of definitions of alcoholism, from the succinctly experiental one used by members of Alcoholics Anonymous, which describes the condition as an "obsession of the mind, coupled with a compulsion of the body," to the lengthier one set forth by Mark Keller of the Center of Alcohol Studies at Rutgers University: "Alcoholism is a chronic disease, or disorder of behavior, characterized by the repeated drinking of alcoholic beverages to an extent that exceeds customary dietary use or ordinary compliance with the social drinking customs of the community, and which interferes with the drinker's health, inter-personal relations, or economic functioning."

Finally, perhaps over a cup of coffee, I'd look that man from Pittsburgh in the eye and lay out my favorite definition. *"Who's the alcoholic? The alcoholic is the person whose drinking interferes with health, job, or studies, relations with his family, community, or social relationships—and yet he, or she, continues to drink."*

Interference need only be felt in *one* of those areas of living for a person to be defined as an alcoholic. Implicit in the fact that the person *continues to drink* is the loss of control, which perhaps more than any other symptom is characteristic of alcoholism.

To be sure, there are numerous other symptoms, not the least of which is denial itself. As noted earlier, alcoholism is a highly predictable illness. Symptomatic progression moves inevitably and almost invariably from point to point to point. The classic downward pattern, perhaps already well under way in my "friend" from Pittsburgh, is worth detailing. It is neither technical nor theoretical, but all too real; and it is unquestionably manifesting itself at this very moment among some twenty to thirty million Americans here, there, and everywhere.

Early symptoms. He promises himself constantly that he'll do better next time, while assuring others that he knows his limit. He lies, minimizing or hiding the amount he drinks; he concocts elaborate "reasons" for drinking. He gulps drinks; he "fortifies" himself before going to social or business functions, even those where alcohol will be served. He must have drinks at certain times—before lunch, after work, at barbecues, and so on; he must have drinks because he's tired, nervous, frantic, harassed, depressed, elated, or angry.

He has a compulsion to drink rather than to "see the situation through" by other means. Although he's often aware that his drinking is inappropriate at a particular time or place, he doesn't seem able to control his urge to drink, or to stop after the first one. He fears that he won't get enough alcohol and often feels inadequate and "apart from."

Chances are, during the first years of drinking, that he has a prodigious capacity and that his drinking goes pretty much unnoticed. However, blackouts often begin at this early stage.

Middle symptoms. The promises, pledges, and lies come faster and more furiously—necessarily so to hide the fact that his drinking is "different," to minimize the amount he drinks, and to perpetuate the myth that he can stop any time he wishes. He also lies to protect his job or keep his marriage or relationships together. He not only gulps drinks, but orders doubles and triples. He's the "bartender" at home or when he's out, making his own the "stiff" one; in any case, he usually has handy his own secret supply.

His eating habits are irregular, and he's always "exhausted," "nervous," "uptight," "hyper," "worried," or "depressed" and, of course, must drink for all these states of mind. The "times" he drinks increase, and he frequently drinks alone or only with other alcoholics, who "understand him," regardless of his interest in them. His drunkenness becomes obvious and, depending on the setting, often embarrassing. Weekend binges begin, along with desperate hangovers and the "Monday-morning flu." He needs a "pick-me-up" in the morning. He begins to "go on the wagon" and becomes increasingly irritable during periods of non-drinking.

His dependence on alcohol changes to compulsion. The last traces of control disappear; a single drink is apt to trigger a chain reaction that will continue without a break until he is totally intoxicated. He talks less and less—and finally not at all—about drinking, hangovers, blackouts, or sickness.

The gulping of drinks is now reinforced by long and secret swigs from his hidden private supply, be it a half pint on the hip or a dozen quarts secreted in the garage—which explains his seemingly inexplicable "quick tightness" on many occasions. He suffers nightmarish hangovers; unlike the "New Year's Day hangover" of the non-alcoholic drinker, his hangovers include physical near collapse, overwhelming remorse, guilt, self-doubt, and extreme anxiety. His blackouts increase and come earlier, sometimes beginning with the very first drink. Physical and mental anguish leads him to make the rounds of hospitals, doctors, and psychiatrists. But because he won't admit the extent of his drinking, he seldom receives any lasting benefits.

Late symptoms. He *must* drink. He gets blindly and helplessly drunk for days at a time, futilely searching for that feeling of alcoholic euphoria he once relished. His tolerance has diminished, so that even a relatively small amount of alcohol causes drunkenness. He utterly disregards everything—family, job, food, and even shelter. His flights into oblivion could well be described as "drinking to escape the problems caused by drinking."

Depending on his physical and financial condition, his drinking bouts increase in frequency and intensity. Now the morning drink is mandatory and he rarely goes on the wagon. He becomes fearful of things he cannot pin down or describe in words—he experiences feelings of impending doom or destruction. He is fired from jobs and sometimes quits for no apparent reason. By any means possible, he must get money to drink, stopping at nothing and often violating his own moral "code" or what is left of it. He observes the devastating effect of his drinking on those around him with seeming indifference. He loses his sense of time.

Drinking or not, his life is now built around alcohol. With apparent obliviousness, he accepts his drinking as natural and inevitable, but he does so with an increased sense of shame and degradation. His isolation, loneliness, and feeling of non-belonging are pronounced. He cannot be convinced that he'll ever be able to feel well and enjoy life without alcohol, for now his few moments without drinking include neither of these reactions.

Now there's an urgent physical need to get and keep a certain amount of alcohol in his system at all times. Hangovers are present whenever he awakens or "comes to," and, if possible, are alleviated by alcohol. He can't lift his head without violent nausea, dizziness, or leaps and shakes. Because of the tremors, he can neither wash his face, shave, nor brush his teeth. The constant presence of alcohol in his system eliminates hunger, and he rarely eats.

Are some people, in fact, born to be alcoholics? Is alcoholism a type of neurosis—symptomatic, perhaps, of an underlying emotional disorder? Is it caused by some physiological malfunction, such as abnormal metabolism of alcohol? Is alcoholism like an allergy?

Professionals and paraprofessionals who deal with alcoholics daily find that the great majority have been conditioned since childhood to look upon alcoholism as the consequence of a particular neurosis or personality defect. And many such persons, once they have conceded that they are indeed alcoholic, have spent literally thousands of dollars and many years trying to unearth and remedy their particular neurotic problem.

Not surprisingly, many of these alcoholics become discouraged, because, even after extensive psychotherapy and apparent resolution of their psychiatric difficulties, they still find they are unable to drink the way a "social drinker" does. Others become even more frustrated, because their years of psychotherapy fail to uncover any significant psychiatric problem.

A number of professionals, along with a growing army of recovering alcoholics, insist that such frustration and discouragement can be wholly eliminated—simply by the realization that there are important *physical* aspects to alcoholism. As a matter of fact, research conducted over the last several years strongly indicates that alcoholism may soon be recognized by the scientific community and the public at large as a metabolic illness, rather than a psychiatric problem.

It has already been determined, for example, that there are a number of systemic metabolic differences between alcoholics and non-alcoholics; as the evidence mounts up, it points over and over to the liver as a major culprit in the disease process. In one recent study, alcoholics and non-alcoholics alike were fed the amino acid tryptophan; it turned out that the livers of the alcoholics broke down the tryptophan into one end product, while the livers of the non-alcoholics broke it down into a different, *normal* end product.

Another experiment involved measurements of one of the body's enzyme systems and the enzyme catalase in particular, which is capable of "breaking down" alcohol. When alcoholics were given various amounts of alcohol, their blood samples showed a significant rise in the level of catalase after *any size* dose of alcohol; once again, the non-alcoholics did not respond in the same manner.

Also, in the past few years, some of the genetic and familial characteristics of alcoholics have been studied. Geneticists and sociologists have discovered, specifically, that the incidence of color blindness in alcoholics is greater than among the general population; that blood group "A" is found in alcoholics far more often than in the general population; that a disproportionately high percentage of alcoholics are unable to taste the chemical phenolthiocarbimide (a characteristic, geneticists have long known, that is inherited as a Mendelian recessive trait).

It has further been determined that abnormalities in such body processes as adrenal gland function, regulation of blood pressure, and metabolism of glucose tend to be constitutional characteristics of alcoholics—even after alcohol intake has been stopped for a number of years. In one important series of recent studies which dealt with endocrine and autonomic nervous function, it was further discovered, not without surprise, that the intake of even small doses of alcohol by the "test" alcoholics tended to restore their various functions toward normal.

A great deal of experimental work on test animals also seems to support the views of those who argue that the causes of alcoholism are essentially physiological rather than psychological or sociological. For example, it is possible to breed strains of mice, rats, and other laboratory animals which prefer alcohol to water, and, in some cases, certain metabolic differences have been noted between the "drinking" animals and the "non-drinking" animals. What is more, there is often a pronounced difference between the alcohol preference of individual animals even from the same litter. This resembles in some ways the responses researchers have also seen in human beings. Treating the animals in various ways may also increase the amount of alcohol they drink voluntarily; certain vitamin-deficient diets, for example, will produce an increased alcohol intake in test animals.

In any case, alcoholism remains a complex and, for the most part, little understood illness; most authorities today seem to agree that it stems from a combination of physiological, psychological, and sociological factors. They further agree that, all things considered, science knows practically nothing about the causes of alcoholism.

In the final analysis, far more is known about what doesn't cause alcoholism than what does cause the illness. To be specific, alcohol alone is certainly not the cause of alcoholism, because the majority of people who drink alcohol never become alcoholics. True, alcoholism would be impossible without alcohol, but alcohol can no more be considered the cause of alcoholism than marriage can be considered the cause of divorce.

It has also been determined that alcoholism is *not* a manifestation of an allergy; that alcoholism is *not* inherited; and that alcoholism is *not* due to any "alcoholic personality." Nor is alcoholism caused by drinking a particular beverage; on the contrary, as we have seen, a person can become an alcoholic by drinking *any* beverage or solution containing *any* amount of alcohol.

And, finally, alcoholics do not *abuse* alcohol. "Although the term 'alcohol abuse' has wide currency," notes the Diagnostic Criteria Committee of the National Council on Alcoholism, "we prefer 'alcohol use,' accompanying this term with a description of effect. This does not anthropomorphize alcohol, which, after all, is a chemical (the 'neutral spirit'). The term 'misuse,' we believe, also carries an unnecessary moral implication."

When all is said and done, to return to the question "Who's the alcoholic?," the answer, obviously, is anyone. The last word should be reserved, in my view, for alcoholics themselves—for those recovering alcoholics who have "been there" and returned.

To be arbitrarily selective, one such individual comes to mind immediately: former golf star Dick Mayer, who, between 1949 and 1957, won sixteen Professional Golfers' Association tournaments and finished second in nineteen others. In 1957, he captured the United States Open and was named PGA golfer of the year. However, in 1962, except for a victory in the New Orleans Open in 1965 and a $50,000 hole-in-one in the Desert Classic at Palm Springs, California, Mayer faded from public view.

"Maybe I'd still be playing today if it had not been for alcohol," says Mayer, now in his early fifties and considered one of the best teaching pros in the country. "Undoubtedly it cost me a lot. My problem was a progressive one, and for a long time it was a periodic type of thing. I'd stop for a while, and then someone would say, 'Let's have a party.' System-wise, though, I was deteriorating. It takes its toll. Finally I realized I did have a serious problem.

"I don't think being in the business I was in had anything to do with my problem," Dick Mayer adds. "I was brought up in a society that drank, and I drank. Some people can drink and some can't. I can't. It's that simple."

Afterword

Where There's Hope,
There's Life

Tacked to a wall of my study is a large road map of America. It is smudged, dog-eared, and torn along one crease; the map has been well used. Rand McNally's official symbols have been supplemented by such personal markings as black triangles, red asterisks, blue X's, and green stars—along with notes, nicknames, and even telephone numbers.

Circled in red, for example, is the small California bayside town of San Rafael. There, inside a medieval fortress called San Quentin, I sat in a locked room talking quietly with six prisoners, each of whom had been convicted of homicide committed "behind booze." Three of the six readily conceded that they drink prison-brewed pruno daily; two said that they are trying to stay sober. The sixth prisoner—who is serving a life sentence—told me he found sobriety eight years ago behind Quentin's gun-turreted walls.

Moving almost due east, one of my larger black triangles encompasses the Bible Belt. There, in Oklahoma's Washita County, the tiny town of Bessie is starred. During a violent nighttime storm in Bessie, I sat cramped and cross-legged for twelve hours within a giant tepee as alcoholic native Americans held a sacred Peyote Meeting at the Cheyenne-Arapaho Alcoholism Rehabilitation Lodge.

Starred also on my map is Center City, Minnesota, from which a country road leads to the world-famous alcoholism treatment center called Hazelden Foundation. Next to Center City's green star is scribbled the phrase "AA slogans"—a reminder to myself of Burma Shave–type signs I had seen along the unpaved road to Hazelden: "EASY DOES IT," "ONE DAY AT A TIME," "FIRST THINGS FIRST."

That map is, of course, a prized possession. Its markings recall not only dozens of cities and scores of places, but, most memorably, hundreds of people. As these pages have made clear, most of those people are my alcoholic brothers and sisters, sober when I last saw them and, I trust, sober still.

Sometimes at night, I pick tapes at random from some two hundred-odd cassettes to hear the voices and picture the faces of my friends, aware that I have learned many things since that day in 1973 when Marty Mann reminded me that we alcoholics should never get too Hungry, Angry, Lonely, or Tired.

I listen to the words of sixty-two-year-old George Hawkins (grandson of Starving Elk, formerly a doorway-sleeper on Oklahoma City's infamous Reno Street, and most recently director of the Cheyenne-Arapaho Lodge), and I'm instantly transported back to that firelit tepee in Bessie, Oklahoma.

I hear the halting voice of newly sober eighteen-year-old Ken. I see Ken as he is on a fall afternoon, blond hair still shower-damp as he proudly displays a Serenity Prayer medallion given to him by his mother and father when they had visited him at Hazelden for the first time just days earlier.

I listen to Danny, a thirty-six-year-old black man—sober today—who remains behind the bars of Lorton Penitentiary in Occoquan, Virginia, charged with felony assault and grand larceny allegedly committed during a drunken blackout.

I turn the recorder switch to "On" and get in touch with Mary Spencer, Bob O'Briant, Riley Regan, Florette Pomeroy, Jim Heath, and so many others.

Listening to their voices and seeing their faces, I travel back in time to halfway houses, hospitals, prisons, and meeting rooms across the length and breadth of America. And I am struck, always, by the same overpowering truths:

There is no such thing as a helpless, hopeless alcoholic.

In a land where The Plague is rampant, ill people *are* getting well.

There *is* hope, and there *is* help.